WHEN HOLLYWOOD RULED THE SKIES

BRUCE W. ORRISS

THE AVIATION FILM CLASSICS OF WORLD WAR II

To my brothers
Donald and Ramon
with
love and respect.

First edition, 1984

Published in the United States of America by Aero Associates, Inc., 4013 W. 120th Street, Hawthorne, Ca. 90250
Printing by Halliday Lithograph Corp., W. Hanover, Mass.
Cover Design by Bruce Orriss, Sergio Gonzalez, Jim Keeshan.
Library of Congress Catalog Card Number: 83-073551
Graphics by Sergio Gonzalez, Jane M. Kalinski
ISBN 0-9613088-0-X

Table of Contents

Acknowledgments

A great many people have generously given me their advise, encouragement and assistance during the preparation of this book. I could not have completed it without them. I'd like to especially thank Dr. Richard Kocher of Loyola Marymount University, who guided this book from its inception to its completion, Sam Gill of the Academy of Motion Picture Arts and Sciences Library, for his expertise on all matters pertaining to film history, Ms. Audree Malkin of UCLA's Theater Arts Library and Dr. Robert Knutson of USC's Performing Arts Library for their kind assistance over the past seven years, Lt. Colonel Art Wildern for his invaluable help on the making of Tora! Tora! Tora!, Mrs. Terry Mantz for her reminiscences of her famed husband, Frank Pine of Tallmantz Aviation and Jim Appleby of Antique Aero, for taking time out of their busy schedules to give me background details of the many films they've worked on, Louise Winkler for her tireless work on the manuscript, and Bonnie Saenz for her many months of editorial expertise.

I would also like to thank the following individuals who were instrumental in helping me to obtain the historical information and photographic illustrations necessary to complete the manuscript: Captain John Crewdson of Helicopter Hire Ltd., Major Norman Ray, Rear Admiral William Moffett, Nick Williams, Paul Groesse, Colonel Charles Birdsall, Gus Gustufson, Denny McFarland, MSgt. Bill Hess, LCDR. Tom Conway, E.J. Pawka, Marion Johnson, Van Johnson, Rick Hilton, Ron Monroe, Robert Mitchum, Dr. Ira Chart, Brigadier General John Dobbin, Donald Hackett, Ernest Wade, Joseph Krueger, Arvid Dahl, Colonel Winton Miller, Captain Clyde Schetter, Colonel Greg "Pappy" Boyington, A.B. Sellards, Tracy Berns, Bob Grier, Lincoln Center's Wallace Athey, T.T. Jackson, Clifford Byrd, D.E. Wingo, Richard Register, Herbert Nusbaum, Joseph Callahan, Mary Corliss, Howard Gregory, Jim Keeshan, Kathee McConnell, Tom Petrus, Martin Caiden, Herbert Strickland, Betty Jo Reed, Captain I.B. Monahan, Brigadier General John Coulter, A.D. McCall, Jr., Maureen Wolchko, Royal Frey, Robert DeHaven, Thomas Smith, William Wagner, Iris Critchell, W. Douglas, Brigadier General Jimmy Doolittle, Captain Dale Lewey, Bud Degler, Larry Powell, Colonel John deRussy, Lt. Colonel Edward Hillery, Steven Birdsall, Melvin Kessler, Commander John Muoio, Captain S.S. Searcy, Colonel Andrew Gordon, Ronald Plante, Barbara "BJ" London, Robert Harvey, Jerry Phillips, Brigadier General Robert Harvey, Captain Robin Lindsey, H.L. Young, Jr., Harold Heisel, Larry Odoms, Robert Middleton, Rear Admiral W.L. Gallery, Rudy Frasca, I.N. Burchinal, Jan Martin, Fred Johnson, James Farmer, Gabrielle Neufeld, Brigadier General Robert Lee Scott, William Larkins, Thomas Dykers, Jr., Dottie George, William Fizer, Rip Starling, Robert Steele, Cliff Byrd, Curt Hanisch, Glen MacWilliams, Dr. David Hatfield, J. McDuffie, Manly Nelson, Ira Matthews, Colonel Robert Stone, Dr. Ira Flowers, G. Christianson, MSgt. Buddy Gordon, Roy Grossnick, Ed Boyle, Anne Shelander, Stan Winchester, James Stewart, Gordon Williams, Al Lloyd, Warren Bodie, Colonel Everett Vaughn, Richard Norton, Zachary O'Kearin, Dan McCarthy, Peter Bowers, Al Morgan, Al Menasco, Colonel R.D. Hughes, Harold Heisel, Robert Lowenberg, Jim Thompson, Stan Reaver, Henry Hathaway, Winston Green, James Davis, Captain James Brown, Bob King, Vince Urban, Robert Surtees, and MSgt. Bill Pierro.

Finally, grateful appreciation is extended to the following organizations for providing invaluable information and photographic material from their historical archives: Museum of Modern Art, Viacom Productions, The Confederate Air Force, Lincoln Center's Library of the Performing Arts, U.S. Air Force Museum, Ryan Aircraft Company, Ontario Film Institute, Library of Congress, Wisconsin Center for Film and Theater Research, University of Wyoming, Hollywood Memories, Public Archives of Canada, Department of the Navy, Department of the Air Force, Boeing Aircraft Company, National Archives, U.S. Marine Corps, Department of Defense, Department of the Army, Academy of Motion Picture Arts and Sciences, Movie Star News, The American Film Institute, National Air and Space Museum, American Aviation Historical Society, Georgia Air National Guard, Movieland of the Air, Northrop University's Aviation History Library, British Film Institute, Eddie Brandt's Saturday Matinee, Michigan Air National Guard, U.S. Naval Audio Visual Center, Collector's Bookshop, Larry Edmund's Bookshop, Clay Lacy Aviation, and Yesterday's Air Force.

Author's Note

The combat films of World War II, whether factual or fictional, have proven themselves to be one of the most enduring and prodigious genres in the history of American motion pictures. Aside from the Western, no subject has been given as much attention by American filmmakers or been so well received by American filmgoers. The scope and purpose of this volume will limit itself to one specific segment of this genre: the aviation films of World War II, from the pre-war recruitment vehicles, the wartime "flag-wavers," the postwar studies in realism, and finally to the more thought-provoking films of the post-1950 era. It will study the radical changes in aim and purpose that these films have undergone in the past forty-two years, and will give special emphasis not only to the stories that these aviation films depicted but also the stories behind their making and the people that made them.

BWO

Hawthorne, Ca.
1984

WHEN HOLLYWOOD RULED THE SKIES

BULLET

Chapter One

The Impending Storm: 1938-1941

By the late 1930's, the shadows of war had rapidly begun to fall across many nations of the world. Blindly ignoring events overseas, the United States remained wrapped in an isolationistic cocoon. Even as Hilter's troops stormed across the face of Europe, the prevailing attitude in America was one of non-involvement, and with few notable exceptions, Hollywood's filmmakers reflected this. They gave the public what it wanted: escape, and with it came an endless stream of entertainment films that consciously avoided topics of a controversial nature. But events overseas would eventually change Hollywood's product of the depression years. The adventure tales, light comedies, and musical extravaganzas would ultimately give way to films that reflected the bleak realities of global conflict. Newsreels and documentaries, with their vivid first-hand accounts of war atrocities, chipped away at America's protective shell and served as an impetus for the movie capital to introduce a different sort of motion picture, one designed to influence and shift a nation's mood from self-centered apathy to one of international involvement.

By the fall of 1939, Hitler's plan for world domination became all too obvious. Germany had seized Austria, Czechoslovakia and Poland, Albania had fallen to the Italians, and to the far east, Japan had invaded China and French Indo-China. World War II would soon become a reality.

Spurred by the loss of most of its overseas markets, film industry leaders decided it was time to end America's complacency with Axis aggression. With government sanction, motion picture studios began increasing their output of patriotic service dramas. Although labeled as war-mongering propaganda by isolationist factions, films like *Test Pilot* and *Wings of the Navy* were well received at the box-office and succeeded in increasing public awareness of the importance of a strong military deterrent.

By mid-1940, France had fallen to Hitler's army, and now only Great Britain and the Atlantic stood between Germany and the United States. Shaken by the world crisis, President Roosevelt requested $1.8 billion dollars to finance the greatest peacetime military buildup in the history of the United States. Having already thrown aside its veil of neutrality, Hollywood's filmmakers turned from anti-Fascist rhetoric towards the pragmatism of national preparedness. *Flight Command* and *I Wanted Wings* were rushed into production following the President's action and became the first of many "cinematic recruiting posters" that extolled the virtues of military service and informed the public of the armed forces' role in defending the nation against possible attack.

As the situation in Europe steadily worsened, the question remained as to how long the British could hold out under repeated Luftwaffe attacks. A Roper Poll taken in the Fall of 1941 indicated that the earlier isolationistic attitude of many Americans had taken a dramatic turn: sixty-eight percent of the nation now favored all-out aid to Great Britain. Impatient for intervention, Hollywood stepped up its attack against the Axis with the first of its pro-British films, *A Yank in the RAF* and *International Squadron*. In releasing such films, the industry sought to inform its viewers of the gallant stand Great Britain was making, and that, somehow, the "Allied cause" had also become our own.

In the three short years since Hollywood had emerged from its escapist seclusion, the aim of American films had been altered to stir the conscience of a nation. Even as powerful isolationist factions accused filmmakers of inciting the American people to war, industry leaders stood resolute in their commitment against fascism. The cries of war-mongering were soon silenced though, as the last vestiges of American neutrality were swept away with the Japanese attack on Pearl Harbor – December 7, 1941.

TEST PILOT

Metro-Goldwyn-Mayer

— 1938 —

CAST

Jim Lane: CLARK GABLE; Ann Barton: MYRNA LOY; Gunner Sloane: SPENCER TRACY; Drake: LIONEL BARRYMORE; General Ross: SAMUEL S. HINDS; Landlady: MARJORIE MAIN; Joe: TED PEARSON; Mrs. Benson: GLORIA HOLDEN; Benson: LOUIS JEAN HEYDT; Sarah: VIRGINIA GREY; Mabel: PRISCILLIA LAWSON; Mrs. Barton: CLAUDIA COLEMAN; Mr. Barton: ARTHUR AYLESWORTH

CREDITS

Director: VICTOR FLEMING; Producer: LOUIS D. LIGHTON; Screenplay: VINCENT LAWRENCE, WALDEMAR YOUNG; Original Story: FRANK WEAD; Cinematographer: RAY JUNE; Aerial Cinematographers: ELMER DYER, CHARLES A. MARSHALL; Air Operations: PAUL MANTZ, FRANK CLARKE, RAY MOORE, FRANK TOMICK, EARL ORTMAN, ART CHESTER; Art Direction: CEDRIC GIBBONS; Set Direction: JOHN DETLIE, EDWIN B. WILLIS; Special Effects: A. ARNOLD GILLESPIE; Film Editor: TOM HELD; Musical Score: FRANZ WAXMAN; Sound Technician: DOUGLAS SHEARER; Wardrobe: DOLLY TREE

As the shadows of war darkened the face of Europe, Hollywood's output of patriotic service dramas took a dramatic turn upward. Notable among these films was MGM's aerial epic, *Test Pilot,* released in 1938, starring Clark Gable, Myrna Loy, and Spencer Tracy.

The story, by former Navy flier turned screenwriter Frank Wead, revolves around a hard-drinking test pilot, Jim Lane (Clark Gable), and his gum-chewing mechanic Gunner Sloane (Spencer Tracy). The opening scene of the film has Jim taking off to break the transcontinental speed record in the *Drake Bullet* race plane. Over Kansas, the aircraft develops an oil leak, and is forced to land on a farm. There he meets and later marries pert farmgirl Ann Barton (Myrna Loy). Long overdue by the time he arrives in New York,

Clark Gable and Myrna Loy listen to Victor Fleming's animated explanation of a scene being shot at San Diego's Lindbergh Field, one of nine airfields used for the film. A Ryan ST sportplane sits in the background.

Jim attempts to bulldoze his way out of the situation and gets fired by boss Howard Drake (Lionel Barrymore). Unable to find a job anywhere, he accepts an offer to fly an experimental racer at the Thompson Trophy Air Race. Despite an engine fire, Jim wins the race and the $10,000 prize. Impressed with his performance, Drake rehires Jim and quickly hands him some of his toughest assignments. In the climactic scene of the film, Jim and Gunner pilot an experimental bomber (actually the YB-17) into the stratosphere to break the world altitude record. At 29,000 feet, the heavily loaded craft unexpectedly stalls and falls into a deadly spin. As Jim struggles to regain control of the stricken aircraft, the sandbag ballast breaks loose, crushing Gunner, and forcing them to crash. Narrowly escaping death, Jim pulls Gunner from the burning wreckage only to have him die in his arms. Gunner's death finally convinces Jim to quit test flying and turn to instructing fledgling pilots for the Army Air Corps.

Seen today, *Test Pilot,* replete with all its Hollywood heroics, remains an exceptional film to watch. Excellent casting, large-scale production, and the authentically staged aerial sequences combined to make it an aviation film classic. More importantly (to the War Department), it introduced American movie-goers to the Army Air Corp's new long-range bomber, the B-17 Flying Fortress, a plane which would soon form the backbone of this nation's strategic bombing force.

Formal production of the film began in December, 1937, with Victor Fleming assigned as director. The three-month shooting schedule included nearly seven weeks of outdoor location work. For the opening scene of the film, MGM's Art Department recreated an entire Kansas-style farm on the Phillips Ranch in Chino, California. Studio technicians trucked in trees, erected fences, and even constructed a farmhouse and silo to give the ranch a proper mid-west appearance. A 100 acre pasture served as a temporary landing field for Gable's *Drake Bullet* race plane.

Well wishers bid Gable luck before the start of the Thompson Trophy Race. The aircraft behind him is the Marcoux-Bromberg "Special."

Gable removes a cowling from the "Drake Bullet" to examine the broken oil line which ruined his chance to break the cross-country speed record.

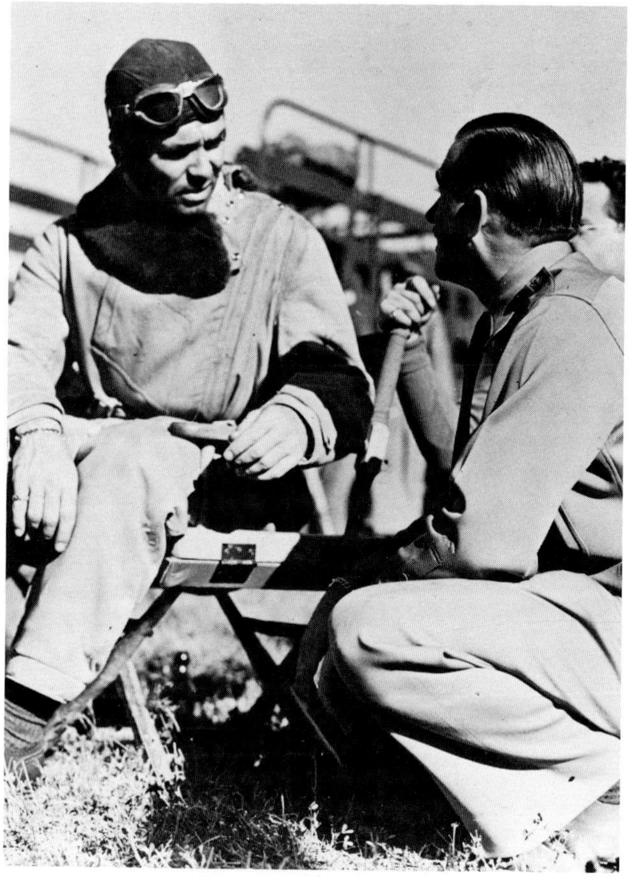

Ace stunt pilot Paul Mantz confers with Clark Gable during filming at the Phillips Ranch in Chino, California.

Lionel Barrymore discusses the testing of his new pursuit ship (actually a Northrop A-17) with Gable and Tracy.

Noted aviation experts, Paul Mantz and Al Menasco, acted as the production's technical advisors throughout the filming of the picture. In his seven years in Hollywood, Mantz had quickly risen to the top of his profession as a movie stunt pilot, and now had cornered most of the flying work in the film capitol. His United Air Services firm provided planes and pilots for all sorts of film productions. Mantz's many responsibilities on *Test Pilot* included coordinating all the stunt flying and aerial camera work for the film.

Former World War I test pilot and air racing authority, Al Menasco, personally arranged the use of Frank Fuller's SEV-S2 race plane to stand in as the *Drake Bullet*. With the exception of some minor refinements, the aircraft was identical to the P-35 pursuits being delivered to the Army Air Corps. Powered by a fourteen-cylinder 1000-hp Twin Wasp engine, it was capable of speeds up to 300 mph at 10,000 feet. Fuller (the paint magnate) had only recently won the 1937 Bendix Air Race in the sleek craft, roaring across the finish line at a record 258.2 mph. It had also placed sixth in the 1937 Thompson Trophy Air Race in the hands of race pilot Ray Moore, who was later contracted to fly in the film, handling all the scenes involving the SEV-S2.

Metro's Special Effects Department, under the aegis of A. Arnold Gillespie, outdid themselves in "Test Pilot." Here Gable prepares to bail out of his stricken pursuit plane following the loss of a wing. The entire scene was shot inside one of MGM's sound stages using rear screen projection.

Some of the most exciting moments in the picture are contained in the excellently staged air racing sequences. Most of this footage was shot on location at the 1937 Thompson Trophy Air Race in Cleveland, Ohio. The day after the race, Fleming and his camera crew restaged their own mock event using actual race planes and pilots. Among them were air racing immortals Rudy Kling, Gus Gotch, Earl Ortman, and the ever flamboyant Roscoe Turner.

Additional scenes, involving the principal actors, were filmed in San Diego and Oxnard, and over the salt flats near

All twelve YB-17 prototypes participated in the making of "Test Pilot." Here number 51, commanded by Major Vince Meloy, poses for the cameras. White engine cowlings identify it as a 20th Bomb Squadron, 2nd Bomb Group aircraft.

Point Mugu, about forty miles northwest of Los Angeles. Race pilot, Earl Ortman, stood in for Gable in these sequences, flying his black and yellow Marcoux-Bromberg *Special,* the plane he had flown to second place in both the 1937 Bendix and Thompson Trophy Air Races.

All the film's special effects were handled by MGM's resident expert, A. Arnold "Buddy" Gillespie. Gillespie first arrived at the studio in 1922, and eventually took over the special effects department after many years as an art director. He later described some of his experiences on *Test Pilot* in Mike Steen's book, *Hollywood Speaks*:

"I remember we used a lot of miniatures in *Test Pilot*. One of the most difficult scenes was a miniature crash of the YB-17. They [MGM's Art Department] had made the full-size set of the crashed bomber, and filmed Gable and Tracy crawling out of the wreckage, before we shot the miniature of the plane actually crashing. That was a bad thing to do, because when you crash a miniature, (that is your miniature is all smashed up) and you have to match that in your full-size set, you have to duplicate, in full-size, the shape and position of the miniature wreckage. Since the full-size set was already shot, we had to reverse that procedure and rehearse for three solid days with five cameras before actually filming the crash of the miniature YB-17 . . . We also used a lot of process shots in the film; stationary sets in the foreground while the scenery and action in the background are actually being projected from the rear of the screen. Most of the close shots of the actors in the airplanes were done in this manner on a sound stage with simulated weather – – snowstorms when necessary. Clark Gable didn't mind going through a certain amount of physical discomfort to get a scene, but Spence [Spencer Tracy] would squawk, although generally with his tongue in cheek."[1]

A great deal of Army Air Corps (AAC) cooperation was given MGM's crew in shooting the final segments of the film at March Field, California. Over 100 military aircraft participated in these scenes, including all twelve of the prototype YB-17 Flying Fortress bombers. The AAC had only recently launched a massive publicity campaign to impress Congress with the unique capabilities of the Flying Fortress, and were anxious to have it participate in the film.

(Above) Gable hauls Tracy from the burning wreckage of their YB-17 bomber. The scene took nearly two weeks to shoot on Metro's backlot (below) and was accomplished using a flying miniature and this fullscale mockup. It is actually a DC-2 transport fitted with dummy engines and a reworked cabin.

The final scene in "Test Pilot" involved this mass flyover of nearly sixty aircraft at March Field, California. Eighteen cameras (nine on the ground and nine in the air) were needed to record the sequence.

Director Victor Fleming (right) and chief cinematographer Ray June (left) line up a shot while on location at March Field, California.

Metro's cameramen position themselves as the 2nd Bomb Group's YB-17's taxi into position for the film's finale.

Under the command of Lt. Colonel Robert Olds, the 2nd Bomb Group's YB-17's were flown cross-country from Langley Field, Virginia, to join aircraft and crews of the 17th Attack and the 19th Bomb Groups, which had temporarily been assigned to MGM's production company. Fleming used many of the AAC crew members as extras in the film during his two-week stay at the base. His leading star, Clark Gable, in turn, was given permission to co-pilot one of the YB-17's assigned to the 20th Bomb Squadron during the filming of the picture. Four years later, Gable would find himself aboard another Flying Fortress, this time for real as an 8th Air Force gunner in the flak-filled skies over Europe.

Test Pilot premiered in April 1938 and became an immediate success with audiences and critics alike. Box-office receipts established it as one of the biggest hits of the year. The Academy of Motion Picture Arts and Sciences later nominated it for three Academy Awards, including Best Picture of 1938, Best Original Story (Frank Wead), and Best Film Editing (Tom Held).

NEW YORK TIMES

"Leo the trade-mark lion, can stop yawning now and roar with some of his old enthusiasm, for Metro-Goldwyn-Mayer has turned out a bang-up aviation drama (and we mean that literally as well as figuratively) in 'Test Pilot.' It is a generous show by any reckoning, long in its running time, star-studded and spectacular, and Victor Fleming, its director, has paced it wisely. Whenever its plot threatened to run down, he has turned his cameras to the skies and let lens and microphone capture anew the excitement of droning motors and sun-glinting wings playing with death above the clouds . . ."

Frank S. Nugent
April 16, 1938

WINGS OF THE NAVY

Warner Brothers

— 1939 —

CAST

Cass Harrington: GEORGE BRENT; Irene Dale: OLIVIA DE HAVILLAND; Jerry Harrington: JOHN PAYNE; Scat Allen: FRANK MC HUGH; Commander Clark: JOHN LITEL; Lt. Parsons: VICTOR JORY; Prologue Speaker: HENRY O'NEILL; Dan Morrison: JOHN RIDGELY; Lt. Harry White: JOHN GALLAUDET; Instructor: DONALD BRIGGS; Ted Parsons: EDGAR EDWARDS; Flight Instructor: REGIS TOOMEY; Armando Costa: ALBERT MORIN; Commandant: JONATHAN HALE; Captain March: PIERRE WATKIN; Officer of the Day: DON DOUGLAS; Drilling Officer: MAX HOFFMAN; Check Pilot: ALAN DAVIS; Aviator: LARRY WILLIAMS

CREDITS

Director: LLOYD BACON; Producer: HAL B. WALLIS; Original Screenplay: MICHAEL FESSIER; Cinematographer: ARTHUR EDESON; Aerial Cinematographer: ELMER DYER; Air Operations: PAUL MANTZ, FRANK CLARKE; Art Direction: ESDRAS HARTLEY; Special Effects: HANS KOENEKAMP; Film Editor: GEORGE AMY; Musical Score: LEO FORBSTEIN; Sound Technician: FRANCIS J. SCHEID; Wardrobe: ORRY-KELLY

By the late 1930's, Warner Brothers Studios had become leaders in the production of films dedicated to the various branches of the military. As war in Europe and Asia became more of an imminent reality, the tone of these films changed to a more serious note, serving to inform the public of the armed forces' role in America's defense efforts. Warner's 1939 release, *Wings of the Navy,* examined the intensive training our Naval air cadets underwent to win their coveted "Wings of Gold."

The screenplay, by Michael Fessier, follows flying cadet Jerry Harrington (John Payne) through the various phases of training at Naval Air Station (NAS) Pensacola, Florida. Upon graduation, he is assigned to a squadron in San Diego for training in the Navy's newest long-range patrol bomber,

Frank McHugh is issued a parachute for his first Navy flight.

the PBY Catalina. With regrets, he ultimately decides to sacrifice his military career to test a new pursuit plane his older brother Cass (George Brent) has designed for the government. The successful demonstration of the aircraft, for Naval authorities, results in Harrington's being recommissioned to full flying status. He rejoins his squadron in time for the film's climactic non-stop flight to Pearl Harbor, Hawaii.

A good deal of time and care obviously went into Warner's production of *Wings of the Navy*. The above

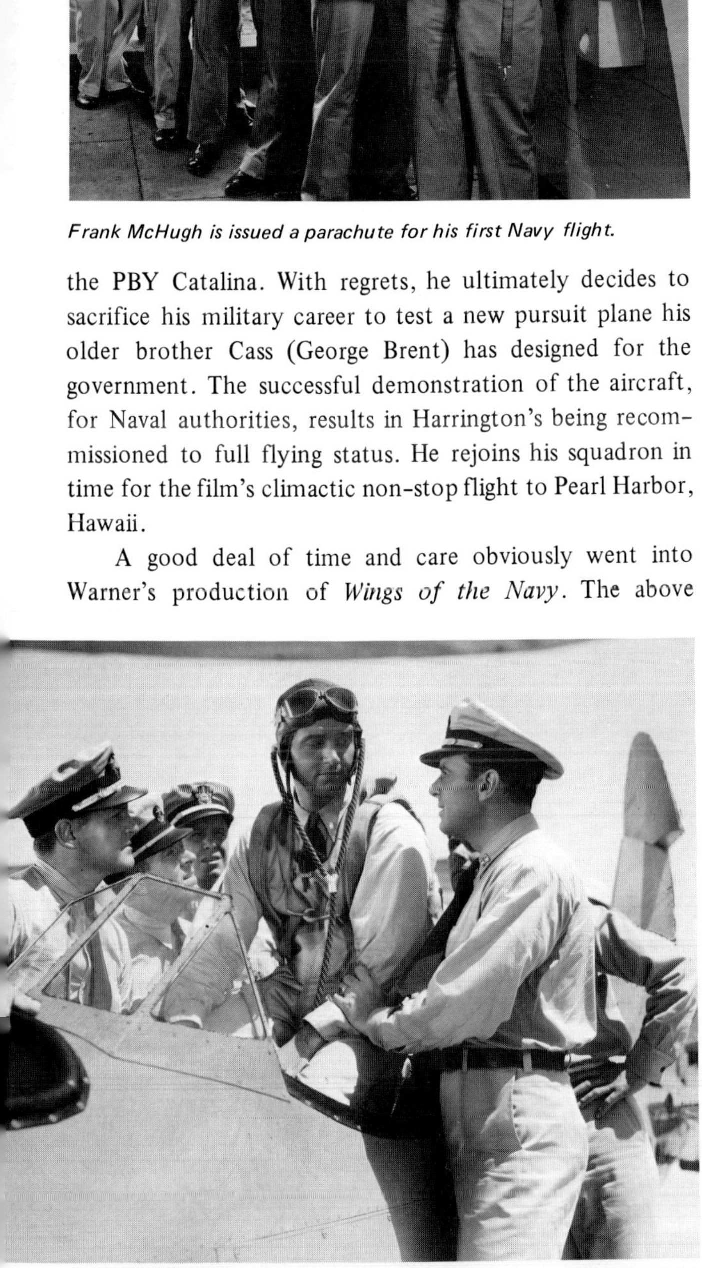

John Payne listens to George Brent explain how not to land his N3N trainer. Brent in real life was a skilled civilian pilot and owned his own Stinson Reliant.

Warner's cast and crew prepare for a scene being shot at NAS Pensacola's Corry Field. The aircraft in the background are Stearman NS-1 trainers from Training Squadron Two.

average script was given a semi-documentary approach and solid execution by veteran director Lloyd Bacon who was, at the time, a Lt. Commander in the U.S. Naval Reserve. Budgeted at over $1,000,000, the picture proved to be one of the more ambitious projects on Warner's film roster for 1939.

Production of the film began on July 5, 1938. Bacon led his cast and crew on two extensive location trips during the picture's nine-week shooting schedule. The first was a cross-country trek to the Navy's flight training facility at NAS Pensacola, Florida (known as "The Annapolis of the Air"), where scenes were filmed against the authentic backgrounds of Pensacola's Corry and Chevalier Training Fields. With less than a dozen actors brought from Hollywood, Bacon relied heavily on actual Navy instructors and trainees to flesh out his script requirements. Five Naval Training Squadrons provided the over 300 aircraft used in the scenes, ranging from N3N and NS-1 biplane trainers to 03U and SU-3 scout planes.

Warner's chief pilot, Paul Mantz, and aerial cinematographer, Elmer Dyer, recorded all the film's air-to-air sequences from Mantz's Lockheed Sirius camera ship. The Sirius Model 8A was one of many specialized aircraft in Mantz's United Air Services fleet and was modified to carry two auxiliary cameras under the wings and a main aerial camera mounted on a 360 degree scarf ring over the aircraft's open rear cockpit.

Following their two-week stay in Florida, the cast and

(L to R) Elmer Dyer, Paul Mantz, George Brent, and Frank Clarke pose atop Mantz's Lockheed Sirius camera ship during filming at NAS North Island in San Diego, California.

crew returned to California to complete the interior soundstage scenes and film additional footage at NAS North Island in San Diego. The Navy granted the full use of its equipment during Warner's ten-day visit to the base. Navy pilots flew all of these aerial sequences with the exception of a number of special stunts performed by Paul Mantz and fellow stunt pilot Frank Clarke.

Included in many of the scenes were the new Consolidated PBY-2 Catalina flying boats assigned to Patrol Wings One and Two. At the time, the "P-Boat" was the pride of the Navy's aerial fleet, with more than fourteen squadrons flying the aircraft. The Catalina normally carried a crew of seven and was capable of speeds of 170 mph and a range of 2700 nautical miles.

Production of the film officially ended on September 7, 1938. To honor the Navy's role in the picture, Warner Brothers premiered *Wings of the Navy* in Pensacola, Florida, on January 6, 1939. The final cut of the film, running a lean ninety minutes, contained some truly excellent aerial footage and met with enthusiastic response from the critics.

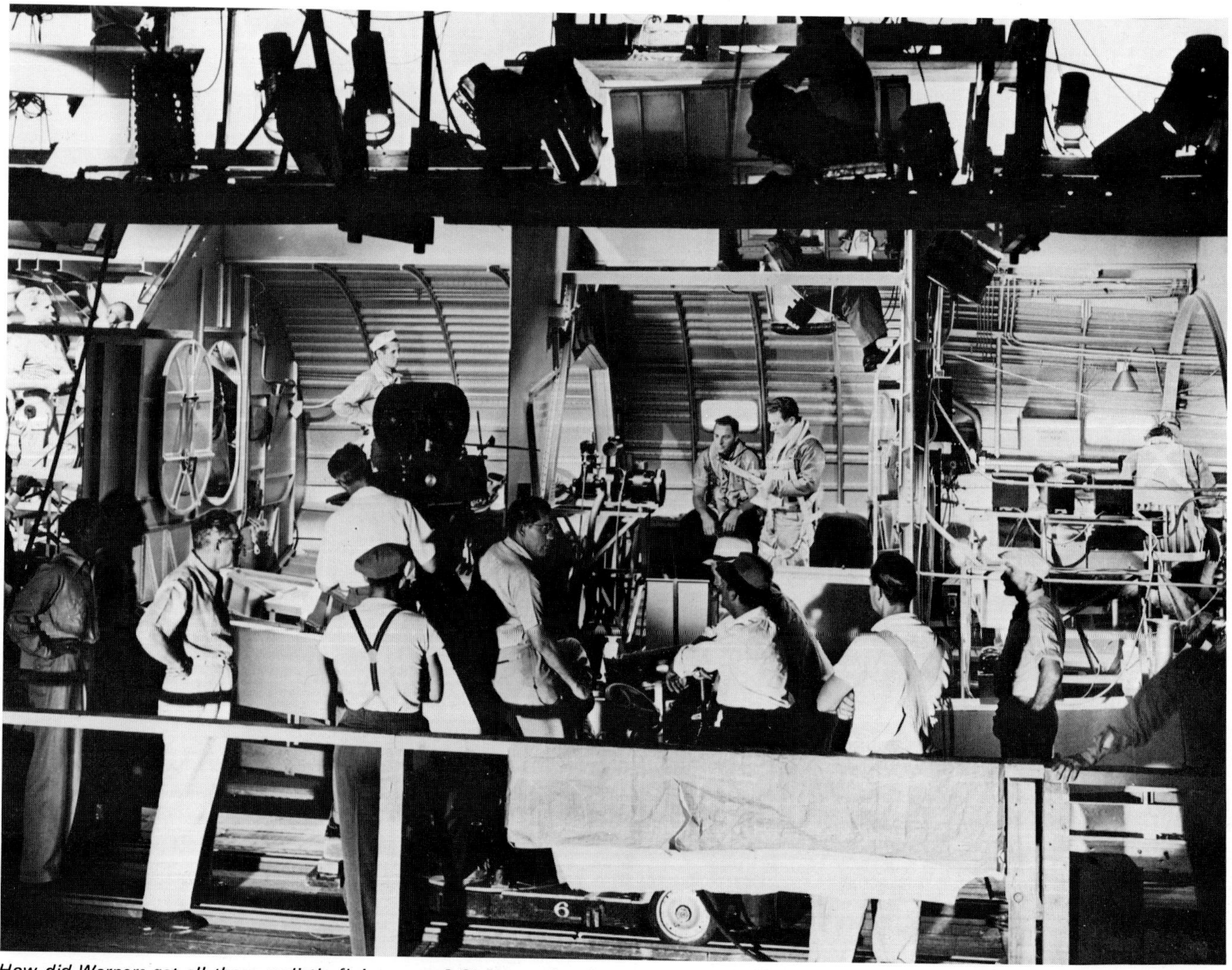

How did Warners get all those realistic flying scenes? Simple – they built an entire PBY inside one of their soundstages. This full-scale replica of a Catalina flying boat and its six compartments was constructed by studio craftsmen at a cost of $20,000.

John Payne breaks the news of his retirement to girlfriend Olivia deHavilland.

Naval Patrol Squadrons VP-9 and VP-10 supplied most of the PBY Catalinas seen in the film.

NEW YORK HERALD TRIBUNE

"The aviation cycle, set in motion with 'Test Pilot' several months ago, hit its stride yesterday when the Warner Brothers set 'Wings of the Navy' down to a neat landing at the N.Y. Strand . . . [the film] is a gala review of the training of the Naval fliers at Pensacola, perhaps with the idea of convincing some timid Americans that Uncle Sam no longer has only a flock of dilapidated crates and a corps of green recruits to man them. The Warners prove instead that American air defenses are attracting hundreds of strapping young fellows, each one of them bitten by the air bug and itching to fly . . . There is plenty of spectacle in all of this, and action galore, especially for the air enthusiasts . . . John Payne one of the newcomers to the Warners roster, confirms early indications that he is fine star material, personable and talented. George Brent, Olivia de Havilland, John Litel and Victor Jory all do workmanlike jobs and Frank McHugh's humor, though mostly on the slap-stick side, is effective relief from the excitement . . ."

Herbert Cohn
January 28, 1939

John Payne and Frank McHugh relax between camera set-ups at NAS Pensacola, Florida.

George Brent and Olivia deHavilland watch as John Payne taxies out in the climactic scene of the film.

FLIGHT COMMAND

Metro-Goldwyn-Mayer

— 1940 —

CAST

Ensign Alan Drake: ROBERT TAYLOR; Lorna Gary: RUTH HUSSEY; Commander Bill Gary: WALTER PIDGEON; Lt. Commandor "Dusty" Rhodes: PAUL KELLY; Lt. Jerry Banning: SHEPPERD STRUDWICK; Lt. "Mugger" Martin: RED SKELTON; CPO "Spike" Knowles: NAT PENDLETON; Lt. "Stitchy" Payne: DICK PURCELL; Lt. Freddy Townsend: WILLIAM TANNEN; Lt. Bush: WILLIAM STELLING; Lt. Frost: STANLEY SMITH; Vice Admiral: ADDISON RICHARDS; First Duty Officer: DONALD DOUGLAS; Second Duty Officer: PAT FLAHERTY; Captain: FORBES MURRAY; Claire: MARSHA HUNT

CREDITS

Director: FRANK BORZAGE; Producer: J. WALTER RUBEN; Screenplay: WELLS ROOT, COMDR. HARVEY HAISLIP; Original Story: JOHN SUTHERLAND, COMDR. HARVEY HAISLIP; Cinematographer: HAROLD ROSSON; Aerial Cinematographer: RICHARD ROSSON, ELMER DYER; Air Operations: PAUL MANTZ, LAURA INGALLS, FRANK CLARKE; Art Director: CEDRIC GIBBONS; Set Decoration: EDWIN B. WILLIS; Special Effects: A. ARNOLD GILLESPIE; Film Editor: ROBERT J. KERN; Musical Score: FRANZ WAXMAN; Sound Technician: DOUGLAS SHEARER; Wardrobe: DOLLY TREE, GILE STEELE

The outbreak of war in Europe awakened Hollywood to the urgent need for national preparedness. MGM's 1940 epic, *Flight Command,* examined in detail the training of a typical Navy fighter squadron and became the first of many "cinematic recruiting posters" to be rushed into production prior to our active involvement in World War II.

The fictional plot, by Wells Root and USN Commander Harvey Haislip (Retired), centers on the "Hell Cats" of VF-8, a crack Navy fighter squadron based in San Diego. One of their pilots has been killed in a training accident and

Mechanic John Sheehan wishes Robert Taylor luck prior to his entry in the aerial gunnery meet. Taylor was so delighted with his role as Ensign Drake that he took flying lessons during the production of the film and later became a Naval aviator.

is replaced by a young Pensacola graduate, Ensign Alan Drake (Robert Taylor). Commanding Officer Bill Gary (Walter Pidgeon) and his wife Lorna (Ruth Hussey) welcome Ensign Drake to the squadron, but the rest of the pilots resent his cocky attitude and feel their outfit is too tough for a mere "shavetail." Drake tries his hardest to impress the men with his ability, but this only succeeds in alienating him further from them. Eventually their behavior convinces the young ensign that he should resign from the squadron. On his last flight with the "Hell Cats," Drake effects the daring rescue of Commander Gary, who has crashed, and flies the injured skipper back to the fog-enshrouded base with the aid of a blind landing device he has helped to develop. Amid apologies, he finally receives the hard-won respect and acceptance of the men of VF-8.

Despite a rather pedestrian love story that was thrown into the script, MGM's *Flight Command* remains an interesting film to watch and very capably depicts the daily training routine of a typical Naval fighter squadron of the period. The carefully choreographed aerial scenes of massed formations of Navy F3F fighter bombers are without a doubt the highlight of the film and surpass anything seen in an aviation epic up till that time.

Pre-production planning for the film began in early 1940. Knowing that Navy cooperation was imperative to the success of the project, producer Jack Ruben worked for several months with screenwriters Root and Haislip to develop a script that would be acceptable to military officials in Washington. "At first the Navy Department didn't approve the script," recalled Ruben. "We had made the fliers just a bit too tough for them. The Navy people asked if we couldn't tone it down, so we did and we soon received approval. They also seemed pleased with the choice of Walter Pidgeon and Robert Taylor as flight officers." [2]

In June 1940, with script approval in hand, Ruben dispatched his production company to Naval Air Station (NAS) North Island in San Diego, where all of the aerial sequences for the film were to be shot. Awaiting them were the eighteen planes and pilots of VF-6, "Fighting Squadron Six," which had been selected by the Navy Department to participate in the film. At the time, the squadron was flying the single-place Grumman F3F-2. Known for its ease of handling and rugged construction, these diminutive fighter bombers were among the last bi-planes to operate with the U.S. fleet.

For two solid weeks, director Frank Borzage and his crew tracked "Fighting Six" with its cameras. NAS North Island would act as the main site for all of the mass take-offs and landings in the film as well as the departure point for the large aerial formations shot over Coronado Island. Paul Mantz, in one of the busiest periods of his career, handled all of the air-to-air photography from three of his specially equipped camera ships: a Boeing Model 100, Lockheed Orion, and Lockheed Vega. Fellow stunt pilot Frank Clarke and noted aviatrix Laura Ingalls assisted him in these chores.

Arrangements had also been made for MGM's crew to film scenes aboard the USS *Enterprise* (CV-6) during Naval maneuvers off the coast of California. While at sea, script requirements called for VF-6 to launch their aircraft with an F3F missing in one of the squadron's three element sec-

The "Hell Cats" give Robert Taylor the cold shoulder for knocking them out of the gunnery meet.

Sheppard Strudwick explains his blind-landing device idea to sister, Ruth Hussey.

The USS Enterprise in Hawaiian waters, circa 1940. F3F's (VF-6), SBC's (VS-6), BT-1's (VB-6) and TBD's (VT-6) line her flight deck. Metro's second unit accompanied VF-6 during fleet maneuvers in the summer of 1940.

tions (a normal squadron consisted of six sections of three aircraft each). Once the air-to-air footage had been shot and returned to the studio, for use in rear projection filming, the missing aircraft would be filled in by an actor flying a wooden soundstage mockup.

Given the highly unstable world situation, the summer of 1940 proved to be quite a busy time for the U.S. Navy. In the midst of filming *Flight Command*, VF-6 was unexpectedly ordered to Pearl Harbor, Hawaii, on emergency fleet maneuvers. Arrangements were hastily made for an MGM camera crew to accompany the squadron aboard the USS *Enterprise*. Second unit director Richard Rosson and his cameramen filmed "Fighting Six" for over six weeks, capturing a great deal of dramatic footage aboard ship and during maneuvers over the Honolulu area. The Navy even supplied a number of aircraft for use as camera ships during this period.

With VF-6 in Hawaii, Marine Fighter Squadron VMF-2 was called in to complete what remained of the NAS North Island sequences. Studio artists temporarily repainted (in watercolor) the squadron's entire complement of Grumman F3F's with Navy markings (a true sacrifice for any red-blooded Marine). Marine Flying Officer, Lt. (j.g.) Winton H. Miller of Spokane, Washington, flew with the squadron during this time and later recalled some of his movie-making experiences:

"I vividly remember a couple of eighteen-plane formation landings that we made on the then small round mat at NAS North Island. As a junior second 'looie', I was one of the 'tail end Charlies' stacked up in the rear of the formation. Coming up the Silver Strand for the formation approach to North Island, we had to take our left hand off the throttle to take the stick, and with our right hand we lowered the landing gear by means of a manual crank that took 33-1/3 turns. Once into that little operation one had to complete it with only the left hand for [both] the throttle and stick. If the cranking were stopped halfway, gravity would take over and the handle would go wild – the close formation must have looked a little wobbly at that point!

"You've got me wrong, Commander – I'm resigning-not quitting," Taylor tells Walter Pidgeon, when the latter excuses him from an air rescue mission the squadron has been called out on.

The F3F's of VF-6 form an echelon of echelons in one of many dramatic scenes shot on location in Hawaii.

Robert Taylor alights from his fighter plane to pick up his injured Commanding Officer. This particular F3F belonged to VMF-2 and was loaned to MGM for use in interior scenes shot at the studio.

Robert Taylor wonders how he will get his injured C.O. back to base safely.

As we approached the base for landing I could see red lights flashing on and off in the cockpits ahead and below me as section and division leaders tried to hold their positions. Now, those red lights went on only when throttles were fully retarded, so you can see our airspeed was dangerously low. Needless to say, that put us in the 'rear ranks' in the delicate position of either overrunning our section leaders or almost stalling out. It was a hairy situation, but we got away with it, and thank goodness we only had to do one retake."[3]

The filming of scenes at NAS North Island were completed by September of 1940. The plan now was to skillfully integrate the many authentic location scenes with those shot at the MGM studios in Culver City, California. The final result was truly impressive. *Flight Command* opened on January 16, 1941, at the Capitol Theater in New York City. It received excellent reviews, and was later nominated for an Academy Award for Best Special Effects (A. Arnold Gillespie and Douglas A. Shearer).

Making the ultimate sacrifice, for any true Marine, the men of VMF-2, commanded by Major Vernon McGee (far right), allowed studio artists to repaint their F3F's in Navy markings for "Flight Command" (note the "Hell Cat" insignia on the aircraft's fuselage). The pilot on the far left is young Lt. Greg "Pappy" Boyington, later to become the Marine's top-scoring ace of World War II.

HOLLYWOOD REPORTER

"Flight Command" smacks of importance from the first scene to the last. It's important because it's educational – pulling back the curtain on a most vital branch of our fighting forces, naval aeronautics. It's important as every foot of it seems real, with never a scene out of gear, so far as audience intelligence is concerned. It's important because of its most effective production, its great direction and the work of its players . . . 'Flight Command' is a triumph for Jack Ruben, its producer; Frank Borzage, its director; Wells Root and Harvey Haislip for the screenplay; Hal Rosson for its photography, and the entire cast, from Robert Taylor on down to Marsha Hunt. It's also a great credit to the U.S. Navy for the co-operation that was so important to the picture's production . . ."

January 17, 1941

Nat Pendleton operates the radio beam landing device as Red Skelton (holding microphone) and the rest of the "Hell Cats" anxiously await their crewmate's arrival at the fog-enshrouded base.

I WANTED WINGS

Paramount

— 1941 —

CAST

Jeff Young: RAY MILLAND; Al Ludlow: WILLIAM HOLDEN; Tom Cassidy: WAYNE MORRIS; Captain Mercer: BRIAN DONLEVY; Carolyn Bartlett: CONSTANCE MOORE; Sally Vaughn: VERONICA LAKE; "Sandbags" Riley: HARRY DAVENPORT; Jimmy Masters: PHIL BROWN; President of the Court: EDWARD FIELDING; Judge Advocate: WILLARD ROBERTSON; Flight Commander: RICHARD LANE; Flight Surgeon: ADDISON RICHARDS; Mickey: HOBART CAVANAUGH; Lt. Hopkins: DOUGLAS AYLESWORTH; Lt. Ronson: JOHN TRENT; Lt. Clankton: ARCHIE TWITCHELL; Cadet Captain: RICHARD WEBB; Radio Announcer: JOHN HIESTAND

CREDITS

Director: MITCHELL LEISEN; Producer: ARTHUR HORNBLOW, JR., Screenplay: RICHARD MAIBAUM, LT. BEIRNE LAY, JR., SIG HERZIG; Original Story: LT. BEIRNE LAY, JR.; Cinematographer: LEO TOVER; Aerial Cinematographer: ELMER DYER; Air Operations: PAUL MANTZ, MAX CONANT, EARL GORDON; Art Direction: HANS DRIER, ROBERT USHER; Special Effects: FARCIOT EDOUART, GORDON JENNINGS; Film Editor: HUGH BENNETT; Musical Score: VICTOR YOUNG; Sound Technician: GENE MERRITT, RICHARD OLSEN

By the Fall of 1940, direct American involvement in the war was judged to be only a matter of time. As part of the national defense effort, President Roosevelt announced the first peace-time draft in U.S. history. The Selective Service Act of 1940 initially called for 800,000 draft-eligible males to be inducted into the armed forces of the United States. Hoping to stimulate the national recruitment effort, Paramount Studios decided to rush its aerial epic *I Wanted Wings* into full production.

Made with the generous cooperation of the Department of War, this cinematic salute to the U.S. Army Air Corps (AAC) examined the flight training given to thousands of young American AAC cadets. The film opens with the following dedication:

"Today, America, the birthplace of man's wings, watches her skies with grave concern. For in these skies of peace, the nation is building the upper battlements of its defense. To the officers and men of the United States Army Air Corps who climb on strong wings to man these high ramparts, and to the young men of America, who will take their places beside them, this motion picture is gratefully dedicated."

The story, developed from Beirne Lay's best-selling novel, follows three young cadets – wealthy socialite Jeff Young (Ray Milland), garage mechanic Al Ludlow (William Holden), and college athlete Tom Cassidy (Wayne Morris) – through the rigors of flight training at the Army Air Corps' school at Randolph and Kelly Fields. The destiny of each is traced through the film as they battle to win their wings under the watchful eyes of their veteran flight instructor Captain Mercer (Brian Donlevy). Veronica Lake (in her screen debut) and Constance Moore provided the love interest between classes.

William Holden walks in on a "surprise," as his fellow flying cadets look on.

Paramount received a great deal of co-operation from the Army Air Corps in making "I Wanted Wings." Here a BT-9 trainer cruises above Randolph Field, "The West Point of the Air," where most of the film was shot.

Mitchell Leisen (on ladder) directs a scene being shot on location at Randolph Field, Texas.

I Wanted Wings ranks as one of the finest aviation films of the pre-war era. Although marred by the improbable romantic sub-plot involving Ray Milland, Veronica Lake, and William Holden, the film's flight training sequences were stunningly effective and no doubt responsible for more than just a few enlistments in the Army Air Corps.

Production of the film began in September of 1940. The authenticity of the picture was greatly enhanced by producer Arthur Hornblow's decision to film most of it on location, with a minimum of soundstage work. In retrospect, his choice of Mitchell Leisen (known for his expertise in light comedies) as director seemed an unusual one. In his biography Leisen later commented on the assignment:

"I never would have picked that one [*I Wanted Wings*] myself, but Ted Reed who was doing it, wasn't making it spectacular enough to suit the front office. They had sent the company all the way to Randolph Field in Texas and they said, 'We could get that much production right here on the backlot.' I knew all about aviation [Leisen was a licensed civilian pilot] so I was called in and told to leave immedi-

Stunt pilot, Paul Mantz, maps out a scene for Captain Tom Dubois and cinematographer Elmer Dyer, as a group of Army Air Corps cadets watch intently.

ately for Randolph Field. That was that. I left within the hour for San Antonio and was on the set the next morning [September 7, 1940] at 11:00 a.m."[4]

Paramount's production company of 130 actors and technicians spent nearly three months in Texas. At Randolph Field (the Army's primary training school near San Antonio), the filming of the picture progressed with the training of students from AAC Flying Class 40D. Over 200 student pilots appeared in scenes shot on the ground or in the air, flying their North American BT-9 and BT-14 basic trainers.

Stunt flier Paul Mantz coordinated all of the production's aerial sequences while on location. Max Conant and Earl Gordon assisted him in piloting the trio of camera ships, which consisted of a Lockheed Vega, a Boeing Model 100, and a Lockheed Orion.

Most of the air-to-air formation footage was shot from the low-winged Orion, which Mantz regarded as one of his best camera ships. Formerly owned by Jimmy Doolittle, the aircraft was equipped with a heated cabin (sheer luxury for pilots and cameramen accustomed to drafty bi-planes)

Chief cinematographer, Leo Tover, captures the action as an Army BT-14 roars by a camera platform erected at Randolph Field.

Paul Mantz closes in on a group of AT-6's high above Kelly Field. His camera ship is a Lockheed Orion, formerly owned by Jimmy Doolittle. The aircraft was a cameraman's delight, equipped with six different camera mounts from which to shoot.

Paramount arranged to use a certain amount of footage from a 1940 AAC recruiting film entitled "Flying Cadets" in "I Wanted Wings." Scenes depicting cadet life at Randolph: taking physicals, marching, eating in the mess hall, etc., were borrowed from the latter.

Ray Milland and Wayne Morris watch as William Holden attempts his first solo flight. Paramount's production crew of 130 actors and technicians spent nearly three months in Texas filming "I Wanted Wings."

and six different camera positions: two door mounts, one emergency exit mount, one landing gear mount, one rear window mount, and one Torrell mount.

While in the air, Mantz and aerial cinematographer Elmer Dyer usually received their directions via a three-way radio communication established between the Orion camera plane, the lead aircraft in the formation that was being filmed and second unit director Hal Rosson on the ground. In this manner, an entire squadron of aircraft could be directed as easily as a group of extras.

From Randolph, the company moved to the advanced training school at Kelly Field (the site of the first major Hollywood aviation epic *Wings*) where 450 cadets, awaiting their commissions, made their Hollywood debut. Among the many scenes filmed at the base, was a mass graduation flyover involving over 500 AT-6 advanced training planes. While at Kelly, the three male stars of the film (Milland, Holden, and Morris) were taken up for a few hours of dual flight instruction to aid their credibility in the close-up scenes that would later be shot at the studio. In all, nearly 1000 AAC aircraft were made available to Leisen and his crew during their stay in Texas.

The remaining scenes in the picture were completed at the Paramount Studios in Hollywood and at March Army Air Field near Riverside, California, where a squadron of B-17B's from the 19th Bomb Group were used in the final segments of the film. Production of the picture officially ended in December of 1940.

I Wanted Wings had its world premier in San Antonio, Texas, on March 22, 1941. Critics praised the picture for its exciting aerial sequences, exceptional special effects, and the forthright performances of its three male stars. It won the 1941 Academy Award for Best Special Effects (Farciot Edouart, Gordon Jennings, and Louis Mesenkop) and became Paramount's top-grossing film of the year.

NEW YORK TIMES

"Any way you look at it, Paramount's 'I Wanted Wings,' which power-dived into the Astor Theatre last evening, amid a smother of boiled shirts and gold braid, is certain to hit the mark . . . in spite of a thread of Class-B story which gets snarled in its whirling propellers before the end, this cinematic salute to the Army Air Corps and to the young men who are entering it today, is a vastly exciting motion picture and a dependable inspiration to the youth of the land . . ."

Bosley Crowther
March 27, 1941

Ray Milland and William Holden prepare their B-17 for a night mission over Los Angeles. Paramount's Prop Department spent over $40,000.00 building this full-sized mock-up for use in interior scenes.

One of March Field's B-17B's (19th Bomb Group) forms-up for the final scene in the film.

DIVE BOMBER

Warner Brothers

— 1941 —

CAST

Doug Lee: ERROL FLYNN; Joe Blake: FRED MAC MURRAY; Dr. Lance Rogers: RALPH BELLAMY; Linda Fisher: ALEXIS SMITH; Art Lyons: ROBERT ARMSTRONG; Tim Griffin: REGIS TOOMEY; Lucky James: ALLEN JENKINS; John Anthony: CRAIG STEVENS; Chubby: HERBERT ANDERSON; Senior Surgeon: MORONI OLSEN; Mrs. James: DENNIE MOORE; Swede Larson: LOUIS JEAN HEYDT; Corps Man: CLIFF NAZARRO

CREDITS

Director: MICHAEL CURTIZ; Producer: ROBERT LORD; Screenplay: FRANK WEAD, ROBERT BUCKNER; Original Story: FRANK WEAD; Cinematographers: BERT GLENNON, WINTON C. HOCH; Aerial Cinematographers: ELMER DYER, CHARLES A. MARSHALL; Air Operations: PAUL MANTZ, FRANK CLARKE, DICK ACKLAND, TONY LE VIER, HOWARD BATT, TEX RANKIN; Art Direction: ROBERT M. HAAS; Set Decoration: FRED MC LANE; Special Effects: BYRON HASKINS, REX WIMPY; Film Editor: GEORGE AMY; Musical Score: MAX STEINER; Sound Technician: FRANCIS J. SCHEID; Wardrobe: DANNY BROWNE

By 1941, a major change was taking place in America's attitude toward the war that was raging in Europe. The country was mobilizing its defenses, and a major rearmament program was underway. Motion pictures were becoming aggressively more patriotic, and Warner Brothers seemed to be leading the way. *Dive Bomber* was Warner's tribute to the Navy's flight surgeons and the work they were doing to keep America's pilots in the air. It was the first film of its kind shot entirely in Technicolor, and its breath-taking aerial sequences, with massed formations of brilliantly colored pre-war airplanes, were indeed classics from the Golden Age of Naval Aviation.

The screenplay, adapted from an original story by USN Commander Frank Wead (Retired), dealt with the medical problems confronting the Navy's dive bomber pilots. One very real problem for aircrews at that time was blackout during high "G" maneuvers. In the absence of pressurized flight suits, pilots were forced to compensate for the phenomenon as best they could.

Following graduation from the U.S. Naval Flight Surgeon School in San Diego, Lt. Doug Lee (Errol Flynn) is assigned to Chief Flight Surgeon Dr. Lance Rogers (Ralph Bellamy), and both men devote their energies to finding solutions to the menace of blackout, pilot fatigue, and aero embolism. Flight Commander Joe Blake (Fred Mac Murray) is skeptical of the doctors' work, and his dislike of the cocky Lt. Lee, blinds him to the importance of Lee's research. Only after one of Blake's close personal friends is killed, due to pilot fatigue, does he agree to help on the project. His cooperation proves invaluable, as research experiments take Lee and Blake from the laboratory to the sky. Ultimately, Blake is killed testing a new pressurized flying suit, but the notes from his final flight enable Lee to perfect the suit's design, thereby making it practical for use by other dive bomber pilots.

Although the script rambles at times, *Dive Bomber's* documentary-like examination of the techniques being

N3N's from the Naval Air Reserve Base in Long Beach enroute to San Diego for the flight training sequences in "Dive Bomber."

High altitude sickness grips one of the carrier pilots in this scene shot aboard the USS Enterprise. The aircraft in the background is one of VB-3's SB2U Vindicators.

Flight surgeons, Errol Flynn and Ralph Bellamy, are questioned by a skeptical Fred MacMurray.

Torpedo Squadron Three (VT-3) participated in many of the scenes in "Dive Bomber." Here camera crews record the action at NAS North Island. Note the mixture of war- and peace-time color schemes on the squadron's TBD dive bombers.

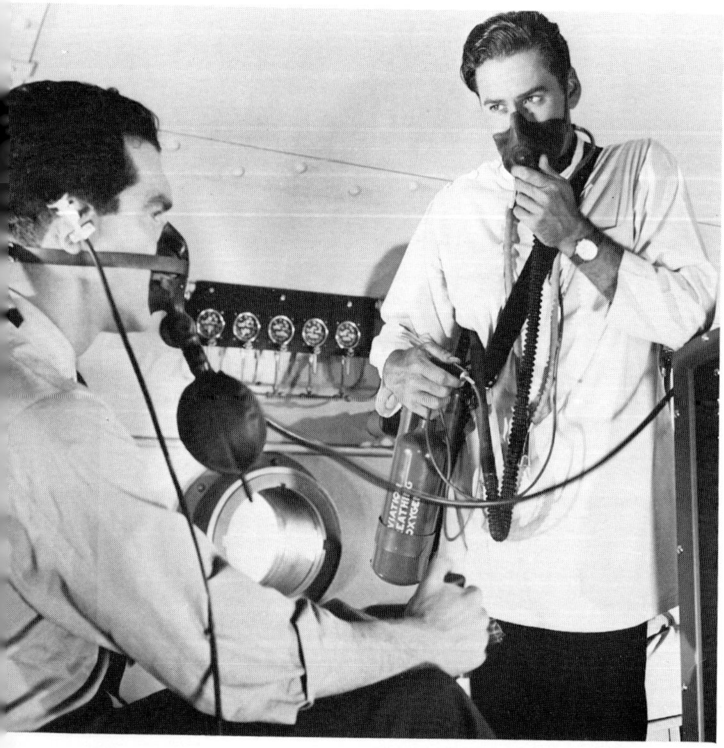

Flynn checks MacMurray's reflexes during tests in a high altitude pressure chamber.

developed to overcome the hazards of high altitude flight is engrossing and was, up till that time a subject untouched by Hollywood's scenarists.

Pre-production planning for the film began in January 1941. *Dive Bomber* was given a then-lavish budget of $1.7 million dollars by the normally cost-conscious Warner executives. The Department of the Navy was also impressed with the film's potential and agreed to lend its full support to the project.

Direction of the film was placed in the competent hands of Michael Curtiz, with Fred Mac Murray and Errol Flynn scheduled to star. This was Flynn's twelfth film with Curtiz, an association which had produced such classics as *Charge of the Light Brigade, The Adventures of Robin Hood,* and *Captain Blood.* The Hungarian-born Curtiz was known as a hard-working perfectionist. His arrogant and sometimes ruthless approach to work – demanding thrills with little regard for the safety of the actors – had caused an ever-widening rift to develop between him and Flynn. By the time *Dive Bomber* went before the cameras, the feud was causing delays in production and resulted in this being their last picture together.

Filming officially commenced on March 20, 1941. Producer Robert Lord had secured the use of Naval Air Station (NAS) North Island in San Diego, California, to photograph the exteriors, and for the next two months the production crew of 150 actors and technicians toiled on a six-day work

The SB2U's of Bombing Squadron Three (VB-3) pose for the cameras in one of many excellently staged aerial scenes in the film.

week to complete their scenes on time.

Although the Navy had agreed to cooperate in the production of the film (over 1000 officers and enlisted men appear in the picture), Warner's production crew had to take care not to interfere with normal flight operations at the base. In light of world events, all Naval air and sea forces had been placed on a full war-readiness alert. Director Curtiz was thus notified, in advance, whenever any of the various squadrons were to take-off on daily maneuvers, so that his camera crews could be prepared to record the action.

Over a dozen Navy and Marine squadrons participated in the film during Curtiz's eight week stay at NAS North Island. This included the "Weekend Warriors" from the Naval Reserve Air Base at Long Beach, who flew their entire complement of N3N trainers to San Diego for the opening scenes in the picture. Most of the specific flying duties for the film (dive bombing and mass formation flights) were performed by the pilots of Bombing Squadron Three (VB-3), and Torpedo Squadron Three (VT-3), flying their Vought SB2U and Douglas TBD dive bombers. In addition to those scenes shot at the base, Curtiz and his company spent a week on board the USS *Enterprise* (CV-6) filming carrier operations off the coast of California.

Interestingly enough, in early 1941, in preparation for possible hostilities, the Navy ordered all of its ship-based

Director Michael Curtiz calls for action while on location at NAS North Island, April 1941.

Fred MacMurray prepares to test a new pressurized flying suit. His aircraft is a Grumman F3F from "Fighting Six" (VF-6).

Errol Flynn, Fred MacMurray, and Regis Toomey pose with some of the Navy and Marine officers that flew in the film.

aircraft painted a non-specular gray. Since *Dive Bomber* was to be filmed in Technicolor, arrangements had to be made to allow a number of the squadron's aircraft to retain their colorful peacetime markings. Therefore, an interesting mixture of war- and peace-time color schemes appear in the final cut of the film.

A great deal of the credit for the picture's excellently staged aerial sequences must go to Warner's chief pilot Paul Mantz and aerial cinematographers Elmer Dyer, Charles A. Marshall, and Winton Hoch. Since the Navy did not indulge in retakes, each scene had to be carefully choreographed and then shot from two of Mantz's camera ships. The resulting Technicolor footage was hauntingly beautiful and surpassed anything seen in an aviation epic up to that time.

Filming of the picture was completed at the Warner Brothers Studios on June 3, 1941. Two months of additional work were needed to edit the North Island sequences and integrate them with those shot on the sound stages. A stirring Max Steiner score, first used in *Submarine D-1,* accompanied the final cut of the film. *Dive Bomber* premiered in San Diego on August 12, 1941. Despite its lengthy running time of two hours and thirteen minutes, reviews of the film were excellent. Bert Glennon later received an Academy Award nomination for his color cinematography.

NEW YORK TIMES

"It is altogether fitting – and highly commendable, too – that the studio which gave us 'The Story of Louis Pasteur' and 'Dr. Ehrlich's Magic Bullet' should turn attention at this time to an experimental branch of medicine which is making remarkable strides and which is of tremendous importance to our preparations for defense. And this the Warners are doing in 'Dive Bomber' . . . not only do the modern experiments in aviation medicine, elaborately detailed herein, have unique and fascinating pictorial interest, but the Warners have photographed this picture in some of the most magnificant technicolor yet seen. And, naturally, they have not forgotten to turn the cameras often upon masses of brilliantly colored planes, ranked in impressive rows about an air base or upon the huge flight decks of carriers, and roaring in silver majesty, wing to wing, through the limitless West Coast skies . . ."

Bosley Crowther
August 30, 1941

MacMurray is carried from the wreckage of his F3F fighter in this scene shot at Pt. Loma near San Diego, California.

(Above) Warner Brother's crew prepares to shoot the final scene in the film. The aircraft in the foreground is a Northrop BT-1 from VB-5, wearing a bogus "High Hat" squadron insignia from VF-1. In the background are some of the many aircraft that participated in the production of the film: BT-1's from Bombing Squadron Six (VB-6) and SB2U's from Bombing Squadron Three (VB-3). (Below) The finished scene as it appeared in the film.

A YANK IN THE R.A.F.

Twentieth Century-Fox

— 1941 —

CAST

Tim Baker: TYRONE POWER; Carol Brown: BETTY GRABLE; Wing Commander Morley: JOHN SUTTON; Roger Pillby: REGINALD GARDINER; Cpl. Harry Baker: DONALD STUART; Thorndyke: RICHARD FRASER; Flight Lt. Redmond: DENNIS GREEN; Flight Lt. Richardson: BRUCE LESTER; Wales: GILCHRIST STUART; Group Captain: LESTER MATTHEWS; Canadian Major: FREDERICK WORLOCK; Al: RALPH BYRD; Mrs. Fitzhugh: ETHEL GRIFFIES; Head Waiter: FORTUNIO BONANOVA; Instructor: JAMES CRAVEN

CREDITS

Director: HENRY KING; Producer: DARRYL F. ZANUCK; Screenplay: DARRELL WARE, KARL TUNBERG; Original Story: DARRYL F. ZANUCK; Cinematographer: LEON SHAMROY; Air Operations: PAUL MANTZ, JERRY PHILLIPS, FRANK CLARKE; Art Direction: RICHARD DAY, JAMES BASEVI; Set Decoration: THOMAS LITTLE; Special Effects: FRED SERSEN; Film Editor: BARBARA MC LEAN; Musical Score: LEO ROBIN, RALPH RAINGER; Sound Technician: BERNARD FREERICKS, ROGER HEMAN; Wardrobe: TRAVIS BANTON

By the summer of 1941, little stood between Germany and the United States except an ocean and the tiny isle of Great Britain. Hitler had vowed to bring the British to their knees, and as part of his plan, the German Navy was now waging indiscriminant submarine warfare in the Atlantic. Any day could bring an incident that would draw the U.S. into the war. Accordingly, the tone of American films began to reflect Hollywood's desire for intervention. Twentieth Century-Fox's *A Yank in the RAF* became the first of many pro-British films that admonished the public to: "defend America by aiding the Allies."

The story (which was originally called "The Eagle Squadron") concerns the exploits of a young American flier who volunteers for duty with the Royal Air Force

Tyrone Power reports for duty with the Royal Air Force. In real life, Power was an experienced civilian pilot and later became a USMC transport pilot during the war.

(RAF). Tyrone Power plays the role of cocky ferry pilot, Tim Baker, who flies Hudson bombers across the Atlantic strictly for the money. While in London, he meets former girlfriend Carol Brown (Betty Grable), who has been working as a volunteer in the Women's Auxiliary Corps. She convinces Tim of the justness of the Allied cause, and he decides to join in the battle by enlisting in the RAF. What follows is a detailed account of his training and eventual assignment to a combat squadron flying missions over Europe.

Although grounded by the stock romantic routine between Tyrone Power and Betty Grable, Fox's *A Yank in the RAF* proved to be of interest when it concentrated on the Royal Air Force aspects of the story – which greatly benefited from a number of excellently staged action sequences. Production of the film began in April 1941, under the personal supervision of Fox Studio chief and screenplay co-author, Darryl F. Zanuck. His choice of Henry King to direct seemed a logical one, since King's love of aviation had earned him the title of "The Flying Director." Box-office success was further ensured with the selection of Fox's top contract players, Tyrone Power and Betty Grable, to star in the film.

Realizing the impact the picture might have on the American public, the Royal Air Force agreed to supply the studio with all the aerial combat footage it needed. Additionally, a Fox camera crew was given permission to film air operations at several RAF bases for use in background scenes.

King, who normally scouted his own movie locations, flew more than 3,000 miles locating areas in Southern California to double for the white cliffs of Dover, the

Stunt pilot Jerry Phillips (in RCAF uniform), acted as a stand-in for Tyrone Power in scenes involving the ferrying of Harvard trainers to Northern Montana.

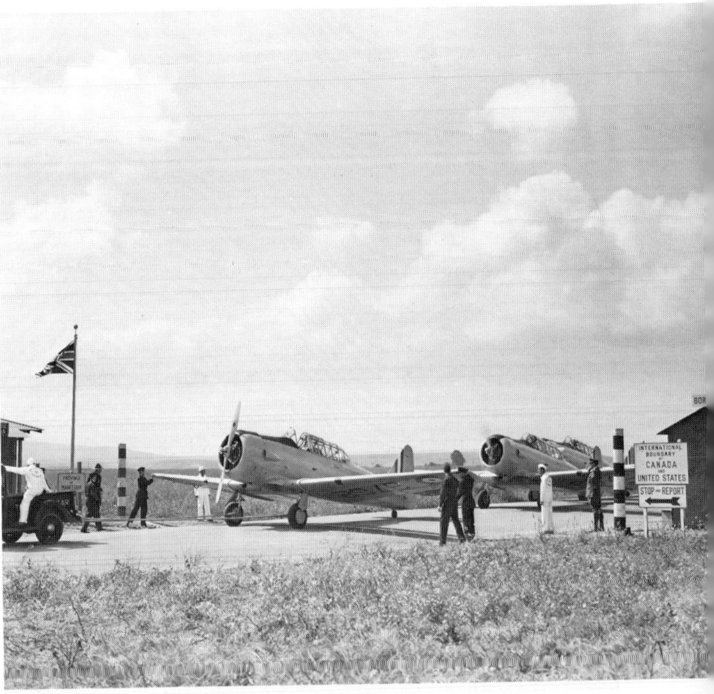

In one of many authentic scenes in the picture, Harvard trainers are towed across the Canadian border following their flight from California. Neutrality laws prevented them from being flown directly into the country.

Henry King and his crew spent a week at the Lockheed Aircraft Plant in Burbank for "A Yank in the RAF." Even Lockheed's employees got into the act by donning RAF coveralls while working on the Hudson bomber flightline.

Betty Grable supplied the romantic interest for RAF fliers John Sutton and Tyrone Power.

Tyrone Power and John Sutton walk past a line of Hudson bombers following their return from a mission.

coast of Holland, and the beaches of Dunkirk. His Waco cabin plane also served as the production's camera ship, photographing formations of Harvard trainers and Hudson bombers being ferried to bases in Canada and England for the opening sequences of the film.

Aside from the stock combat footage shot in England, all of the film's aerial battles took place inside the Fox soundstages in Hollywood. Special effects experts, Fred Serson and Lou Witte (later nominated for an Academy Award), worked closely with King in creating the desired atmosphere for these scenes. A half-dozen wood and sheet metal replicas of Spitfires, Messerschmitts, and Hudson bombers were constructed for use on the studio's backlot. These same airplanes would later appear in numerous productions throughout the war, including *Captains of the Clouds, Eagle Squadron*, and *Desperate Journey*.

The evacuation of Dunkirk, which climaxes the film, proved to be the most difficult and costly ($190,000) scene to recreate during the three months of shooting. Nearly five weeks were needed to complete the fifteen minute sequence, which was shot on the beach at Pt. Mugu, California, and in a twenty-seven acre lake on the studio's backlot. Scores of small boats were rented in Santa Monica and trucked to the studio for "atmosphere." Unlike the real evacuees of Dunkirk, things were made considerably more comfortable for the over 800 extras used in the scene, since the water in the studio's "English Channel" had been heated to a mild 70 degrees.

Bowing to pressure from the British government, Zanuck decided to change the original ending of the film,

The evacuation of Dunkirk proved to be the highlight of the film. This particular scene was shot in a twenty-seven acre lake on Fox's backlot.

which had Tyrone Power killed in a German air raid. Apparently the British were worried about giving moviegoers the impression that Americans aiding Britain might be killed. Therefore, Power was ordered back to the lot in July 1941 to shoot a revised version of the film, which allowed him to live on and win the heart of his girlfriend, Betty Grable.

This final version of the film premiered on September 25, 1941, at Grauman's Chinese Theater in Hollywood. Critical reviews of the picture were excellent and the film won an Academy Award nomination for Best Special Effects (Fred Sersen and Lou Witte).

John Sutton briefs his men on the merits of the ME-109 as Tyrone Power looks on.

NEW YORK TIMES

"Never have Darryl F. Zanuck and Twentieth Century-Fox owed so much to so few as they do for the pulsing excitement contained in their new film, 'A Yank in the RAF.' For most of the thrilling action, most of the tingling suspense, paced through this lively adventure-romance, is creditable to the lads of the Royal Air Force, who made it possible. If it weren't for the fact that those boys saved England when and as they did; if they hadn't anticipated fiction with one of the most dramatic climaxes on record, and if someone hadn't permitted Fox to photograph their planes in action for some vivid background shots, there would never have been 'A Yank in the RAF.' And we would all have missed a thoroughly enjoyable show . . ."

Bosley Crowther
September 27, 1941

A Twentieth Century-Fox camera unit spent six months in England filming the many authentic combat scenes that appeared in the picture.

INTERNATIONAL SQUADRON

Warner Brothers

— 1941 —

CAST

Jimmy Grant: RONALD REAGAN; Squadron Leader Charles Wyatt: JAMES STEPHENSON; Mary: JULIE BISHOP; Omaha McGrath: CLIFF EDWARDS; Wing Commander Severn: REGINALD DENNY; Jeanette: OLYMPE BRADNA; Lt. Roger Wilkins: WILLIAM LUNDIGAN; Bill Torrence: JOHN RIDGELY; Connie: JOAN PERRY; Saunders: SELMER JACKSON; Sir Basil Wryxton: HOLMES HERBERT; Major Fresney: CRAWFORD KENT; Biddle: CHARLES IRWIN

CREDITS

Director: LEWIS SEILER; Producer: HAL B. WALLIS; Screenplay: BARRY TRIVERS, KENNETH GAMET; Original Story: FRANK WEAD; Cinematographers: JAMES VAN TREES, TED MC CORD; Air Operations: PAUL MANTZ, JERRY PHILLIPS, HOWARD BATT; Art Direction: ESDRAS HARTLEY; Special Effects: ROBERT BURKS; Film Editor: FRANK MAGEE; Sound Technician: ROBERT B. LEE; Wardrobe: HOWARD SHOUP

Warner Brothers jumped on the pro-British bandwagon in late 1941 with its own story of an American flier who volunteers for duty with the Royal Air Force in its low-budget 1941 air epic entitled *International Squadron.*

The story, loosely based on an old Jimmy Cagney feature, *Ceiling Zero,* has brash American flier Jimmy Grant (Ronald Reagan) ferrying bombers to England. While in London, he's caught in a German air raid and witnesses the death of an innocent young girl. Vowing revenge, Grant enlists in the RAF's International Squadron, composed of volunteers from all over the world. He immediately incurs the displeasure of the entire squadron with his selfish heroics and subsequently intensifies their dislike by causing the death of two of the pilots. In an effort to square himself with his comrades, he undertakes a dangerous bombing mission to destroy an enemy munitions dump and dies a hero's death.

Although *International Squadron's* plot is a bit time-worn, director Louis Seiler kept the film's pace moving and managed to extract some effective performances from his actors. Production of the picture began in March 1941. Due to a limited budget, producer Hal Wallis decided to shoot most of the film at three airfields close to the home studios and rely on actual RAF combat footage to fleshout the action scenes.

The majority of the scenes were shot at Alhambra's Municipal Airport, which was temporarily camouflaged to look like a typical RAF air base for the duration of filming. Gathered there were six of the "latest British fighters" for use in the aerial sequences: a Boeing Model 100, the Brown B-3 Racer, a trio of Ryan STA's, and the Travel Air Mystery Ship. Studio technicians had modified and repainted each of the aircraft to blend in with the combat footage supplied by the British Ministry of Defense. The remaining sequences were staged at Van Nuys' Metropolitan Airport, Lockheed's Hudson bomber facility, and the Warner Brothers Studios in Burbank.

When completed in May 1941, this "bread and butter" air epic so closely resembled Twentieth Century-Fox's *A Yank in the RAF* that Fox studio chief Darryl F. Zanuck threatened to sue Warner's if their film was released before his own. Consequently, the premier of *International Squadron* was delayed six months until October 1941.

The death of an innocent young girl in a London blitz inspires Ronald Reagan to volunteer for duty with the Royal Air Force.

Ronald Reagan is welcomed to England by RAF officers Reginald Denny and James Stephenson. The scene was shot at the Lockheed Aircraft Plant, which proved to be a favorite location site of Warner's, since it was just a few blocks from the studio.

NEW YORK TIMES

"For all its flaming crashes and for all its shots of helpless planes spinning clumsily earthward, credit 'International Squadron' with a neat three point landing at high speed. As another aerial and romantic dogfight in the hurtling succession of epics about the Royal Air Force, it breezes along with dash and bravado and not too much self-importance. Its emotional upheavals are tossed off with a wisecrack; it doesn't belabor its story with inspirational organ music and it keeps its wheels well off the ground . . . "

Theodore Strauss
November 14, 1941

Reagan returns to base following his first mission over Europe. In the background is the Brown B-3 racer dressed in RAF markings.

Reagan's squadron prepares for takeoff in this scene shot at Alhambra Airport. Modified as British fighters are (L to R) the Brown B-3 racer, two Ryan STA sport planes, and the Travel Air Mystery Ship. Note that wheel wells have been painted on the bottom of the wings.

KEEP 'EM FLYING

Universal

— 1941 —

CAST

Blackie Benson: BUD ABBOTT; Heathcliff: LOU COSTELLO; Gloria: MARTHA RAYE; Barbara: MARTHA RAYE; Linda Joyce: CAROL BRUCE; Jinx Roberts: DICK FORAN; Craig Morrison: WILLIAM GARGAN; Jimmy Johnson: CHARLES LANG, Butch: TRUMAN BRADLEY; Gonigle: WILLIAM DAVIDSON; Major Barstow: LORING SMITH

CREDITS

Director: ARTHUR LUBIN; Producer: GLENN TRYON; Screenplay: TRUE BOARDMAN, NAT PERRIN, JOHN GRANT; Original Story: EDMUND L. HARTMANN; Cinematographer: JOSEPH VALENTINE; Aerial Cinematographer: ELMER DYER; Air Operations: PAUL MANTZ; Art Direction: JACK OTTERSON; Set Decoration: R.A. GAUSMAN; Special Effects: JOHN FULTON; Film Editor: PHILLIP CAHN, ARTHUR HILTON; Musical Score: FRANK SKINNER; Sound Technician: BERNARD B. BROWN; Wardrobe: VERA WEST

In an effort to make the draft more palatable to thousands of new inductees and their families, Hollywood began filling the silver screen with service comedies of every description. These films proved to be a perfect vehicle for the particular kind of humor of the new comedy team of Bud Abbott and Lou Costello. In 1941 alone they had taken on the Army in *Buck Privates,* the Navy in *In the Navy,* and finally the U.S. Army Air Corps in a Universal release entitled *Keep 'Em Flying.*

The story, which is incidental, revolves around former circus stunt pilot Jinx Roberts (Dick Foran), who decides to do his part for the country and joins the Army Air Corps. His pals, Blackie and Heathcliff (Abbott and Costello), follow suit, hoping for jobs as ground crew mechanics. All three report for duty at the Cal-Aero Academy, a government flying school, and immediately get into trouble for stunt flying over the field. Knowing that he can out-fly most of his instructors, Jinx breaks every regulation in the book and eventually is "washed out." Before he leaves the field though, he effects the daring rescue of his instructor and wins a reprieve from the school's commandant. Amidst all of this, Blackie and Heathcliff have wrecked as much havoc on the base as is humanly possible, but are kept on "for the good of the service"!

Aside from all the comedy, *Keep 'Em Flying* features a good deal of excellent flying by veteran stunt pilot Paul Mantz (in his Stearman C-3R and Boeing Model 100) and the 500 officers and cadets of the Cal-Aero Academy in Chino, California. Universal's crew spent three weeks on location at the school, which was the first of its kind to be established for the civilian training of Army Air Corps (AAC) cadets. The AAC supplied the studio with nearly 200 PT-13 and BT-13 training planes for use in the aerial sequences and even school commandant, Major Robert Lee Scott, got into the act by assisting Mantz in a number of

Bud and Lou bid farewell to Dick Foran and Charles Lang who are quitting the Air Corps for good. Their aircraft is Paul Mantz's Stearman C-3R.

A shaken Charles Lang climbs out of his Stearman biplane following a crash landing.

The cadets and BT-13's of the Cal-Aero Academy line up for the film's finale. Cal-Aero was the first school of its kind for the civilian training of military pilots and served as an architectural model for others built during the war.

stunts for the film. Scott later gained fame with Chennault's Flying Tigers and authored the best-selling *God is My Co-Pilot.*

Keep 'Em Flying opened in November of 1941 to packed houses and received enthusiastic response from audiences and critics alike.

NEW YORK TIMES

"The Messrs. Bud Abbott and Lou Costello and Messrs. is the word for them, all right – have summed up our major armed services so effectively but cheerfully of late that a little additional damage to the Air Corps can't do any harm. And confusion is what they are creating, wildly and without the slightest sense, upon a comfortingly fictitious training air field in 'Keep 'Em Flying.' So chalk up another mad antic for these two harum-scarum clowns, and give Universal credit for the third of its series of rowdy service films . . . "

Bosley Crowther
November 27, 1941

Dick Foran effects the daring rescue of instructor William Gargan in the last scene of the film. Carol Bruce greets them upon landing.

CAPTAINS OF THE CLOUDS

Warner Brothers

— 1941 —

CAST

Brian Mac Lean: JAMES CAGNEY; Johnny Dutton: DENNIS MORGAN; Emily Foster: BRENDA MARSHALL; Tiny Murphy: ALAN HALE; Blimp LeBec: GEORGE TOBIAS; Scrounger Harris: REGINALD GARDINER; Commanding Officer: REGINALD DENNY; Prentiss: RUSSELL ARMS; Group Captain: PAUL CAVANAUGH; Store-Teeth Morrison: CLEM BEVANE; Foster: J.M. KERRIGAN; Dr. Neville: J. FARRELL MAC DONALD; Fyffe: PATRICK O'MOORE; Carmichael: MORTON LOWRY; Chief Flying Instructor: OWEN CATHCART-JONES; President of Court Martial: FREDERIC WORLOCK; Popcorn Kearns: BENNY BAKER; Nolan: CHARLES HALTON; Provost Marshal: LOUIS JEAN HEYDT

CREDITS

Director: MICHAEL CURTIZ; Producer: HAL B. WALLIS, Screenplay: ARTHUR T. HORMAN, RICHARD MACAULAY, NORMAN REILLY RAINE; Original Story: ARTHUR T. HORMAN, ROLAND GILLETT; Cinematographers: SOL POLITO, WILFRED M. CLINE; Aerial Cinematographers: ELMER DYER, CHARLES MARSHALL, WINTON C. HOCH; Air Operations: FRANK CLARKE, HOWARD BATT, GARLAND LINCOLN, JERRY PHILLIPS, HERB WHITE, PAUL MANTZ; Art Direction: TED SMITH; Special Effects: BYRON HASKIN, REX WIMPY; Film Editor: GEORGE AMY; Musical Score: MAX STEINER; Sound Technician: C.A. RIGGS; Wardrobe: HOWARD SHOUP

Captains of the Clouds, Warner Brothers' Technicolor salute to the men of the Royal Canadian Air Force (RCAF), was yet another contribution to the then current cycle of motion pictures glorifying the Allied cause.

The story centers on the exploits of a group of North Woods bush pilots, who, upon hearing an inspirational speech by Prime Minister Winston Churchill, decide to volunteer for duty with the RCAF. One of the pilots, Brian Mac Lean (James Cagney) is somewhat chagrined to learn he's too old for combat and is given the task of training fledgling pilots for duty overseas. Used to flying by the seat of his pants, his complete disregard for rules and regulations nearly causes the death of one of his students and results in his dismissal from the service. Still anxious to get overseas, he bluffs his way into a ferry squadron flying Hudson bombers to England. During the trans-Atlantic flight, the unarmed squadron is intercepted by a Messerschmitt fighter plane. In one final act of courage, Mac Lean rams the attacker with his aircraft and sacrifices his life so that the others can get through to England safely.

Although the first half of *Captains of the Clouds* is rather routine, it prepares the viewer for the film's semi-documentary account of Canada's role in the Commonwealth Air Training Program. The scenes depicting the training of RCAF flying cadets for combat overseas are visually very impressive and are marked by the authenticity and beauty of their locale.

From the outset of the project, Warner's executives had decided to shoot most of the film on location in Canada. Producer Hal B. Wallis worked for several months with Canadian Department of National Defense officials, selecting suitable sites for shooting the picture. Agreement was finally reached to film the bush-flying scenes in North Bay, Ontario, and the military sequences at the RCAF's Uplands, Trenton, Dartmouth, and Mountain View Air Stations.

Production officially began on July 16, 1941, under the direction of Michael Curtiz (fresh from his assignment on *Dive Bomber*). The cast and crew, approximately 200 people in all, spent three long months on location, shooting the film in rough weather and under the strictest of wartime conditions.

Brenda Marshall provided the romantic interest for bush pilots James Cagney and Dennis Morgan.

Alan Hale, George Tobias, and James Cagney report for duty with the Royal Canadian Air Force.

Studio agents rounded up five seaplanes and five identical landplanes in Canada for use in the film's bush flying sequences. Here, a Norseman seaplane takes off from a lake in Northern Ontario.

Dennis Morgan and Jimmy Cagney pause for a moment with Warner's stunt pilots, at the Woodcliffe Camp in North Bay, Ontario. First row: (L to R) Garland Lincoln, Dennis Morgan, Jimmy Cagney, Frank Clarke. Second row: Howard Batt (in white shirt). Third row: Jim Barton (in coveralls) and Herb White (far right). The rest are Canadian pilots hired to fly some of the bush planes.

Among the first scenes to be filmed in Canada was the "Presentation of Wings Ceremony", shot at the No. 2 Service Flying Training School in Uplands, Ontario. World War I flying ace, Air Marshall W.A. "Billy" Bishop, presided over the ceremonies as 110 actual RCAF cadets (including many American volunteers) received their wings as commissioned flying officers. A mass fly-over of nearly 100 bright yellow Harvard training planes ended the proceedings as four cinematographers recorded the action from the air and ground.

The bush-flying sequences, which comprise roughly the first half of the picture, were all filmed at the Woodcliff Camp in North Bay, Ontario. Warners' advance agents had leased five seaplanes and five identical land planes for use in these scenes and had them repainted in bright colors for the benefit of the Technicolor cameras.

Elmer Dyer was in charge of aerial cinematography for the film and later described some of his bush-flying experiences in a 1942 issue of *American Cinematographer*:

". . . Getting these scenes, with a group of picture-trained Hollywood pilots flying seaplanes (some of them

All of the aerial footage in the film was shot from Paul Mantz's Stinson Model "A" camera ship. It carried the main Technicolor camera complete with its 600 pounds of support equipment.

for the first time) while we photographed them from a land plane, was quite a thrill in itself. We had plenty of spectacular "chase" action which called for hedge-hopping over the forest's tree tops, and skimming close above the surface of the lakes with which Canada is dotted. That was all right for stunt pilots flying solo in float-equipped seaplanes, which could land safely on the lake in case of trouble, but following them in a land plane was another story. There were plenty of times when each of us was very happy indeed that the studio had been kind enough to give us a camera ship equipped with three husky motors [Paul Mantz's Stinson Model A] rather than a single one. We can hardly pay too much credit too, to the pilots, who, under the direction of chief pilot Frank Clarke, flew all of this part of the picture. They indulged in a lot of really dangerous flying, doing it, too, in unfamiliar float seaplanes, yet came through it as though they had been flying seaplanes for years . . ."[5]

A long-time associate of Paul Mantz's, Clarke had stepped in for Mantz as Warner's chief pilot when the latter was grounded with a broken hip suffered in an automobile accident. This would be the veteran stunt pilot's (flying in films since 1918) most important assignment since making *Hells Angels* for Howard Hughes in 1930.

From North Bay, Curtiz and his crew proceeded to the Trenton Air Station in Bellville, Ontario, where most of the aerial scenes involving the RCAF were to be shot. Situated on the North shore of Lake Ontario (170 miles east of Toronto), Trenton was home to the No. 1 Central Flying School, where RCAF cadets received their advanced flight training. During the seven days of shooting, 110 students

Director Michael Curtiz lines up a shot at the RCAF's Uplands Air Station, as a Norseman and Waco Cabin ship "buzz" the field.

Cagney discusses the finer points of aerial gunnery with a student in the rear cockpit of a Fairey Battle.

Camera crews capture the "Presentation of the Wings" ceremony at the No. 2 Service Flying Training School at Uplands Air Station in Ottawa, July 1941. Famed WW I air ace "Billy" Bishop presided over the ceremonies.

James Cagney prepares to exit his Harvard training plane following a crash landing. The scene was shot in a water tank on one of Warner's soundstages. The rear projection screen (in the background) provides a backdrop for the action being filmed in the foreground.

and instructors participated in the film, flying a myriad of aircraft ranging from the diminutive Fleet Finch training plane to twin engine Avro Anson transports.

The last scenes to be shot in Canada were those involving the film's climactic ferry flights to England. Most of the air-to-air footage was shot 150-200 miles out to sea using six Hudson Mk. V bombers from the Dartmouth Air Station in Halifax, Nova Scotia. In holding with the script, one of Dartmouth's Hurricane fighter planes was repainted to represent the German Messerschmitt that attacks the flight. Since Canada was at war, it was necessary to issue warnings each time the aircraft took off to prevent it from being shot down by the numerous anti-aircraft batteries that dotted the area's coastline.

Another six weeks of backlot shooting lay ahead of the cast and crew upon their return to California in early September. Filming officially ended on November 8, 1941. Unbeknown at the time of its production, *Captains of the Clouds* would become the last aviation epic to be made before America's entry into World War II. The film's release in January 1942 met with excellent reviews from the critics and was later nominated for two Academy Awards for Best Color Cinematography (Sol Polito) and Best Interior Decorating (Ted Smith and Casey Roberts).

NEW YORK TIMES

"The thunderous roar of engines in giant bombers, the thrilling sweep of planes across the sky and the strong and eager faces of young airmen are now familiar in the vocabulary of the screen. But they can be eloquent and exciting when properly used in a film. And properly is but a mild word for the way in which they and other aerial shots are packed into the Warners' stoutly heroic and exceedingly masculine 'Captains of the Clouds' a salute to the Royal Canadian Air Force . . ."

Bosley Crowther
February 13, 1942

Warner's crew prepares to film one of the pictures most exciting scenes: the mass takeoff of the ferry squadron for England. The sequence was shot at night at Lockheed's facility in Burbank, at considerable expense to the studio.

Cagney prepares to save the ferry squadron by ramming a Messerschmitt fighter plane with his Hudson bomber.

Chapter Two

The War Years: 1942-1945

With war an outright reality, Hollywood set aside its preparedness themes and "geared-up" for the long fight ahead. "Remember Pearl Harbor" became the national battle cry, as President Roosevelt declared the film industry a vital resource in winning the fight with our Axis foes. Studio officials were now openly encouraged to create cinematic icons to lift the morale of the nation and stimulate the total war effort. There no longer was any need to tread lightly where fascism was concerned, as the cries of "war-mongering" had been silenced for the duration.

Swept away with a new sense of unity and purpose, the studios swiftly mobilized for the national defense effort. In June of 1942, the government established the Office of War Information to act as its liaison with the film industry. It was through this agency that Hollywood and Washington worked together to make the best possible use of the motion picture as a "weapon of democracy." Prints of all first-run feature films were made available, free of charge, to troops stationed everywhere. In addition, the studios turned over their huge facilities to produce thousands of vitally needed training films, documentaries, newsreels, and propaganda shorts of all kinds.

Although the "positive propaganda" that the studios created could not provide actual victories, it could supply the American people with a great deal of information about the war and how their husbands, sons, wives, and daughters were winning it. It also provided morale-boosting evidence to war industry workers of the importance of the arms and equipment they were making, and to keep up the good work.

The War Department in particular gave filmmakers a considerable amount of assistance in their films about the armed forces. Motion picture productions that were deemed important to the war-effort were given technical advisors, military personnel, and, where priorities allowed, combat equipment of every description – allowing movies a scope never before known. This cooperation was not without its price though. While censorship was not practiced per se, the military did exercise a great deal of control over films to which it lent its assistance. Any films with a military theme had to be cleared by the War Department, where scripts were analyzed for accuracy and authenticity before the official approval was given.

In addition to these restrictions, the studios were also faced with numerous war-related production problems. Severe manpower shortages existed in all of its departments – over one-quarter of the industry's male employees, from stars to grips, had gone into the service. Motion picture budgets were restricted. A price ceiling of $5,000 had been placed on the construction of sets (prompting some studios to swap major set constructions), and film stock was rationed for the duration – the war took priority over everything.

Despite these setbacks, the industry worked tirelessly to meet or exceed its production and distribution deadlines following the outbreak of hostilities. Films with a post-Pearl Harbor background began to appear in June 1942. Unfortunately, few of the pictures made during the first year of the war attempted to treat the conflict in a thoughtful or serious way. The majority simply combined propaganda with entertainment and were generally transformations of old "B" melodramas updated with topical wartime settings.

How little Hollywood understood the realities of the war at this point could easily be seen in the first aerial epics to hit the screen. Universal's *Eagle Squadron*, with its British setting and sizeable cast, headed by Robert Stack and Diana Barrymore, was "loosely based" on the exploits of the American volunteers serving with the Royal Air Force. In Warner Brother's *Desperate Journey*, RAF bomber pilots Errol Flynn and Ronald Reagan rewrite history as they take on the Luftwaffe, Gestapo Chief Raymond Massey, and the whole of Germany, and end up the victors. Republic's *Flying Tigers* has AVG hero John Wayne and his outnumbered band of fliers sweeping the skies of Zero's and blasting Jap supply trains with nitro at zero altitude.

Among these early "flag-wavers" came the first attempts to sort fact from fiction. Paramount's *Wake Island* reenacted the heroic last-stand on that island by the U.S. Marines. Shot along California's inland Salton Sea, the film stood out for its realism and lack of false heroics. In Warner Brother's film *Air Force*, American audiences got their first good look at how the air war was really being fought. Made at the suggestion of Army Air Force Commanding General "Hap" Arnold, the picture was based on the true exploits of AAF aircrews during the first dark months of war in the Pacific. These films proved that Hollywood could effectively combine propaganda with entertainment and still have a box-office success.

By late 1942, motion pictures that glorified our combat forces were rolling off the cinematic assembly lines by the dozen. Typical of these were the films that dramatized the training of America's fledgling airmen. They ranged from the training of air cadets from three allied nations in Twentieth Century-Fox's *Thunderbirds*, to the Army Air Forces' gunners in Universal's *Aerial Gunner*, to the Navy's Lighter-Than-Air pilots in Metro-Goldwyn-Mayer's *This Man's Navy*. Designed primarily to stimulate recruitment, these pictures had the strong backing of military planners who were charged with providing qualified aircrews to the air arms of the Army, Navy, and Marine Corps.

As the war progressed, motion pictures that showed the actuality of war in terms of battle and loss of life began to emerge from the cameras of front-line GI filmmakers. An altogether superior film of this genre was Major William Wyler's *Memphis Belle*, released in the spring of 1944. Produced by the AAF's First Motion Picture Unit, it followed the fortunes of one 8th Air Force bomber crew and the part they played in the war against Germany. Equally impressive was Captain Edward Steichen's Academy Award winner, *The Fighting Lady*, a graphic account of life aboard the aircraft carrier USS *Yorktown*, from the time of its commissioning through combat in the South Pacific. A combination of powerful images and thoughtful commentary, these feature-length documentaries brought the real air war home to American movie audiences for the first time.

Inspired by the work of these filmmakers, Hollywood began to develop more realistic film themes. The last twelve months of the war saw the release of a number of pictures that dramatized, honestly and constructively, the fine job being done by America's fighting airmen. Henry Hathaway's film *Wing and A Prayer* gave moviegoers their first good look at carrier warfare in the Pacific during the first crucial months of the war. Mervyn LeRoy's *Thirty Seconds Over Tokyo* was a blow-by-blow account of the preparation, execution, and aftermath of the first bombing raid on Tokyo in April 1942. Robert Florey's film *God Is My Co-Pilot* recounted the exploits of P-40 ace Colonel Robert Lee Scott while he was a member of General Claire Chennault's legendary "Flying Tigers." These motion pictures were a credit to the studios that made them and a high note on which to end Hollywood's contribution to the war-effort.

Looking back, one must be impressed with the sense of unity the war seemed to foster throughout America. Swept by the same currents as the rest of the nation, Hollywood rolled up its sleeves and pitched in "to do its part." Of the 1700 motion pictures made during this period, more than 500 were directly related to some aspect of the war. Although the images these films conveyed were not always realistic, they did convey some sense of the complexity of a global conflict, while engendering in the American people the patriotism and determination needed to see the war through to a victorious end.

EAGLE SQUADRON

Universal

— 1942 —

CAST

Chuck Brewer: ROBERT STACK; Anne Partridge: DIANA BARRYMORE; Hank Starr: JON HALL; Leckie: EDDIE ALBERT; Lt. McKinnon: NIGEL BRUCE; Nancy Mitchell: EVELYN ANKERS; Johnny Coe: LEIF ERIKSON; Paddy Carson: JOHN LODER; Borowsky: EDGAR BARRIER; Dame Elizabeth: ISOBEL ELSOM; Aunt Emmie: GLADYS COOPER; Sir John Partridge: PAUL CAVANAGH; White: RICHARD DAVIES; Phyllis: JILL ESMOND; The Kid: GENE REYNOLDS; Peder Olesen: ALAN HALE, JR.; Captain Grenfall: FREDERICK WORLOCK

CREDITS

Director: ARTHUR LUBIN; Producer: WALTER WANGER; Screenplay: NORMAN REILLY RAINE; Original Story: C.S. FORESTER; Cinematographer: STANLEY CORTEZ; Art Direction: JACK OTTERSON; Set Decoration: R.A. GAUSMAN; Special Effects: JOHN FULTON; Film Editor: PHILIP CAHN; Musical Score: FRANK SKINNER; Sound Technician: BERNARD B. BROWN; Wardrobe: VERA WEST

Universal's *Eagle Squadron,* released in June of 1942, became the first aviation film to go into production following America's entry into the war. Designed as a tribute to the American fighter pilots serving with the Royal Air Force, the picture was a continuation of the pro-British trend begun before the war with *A Yank in the RAF.*

The plot, based on a *Cosmopolitan Magazine* story by C.S. Forester, centers on a young American test pilot Chuck Brewer (Robert Stack), who, with his pal Johnny Coe (Leif Erikson), volunteers for combat duty with the RAF's Eagle Squadron. On their first sortie across the English Channel, Coe disobeys orders and is shot down.

Robert Stack signals "thumbs-up" before taking off on his first sortie across the Channel. His plywood Spitfire had originally been constructed for use in Fox's "A Yank in the RAF."

Upon return to base, Brewer is angered and disillusioned by what he believes is the callousness of his fellow pilots over the death of his friend. In time, and with the help of WAAF member Ann Partridge (Diana Barrymore), he realizes he has mistaken callousness for courageous stoicism. Inspired by their "chin up and carry on" attitude, Brewer volunteers for a dangerous commando raid on the coast of France. With little regard for his own safety, he captures a newly-designed Messerschmitt fighter plane and spirits it away to England, where he is decorated for heroism.

Although sincere in its attempt to stimulate audience awareness of what was happening "over there," *Eagle Squadron* offered little in the way of reality and was typical of many films released during the first year of the war. Interestingly enough, the film did contain some fine combat footage, which saved it from being little more than a grade "B" adventure story.

Second unit director Ernest Schoedsack spent nearly six months in England photographing actual Eagle Squadron operations for use in background scenes. The aerial

Ambulance crews rush into action following the crash of Edgar Barrier's Spitfire.

Robert Stack and a group of British Commandoes prepare to capture a newly-designed Messerschmitt fighter plane at an airfield in France.

combat sequences were provided by the British Air Ministry and were taken from 16mm gun camera footage shot during RAF missions over Europe. The remainder of the picture was filmed on Universal's backlot outside of Los Angeles.

Eagle Squadron had its world premier at the Globe Theater in New York City on July 2, 1942, with selected members of the actual Eagle Squadron in attendance. Although popular with wartime audiences, critical reviews of the film were generally disappointing.

MOTION PICTURE HERALD

"Walter Wanger's account of the activities of American pilots in the RAF prior to America's entry into the war combines the essentials of documentary, tribute and fiction in a blending which makes in many respects a striking wartime subject . . . The picture is at its best in the sequences which are in effect documentaries . . . the RAF planes engaging in battle with the enemy and returning to base after sustaining some losses and inflicting more, commands and holds attention and admiration . . ."

July 20, 1942

The men of the Eagle Squadron snap to attention as Robert Stack is decorated for heroism.

WAKE ISLAND

Paramount

— 1941 —

CAST

Major Caton: BRIAN DONLEVY; Joe Doyle: ROBERT PRESTON; Lt. Bruce Cameron: MAC DONALD CAREY; Shad McCloskey: ALBERT DEKKER; Aloysius Randall: WILLIAM BENDIX; Commander Reynolds: WALTER ABEL; Ivan Probenski: MIKHAIL RASUMNY; Sgt. Higbee: BILL GOODWIN; Sally Cameron: BARBARA BRITTON; Captain Patrick: DAMIAN O'FLYNN

CREDITS

Director: JOHN FARROW; Producer: JOSEPH SISTROM; Screenplay: FRANK BUTLER, W.R. BURNETT; Original Story: U.S.M.C. RECORDS; Cinematographer: THEODOR SPARKUHL, WILLIAM MELLOR; Aerial Cinematographer: ELMER DYER, WALLACE KELLEY; Air Operations: FRANK CLARKE, HERBERT WHITE, PAUL GUSTINE, PAUL PENROSE, DANA BOLLER; Art Direction: HANS DRIER, EARL HEDRICK; Special Effects: GORDON JENNINGS, FARCIOT EDOUART; Musical Score: DAVID BUTTOLPH

The Fall of 1942 saw the release of one of the first motion pictures to deal with the war in an accurate and sincere manner, Paramount's *Wake Island*. The film was a major departure from Hollywood's recruiting poster approach to the fighting and told of the heroic, but doomed, defense of Wake Island by a contingent of hopelessly-outnumbered U.S. Marines.

The screenplay, by Frank Butler and W.R. Burnett, is a deft account of the actual battle with few of the usual Hollywood embellishments. Except for the fictional names and a slight contrivance in the plot, it accurately portrays the day-to-day events in the two week siege of Wake Island by Japanese invasion forces.

Planes of the Imperial Japanese Navy attacked the tiny outpost on December 8, 1941, one day after the bombing

Japanese planes attacked Wake Island on December 8, 1941, one day after the raid on Pearl Harbor.

Macdonald Carey alights from his F4F upon arrival at Wake. His real-life counterpart was Major Henry Elrod of VMF-211, the first American pilot to sink a Japanese ship during World War II.

of Pearl Harbor. The surprise raid left the base in shambles. Eight of the twelve F4F's that defended the installation were destroyed or damaged before any American pilots could get into the air. For the next two weeks, the small garrison of Marines held out against continual air and sea bombardment. During this period, the men of VMF-211 fought valiantly to keep their remaining planes in the air – breaking up numerous attacks and routing a seaborne invasion attempt in which they sank a Japanese destroyer and damaged a medium transport. Finally, on December 22nd, the last two F4F's were destroyed and the Island's defenses overrun.

Wake Island roused the emotions of the American public as few films had done before it, and marked the beginning of a short but welcome cycle of realistic motion pictures about the war. In bringing the story to the screen, producer Joseph Sistrom faced, what was for him and others in Hollywood, the new experience of making a motion picture under wartime conditions. Since the entire West Coast area had been alerted for a possible invasion, he decided to film most of the picture on the shores of California's inland Salton Sea, about 200 miles from Los Angeles. Topographically and climatically, the area bore a striking resemblance to conditions found on Wake. To further ensure the film's accuracy, the construction firm that built the original Wake Island installation was contracted to build Paramount's set, complete with barracks, seaplane base, shore batteries, civilian construction camp, and a 4000 foot airfield.

Actual filming got underway on April 13, 1942. Paramount's production company of 200 actors and technicians spent nearly a month on location in the Salton Sea area. During this time, director John Farrow (who had only recently been relieved of combat duty with the Royal Canadian Navy) worked closely with the U.S. Marine Corps advisors who had been assigned to the project. Accordingly, the battle sequences took on a tough, literal quality seldom achieved in motion pictures of this period.

Stunt pilot Frank Clarke coordinated all of the production's flying scenes during the two months of filming. Due to coastal defense restrictions, the aerial combat scenes were staged over the Great Salt Lake in Northern Utah. Five low-winged Ryan SC sport planes doubled as Nakajima 97's in the air battles with the F4F-3's supplied by the Marine Corps. Advance notice of the filming had to be broadcast throughout the area to warn local residents about the "Japanese" dive bombers flying in the Salt Lake vicinity.

Five Marine Corps F4F-3's buzz the Salton Sea during location filming, April 1942. Located 200 miles from Los Angeles, the "Wake Island" set included a 4000 foot runway, which was later turned over to the military upon completion of the film.

Production of the film ended on June 8, 1942. *Wake Island* premiered three months later and became an immediate success with audiences and critics alike. The Academy of Motion Picture Arts and Sciences nominated it for four awards, including Best Picture of 1942, Best Director (John Farrow), Best Supporting Actor (William Bendix), and Best Original Screenplay (Frank Butler and W.R. Burnett).

Brian Donlevy discusses the Island's defense with Macdonald Carey as Mikhail Rasumny makes some last-minute repairs on an F4F.

NEW YORK TIMES

"Now that the United States Marine Corps has given the Japs a dose of medicine in the Solomons and is poising from all accounts, for further thrusts, this is a time for grim reflection upon a score which the Leathernecks have to pay off. Such a stern mediation – and a rousing tribute, too – is Paramount's new film, 'Wake Island.' Here, in all its harsh and bitter detail, in all its deathless gallantry, is the story of the small Marine garrison which held that tiny Pacific Isle for the two terrible weeks after Pearl Harbor and went down fighting, brave and defiant to the end . . . Credit Director John Farrow with giving the film much brutal suspense, for drawing the story taut with screaming action and intervals of breathless quiet . . ."

Bosley Crowther
September 2, 1942

A flight of Ryan SC sport planes form-up over the Great Salt Lake during aerial combat scenes with Marine Wildcats. The studio leased five of the low-winged monoplanes, which bore a remarkable resemblance to the Nakajima 97's that attacked Wake.

The end is near as invasion forces prepare to overrun the Island. Since all of the Japanese extras in Hollywood had been interned for the duration, the studio was forced to hire 200 Filipino farm workers to impersonate the Emperor's soldiers.

DESPERATE JOURNEY

Warner Brothers

— 1942 —

CAST

Flight Lt. Terence Forbes: ERROL FLYNN; Flight Lt. Johnny Hammond: RONALD REAGAN; Kaethe Brahms: NANCY COLEMAN; Major Otto Baumeister: RAYMOND MASSEY; Flight Sgt. Kirk Edwards: ALAN HALE; Flying Officer Jed Forrest: ARTHUR KENNEDY; Flight Sgt. Lloyd Hollis: RONALD SINCLAIR; Dr. Mather: ALBERT BASSERMAN; Preuss: SIG RUMANN; Squadron Leader Lane Ferris: PATRICK O'MOORE; Hermann Brahms: FELIX BASCH; Frau Brahms: ILKA GRUNING; Frau Raeder: ELSE BASSERMAN; Captain Coswick: CHARLES IRWIN; Squadron Leader Clark: RICHARD FRASER; Kruse: ROBERT O. DAVIS; Heinrich Schwartzmueller: HENRY VICTOR; English Officer: BRUCE LESTER; Wing Commander: LESTER MATHEWS

CREDITS

Director: RAOUL WALSH; Producer: HAL B. WALLIS; Original Screenplay: ARTHUR T. HORMAN; Cinematographer: BERT GLENNON; Air Operations: PAUL MANTZ; Art Direction: CARL JULES WEYL; Special Effects: EDWIN DU PAR; Film Editor: RUDI FEHR; Musical Score: MAX STEINER; Sound Technician: C.A. RIGGS; Wardrobe: MILO ANDERSON

Apparently Warner Brothers saw little harm in applying their particular action formula to a film dealing with a contemporary war theme. The result was *Desperate Journey,* a 1942 release in which Errol Flynn and the crew of a B-17 single-handedly take on the whole of Germany – and win.

Arthur T. Horman's script has Flight Lt. Terence Forbes (Errol Flynn) leading the four surviving crewmen of B-17, "D for Danny," out of Germany following the crash of their bomber in the Black Forest. Unfortunately, their escape plans are cut short when they walk into the hands of sneering Gestapo Major Otto Baumeister (Raymond Massey). The delay is only temporary though, as the crew leads the Nazis on a merry chase across the entire Third Reich, lingering occasionally to blow up some key military installations. Despite the efforts of Baumeister and his henchmen, the fliers make it to Holland, commandeer a Hudson bomber, and return to England, carrying information vital to the Allied cause.

The fast-paced action of this film compensates for what it lacks in serious story content. Directed by Raoul Walsh, *Desperate Journey* contains many exciting moments typical of the director's adroit handling of such melodramas (his third with Flynn). Walsh staged all of the action at the Warner Brothers' Studios in Burbank, with the exception of a hair-raising chase scene between Flynn's crew and the Nazis, which was shot along the California coast (doubling for Holland) near Pt. Mugu and Pt. Hueneme.

Released in September 1942, *Desperate Journey* proved to be extremely popular at the box-office and earned itself one Academy Award nomination for Best Special Effects (Byron Haskin, Nathan Levinson).

The crew of "D for Danny" following the crash of their bomber in Germany's Black Forest (actually Warner's Sound Stage 16). If the B-17 looks familiar – it's the mockup from "I Wanted Wings."

A German sentry draws a bead on RAF fliers (L to R) Alan Hale, Ronald Reagan, Arthur Kennedy, Ronald Sinclair and Errol Flynn. This was Reagan's last role before reporting for duty with the U.S. Army Air Force.

Hot on the trail of the RAF fliers, this German soldier is about to hit the drink in one of the most exciting chase scenes ever filmed for a motion picture. All the action took place along the beaches of Pt. Mugu and Pt. Heuneme in California.

NEW YORK TIMES

". . . 'Desperate Journey' is an action melodrama of the wildest stripe, deprived of the intensity its subject should have by the bravado of its story and characters. Obviously, the author filched freely from 'Target for Tonite' and 'Man Hunt,' but the consequence is little more than a parody of those two striking films. Folks who will sacrifice reason for fast action and the joy of seeing "Nazis" foiled should find it entirely gratifying . . ."

Bosley Crowther
September 26, 1942

Errol Flynn and his crew commandeer a Hudson bomber with Gestapo Major Raymond Massey, et. al. in pursuit.

FLYING TIGERS

Republic

— 1942 —

CAST

Jim Gordon: JOHN WAYNE; Woody Jason: JOHN CARROLL; Brooke Elliott: ANNA LEE; Hap: PAUL KELLY; Alabama: GORDON JONES; Verna Bales: MAE CLARKE; Colonel Lindsay: ADDISON RICHARDS; Blackie Bales: EDMUND MAC DONALD; Dale: BILL SHIRLEY; Reardon: TOM NEAL; McCurdy: MALCOLM MC TAGGART; Barton: DAVID BRUCE; Mike: CHESTER GAN; McIntosh: JAMES DODD; Tex: GREGG BARTON; Selby: JOHN JAMES

CREDITS

Director: DAVID MILLER; Producer: EDMUND GRAINGER; Screenplay: KENNETH GAMET, BARRY TRIVERS; Original Story: KENNETH GAMET; Cinematographer: JACK MARTA; Air Operations: CLARENCE BRAGUNIER; Art Direction: RUSSELL KIMBALL; Set Direction: OTTO SEIGEL; Special Effects: HOWARD LYDECKER, TED LYDECKER, DON BLOOMBERG; Film Editor: ERNEST NIMS; Musical Score: VICTOR YOUNG; Wardrobe: ADELE PALMER

By late 1942, Hollywood was hard at work cranking out its own version of the struggle overseas. As part of the effort, Republic Studios ordered its star performer, John Wayne, out of the saddle and into the cockpit of a P-40 for its first major production of the war, *Flying Tigers.* The picture was loosely based on the exploits of China's American Volunteer Group, the Flying Tigers, who had been fighting the Japanese long before the attack on Pearl Harbor.

The screenplay, by Barry Trivers and Kenneth Gamet (*International Squadron*), followed the typical Hollywood service-film formula. Hardbitten AVG leader Jim Gordon (John Wayne) has been fighting against tremendous odds to keep his planes and pilots in the air. In an effort to fill

John Wayne briefs his men on an upcoming mission. "Flying Tigers" was one of a long series of films Wayne did for the Republic Studios.

his rapidly depleting ranks, he recruits cocky transport pilot Woody Jason (John Carroll). Unbeknown to Jim, Woody's sense of loyalty goes no further than the $500 bonus paid for every Japanese plane shot down. Anxious for a "kill," he causes the death of two of the "Tigers." In an effort to redeem himself with the rest of the fliers, he accompanies Jim on a dangerous bombing mission to destroy an enemy supply train. During the attack, their aircraft is hit and catches fire. Badly wounded, Woody forces Jim to bail-out and in one final act of heroism, dives the plane head-long into the train.

Although long on heroics and short on realism, *Flying Tigers* proved popular with wartime audiences anxious to see Americans on the winning side of the battle. Most of the film was shot at the Russell Ranch (frequently used in Republic's westerns) some twenty miles from Republic's lot in Studio City, California; there construction crews had built an exact reproduction of AVG Headquarters, complete with barracks, aircraft hangars, and an operational airstrip.

Since wartime priorities prohibited the use of actual P-40's on the set, the studio was forced to build its own. Seven wood and canvas replicas were constructed under the

Republic recreated AVG Headquarters at the Russell Ranch, twenty miles from their lot in Studio City. Included were an airstrip, barracks and even a Chinese Temple.

guidance of United Air Services' (Paul Mantz's operation) chief pilot Clarence "Ace" Bragunier and chief mechanic Robert King. Two of the aircraft were equipped with OX-5 engines and capable of taxiing up to 60 mph. The rest had high torque electric motors to turn the propellers during ground run-up sequences.

Arrangements were made to photograph all of the film's aerial scenes at the Curtiss Aircraft Company in Buffalo, New York. A number of Army Air Force P-40E's, awaiting delivery, were temporarily repainted in AVG markings and flown for the cameras by Curtiss' test pilots. Supplementing this footage, were some excellent miniature scenes staged by Republic's special effects wizards Howard and Ted Lydecker.

Flying Tigers premiered in Los Angeles on September 23, 1942. Critics in general praised the film as one of Republic's best, and the Academy of Motion Picture Arts and Sciences nominated it for three awards: Best Sound Recording (Daniel Bloomberg), Special Effects (Howard Lydecker), and Musical Score (Victor Young).

The film's romantic interest was supplied by Red Cross Nurse Anna Lee. Here the actress runs through a scene with John Wayne. The padded cover on the camera is known as a "barney," designed to muffle the noise of the camera's motor.

A number of P-40's, about to be delivered to the Army Air Force, were repainted in AVG markings for the film. These sequences were shot at the Curtiss Aircraft Plant in Buffalo, New York.

Director David Miller discusses a scene with actor Addison Richards.

NEW YORK TIMES

"On a patch-work story frame, Republic Pictures has strung a first-rate aerial circus chock-full of exciting dog-fights in 'Flying Tigers' . . . Though the film has a heartfelt foreword by Generalissimo Chiang Kaishek, it is first and foremost a romantic adventure tale and only incidentally a record of the famous American Volunteer Group that wrote history in the China sky against an overwhelmingly superior enemy during the two years prior to the attack on Pearl Harbor . . . 'Flying Tigers' is all that its title implies and a good bit more at times, while the camera is following the aerial acrobatics. Happily it is doing just that most of the time."

Thomas Pryor
October 23, 1942

Four of the seven P–40 replicas built for the film prepare to "take-off." Two of the planes were capable of taxiing, while the rest were equipped with electric motors to turn the props.

Wayne's XC–12 transport swoops low over a railroad bridge with a load of nitroglycerine. This scene, done in miniature, was typical of the excellent work accomplished by Republic's Special Effects crew, headed by Howard and Ted Lydecker.

THUNDERBIRDS

Twentieth Century-Fox

— 1942 —

CAST

Kay Saunders: GENE TIERNEY; Steve Britt: PRESTON FOSTER; Peter Stackhouse: JOHN SUTTON; Colonel Mac Donald: JACK HOLT; Lady Stackhouse: DAME MAY WHITTY; Gramps: GEORGE BARBIER; George Lockwood: RICHARD HAYDN; Barratt: REGINALD DENNY

CREDITS

Director: WILLIAM A. WELLMAN; Producer: LAMAR TROTTI; Screenplay: LAMAR TROTTI; Original Story: MELVILLE CROSSMAN; Cinematographers: ERNEST PALMER, HARRY JACKSON; Air Operations: PAUL MANTZ; Art Direction: RICHARD DAY, JAMES BASEVI; Set Decoration: THOMAS LITTLE; Film Editor: WALTER THOMPSON; Musical Score: DAVID BUTTOLPH; Sound Technicians: ALFRED BRUZLIN, ROGER HEMAN; Wardrobe: DOLLY TREE

Few aspects of military preparation went unnoticed by Hollywood's filmmakers during the first year of the war. In late 1942 the Army Air Force's Flight Training Program became the subject of a Twentieth Century-Fox release entitled *Thunderbirds*. Directed by World War I flying ace William Wellman (*Wings*), the film dramatized the training of air cadets from three allied nations: China, Great Britain, and the United States.

The screenplay, developed from an original story by Fox studio chief Darryl F. Zanuck, centers on British Air

Ace flier Preston Foster is greeted by Commanding Officers Jack Holt and Reginald Denny upon his arrival at Thunderbird Field.

Cadet Peter Stackhouse (John Sutton) and veteran flight instructor Steve Britt (Preston Foster), who served with Peter's father in World War I. At the onset of training, Peter finds that he has the unfortunate tendency to get air sick while flying, a fact that nearly gets him "washed out" of flying school. Britt, knowing that the young cadet is basically a good pilot, covers for him until he can overcome this problem. Perseverance rewarded, Peter finally solos and returns his instructor's kindness by saving his life during a freak desert sandstorm.

When *Thunderbirds* remained in the air and concentrated on the training of the Allied cadets, it proved to be an interesting film. Most of it was shot on location at the Army Air Force's training facilities at Thunderbird and Falcon Fields in Arizona. The scenes of actual American, British, and Chinese cadets flying their PT-13, BT-13 and AT-6 training planes (filmed in Technicolor) were visually very impressive and lent an air of credibility to the entire production. Unfortunately, most of the action took place on the ground in the form of a romantic triangle between John Sutton, Gene Tierney, and Preston Foster. Even William Wellman's aerial expertise could not make up for the film's hackneyed story content.

John Sutton prepares for his first flight in a Stearman training plane as Preston Foster runs through the preflight.

Thunderbirds premiered at Grauman's Chinese Theater in Hollywood on October 28, 1942. Critical reviews of the film were decidedly mixed.

In holding with the film's United Nations theme, many of the actual cadets that appeared in the picture were from China and Great Britain.

NEW YORK TIMES

"Thunderbird Field in Arizona must be a pretty spectacular place, with its layout of colorful buildings on the desert floor under a beetling mountain range and its interesting assortment of youngsters from China, Britain and America training to fly. It should, indeed, be a tempting topic for a first class factual wartime film. But precious little sense of its significance in the general scheme of things has been realized to any advantage by Twentieth Century-Fox in its latest Technicolor epic 'Thunderbirds.' Rather Producer Lamar Trotti, who also co-authored the script, has simply dished up another one of those tales about an American instructor and a British flying cadet who, in love with the same American lassie, vie to see which one can be the nobler goof . . . "

Bosley Crowther
October 28, 1942

A gaggle of AT-6's lift off from Thunderbird Field No. 1. Located outside of Scottsdale, Arizona, the facility was the largest of its kind in the AAF's Flight Training Command and was the only school used to instruct Chinese air cadets. Additional scenes were filmed at the Falcon Field Training Facility in Mesa, Arizona.

AIR FORCE

Warner Brothers

— 1943 —

CAST

Captain Quincannon: JOHN RIDGELY; Lt. Williams: GIG YOUNG; Lt. McMartin: ARTHUR KENNEDY; Lt. Hauser: CHARLES DRAKE; Sergeant White: HARRY CAREY; Corporal Weinberg: GEORGE TOBIAS; Corporal Peterson: WARD WOOD; Private Chester: RAY MONTGOMERY; Sergeant Winocki: JOHN GARFIELD; Lt. Rader: JAMES BROWN; Major Mallory: STANLEY RIDGES; Colonel: WILLARD ROBERTSON; Commanding Officer: MARONI OLSEN; Sergeant J.J. Callahan: EDWARD BROPHY; Major W.G. Roberts: RICHARD LANE; Lt. P.T. Moran: BILL GRAGO; Susan McMartin: FAYE EMERSON; Major Daniels: ADDISON RICHARDS; Major A.M. Bagley: JAMES FLAVIN; Mary Quincannon: ANN DORAN; Mrs. Chester: DOROTHY PETERSON

CREDITS

Director: HOWARD HAWKS; Producer: HAL B. WALLIS; Screenplay: DUDLEY NICHOLS; Original Story: U.S. AIR CORPS RECORDS; Cinematographer: JAMES WONG HOWE; Aerial Cinematographers: ELMER DYER, CHARLES A. MARSHALL; Air Operations: PAUL MANTZ, PAUL GUSTINE, HARRY CROSBY; Art Direction: JOHN HUGHES; Set Decoration: WALTER F. TILFORD; Special Effects: ROY DAVIDSON, H.G. KOENEKAMP, REX WIMPY; Film Editor: GEORGE AMY; Musical Score: FRANZ WAXMAN; Sound Technician: OLIVER S. GARRETSON; Wardrobe: MILO ANDERSON

By 1943, much of the glamour and escapism found in earlier Hollywood war films was being replaced by films of greater honesty and realism. American audiences got their first perceptive look at how the air war was really being fought in Warner Brothers' multi-million dollar epic *Air Force.* Made at the suggestion of USAAF Commanding General "Hap" Arnold, and directed by former World War I pilot Howard Hawks (*Dawn Patrol, Ceiling Zero, Only Angels Have Wings*), the film follows the exploits of the crew of the B-17 "Mary Ann" during the first dark months of war in the Pacific.

Their story begins in the early morning hours of December 7, 1941. During a routine training flight to Hawaii, the crew picks up the first radio reports that Pearl Harbor is under attack. Landing at Hickam Field, they find the base in smoldering ruin and hurriedly refuel for a flight to Wake Island. Once there, the Marines order the "Mary Ann" and her crew to the Philippines, where they'll at least have a fighting chance to survive. Reaching Manila, the plane is armed and takes off on its first bombing mission. Three Japanese ships are sunk during the attack, but the Fortress is strafed by Zero fighters and abandoned by all, except her injured pilot and one of the crew, who bring her in for a belly landing at Clark Field. Ignoring orders to burn their ship, to prevent it from falling into enemy hands, the men work through the night to rebuild the bomber. Taking off as Japanese troops overrun the airfield, the "Mary Ann" sights an invasion fleet steaming toward Australia and guides a force of bombers to the site for the film's climactic Battle of the Coral Sea. Its mission complete, the heroic bomber limps to a final crash landing on an Australian beach, where the crew regroups to continue their fight against the enemy.

Although heavy-handed on the propaganda at times, *Air Force* remains one of the finest and perhaps one of the

The squadron prepares to takeoff for Hawaii. The "Mary Ann," a B-17C, was one of ten Flying Fortresses obtained from Hendrick Field in Sebring, Florida, for use in the film. The individual aircraft number on the nose indicates the aircraft is attached to a Combat Crew Training Center.

Pilots of the "Mary Ann," John Ridgely and Gig Young, receive their orders prior to takeoff for Hickam Field, Hawaii.

By the time the "Mary Ann" arrives at Hickam Field, the base is a smoldering ruin.

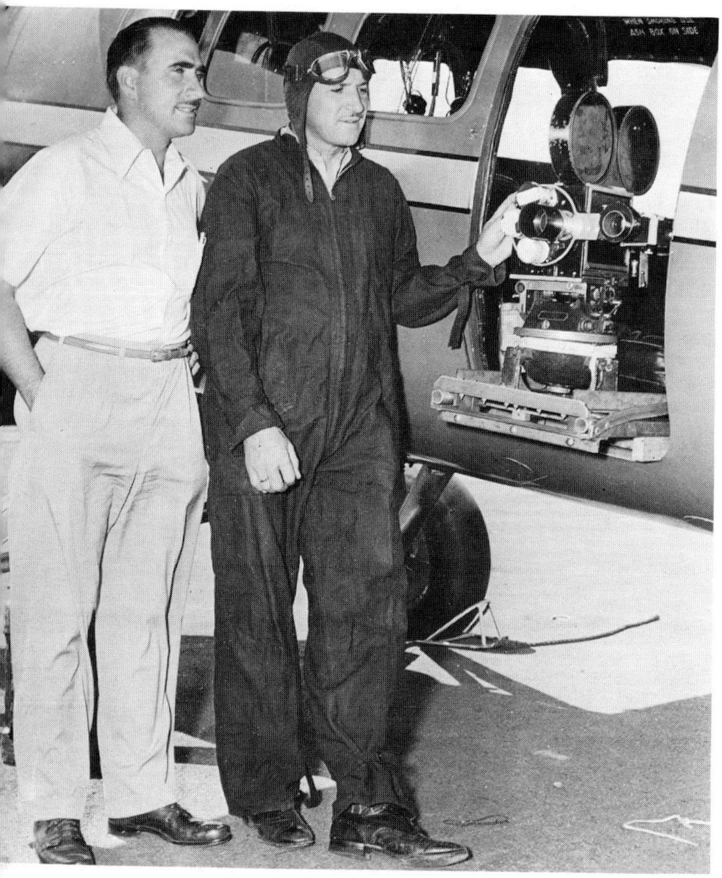

Famed stunt pilot Paul Mantz (left) and aerial cinematographer Elmer Dyer (right) co-ordinated all of the air-to-air camera work for the film. This was the last film assignment for both men before reporting to the AAF's First Motion Picture Unit in Culver City, California.

noblest films to come out of Hollywood during the war years. Work on the picture began soon after the Japanese attack on Pearl Harbor. In offering USAAF assistance on the project, General "Hap" Arnold insisted that Warners use historical fact as the basis for its story. Placed at screenwriter Dudley Nichols' disposal were the combat records of the 19th Bomb Group, which distinguished itself in the early months of fighting in the Pacific. In composing his scenario, Nichols drew heavily on the heroics of such 19th Bomb Group pilots as Captain Colin Kelly and Lt. Hewitt T. Wheless. Assisting him with the technical aspects of the story were USAAF Captains John Coulter and Samuel Triffy, who had been assigned to the studio for the duration of the project. Nearly $3,000,000 (a large budget by 1942 standards) and six months of back-breaking work would be needed to turn the screenplay into a finished motion picture.

Formal production of the film began on May 18, 1942, following War Department approval of the script. One of the first chores facing Hawks and his crew was the recreation of the Coral Sea battle that climaxes the film. Relying on Warner's Special Effects Department to supply the spectacle, Hawks dispatched a camera crew to the Santa Barbara Channel, where the entire air-sea battle was filmed using a flotilla of miniature Japanese warships. This sequence alone cost the studio a half-million dollars. The model battleships were so large (in order to fit all the intricate mechanisms needed to maneuver the ship, swivel the turrets, and fire the guns) that two of them completely filled a fifty-foot railroad flatcar enroute to the location.

Gig Young, James Brown and John Ridgely prepare to takeoff from Wake Island. This scene was shot in the elaborate mockup originally constructed for Paramount's "I Wanted Wings." Cinematographer James Wong Howe used minute lighting units, called peanut globes, throughout the ship, so that every detail could be seen on the screen.

While this unit completed the miniature sequences in Santa Barbara, Hawks concentrated on shooting the interior scenes at the Warner Brothers Studios in Burbank. The elaborate B-17 mockup used in *I Wanted Wings* was leased from Paramount and used for the process shots filmed on the backlot. At the same time, arrangements to shoot the exterior flying scenes were being finalized with USAAF officials in Washington, D.C. West Coast defense restrictions on flying and Hawks' desire to simulate the South Pacific war zone as closely as possible influenced the studio's decision to shoot all of the exteriors in Florida.

On July 24th, Hawks and his production company of 150 actors and technicians entrained for the 2600 mile trip to Drew Army Air Field near Tampa, Florida. Located on the shores of Tampa Bay, Drew normally served as a Third Air Force training facility for combat aircrews being sent overseas. For Hawks and his crew, the base would function as the main site for staging all of the production's air and ground sequences.

While on location, Captains Coulter and Triffy acted as Warner's liaison with the military. Among their many responsibilities was the acquisition of planes, pilots, and equipment for the proposed air and ground sequences. Working closely with local base commanders, the two men requisitioned nearly thirty aircraft for use in the film. From the Combat Crew Training Center at Hendrick Field in Sebring, Florida, came the ten B-17 Flying Fortresses (a mixture of "C" and "D" models) which figured so prominently in the story. Drew Field provided the pursuit ships,

Rearmed and ready to fight, the crew takes off on their first bombing mission.

Despite a War Department edict prohibiting this practice, a number of AAF aircraft doubled for Japanese fighters and bombers in the film. Here, technical advisor Captain Sam Triffy roars over the "Manila" set in a "Japanese" P-43A. The scene was staged on the outskirts of Drew Field, Florida.

One of the most poignant moments in the film comes when John Ridgely must inform his crew chief Harry Carey of his son's death. Director Howard Hawks (seated beside camera) and Chinese cinematographer James Wong Howe (behind him) observe as cameramen record the scene beneath the "Mary Ann."

which included varying numbers of P-39D's, P-40C's and P-43A's from the base's combat training program. The balance of "Hawks Air Force" represented aircraft from the Imperial Japanese Navy. Despite a War Department directive prohibiting this practice, a half-dozen B-26C's (397th Bomb Group) from nearby Mac Dill Field and a like number of P-43's and AT-6's from Drew were repainted with Japanese markings for the duration of the filming schedule.

For five long weeks, Drew Field resounded to the sounds of battle, as the cast and crew struggled, in intense heat and humidity, to complete their shots in the time allotted. The smoking ruins of Hickam Field, Wake Island, and Clark Field were recreated on a half-mile section of swamp land adjacent to Drew, allowing the filmmakers a free hand in shooting their scenes without interfering with normal base operations.

Most of the major aerial sequences were staged over Tampa Bay, which doubled for the Pacific Ocean in the film. Paul Mantz (in his last assignment before reporting for duty with the AAF) and fellow stunt pilots Harry Crosby and Paul Gustine recorded the action from three of Mantz's camera planes: a Lockheed Orion, Boeing 100, and Stinson Model "A." Notice of the filming had to be broadcast throughout the Southeastern United States to warn military units of the "Japanese" fighters and bombers flying over the Tampa Bay area.

Hawks' single-minded pursuit of authenticity nearly proved to be the undoing of a number of Army pilots at the time of the filming. One major, who led a dive-bombing attack in a "Japanese P-43," got to within thirty feet of the ground when a charge was prematurely set off, nearly causing him to crash. Another incident occurred one day while filming a flight of B-17's at dusk. As the aircraft turned onto base leg to land, the generators for the runway lights failed. Cinematographer James Wong Howe excitedly turned to Hawks saying, "What shall we do now? We can't light the airstrip." Hawks retorted, "That's not my problem – keep shooting." Howe obtained the help of several special effects people and lined the runway with flares so the aircraft could land safely.

Technical advisor, Captain Sam Triffy, himself, was shaken badly when one of the disguised fighters he was flying experienced a landing gear malfunction. When Hawks found out about the incident, he suggested that Triffy should have made a belly-landing – after making sure the cameras were rolling. Triffy later stated that "the filmmakers were ruthless, absolutely ruthless. If they could have damaged a plane in flight so that I would have had an accident, they would have done it. I couldn't trust them at all!"[1]

A surprise air raid on Clark Field brings the call to action. Pilots race to their positions as ground crews prepare their P-39's (under camouflage nets) for flight.

Whatever the motivation for his actions, Hawks achieved a realism in these battle scenes seldom seen in war films of the period. With the completion of filming in Florida, the company returned to California to finish what remained of the interior scenes at the studio. Production officially ended on October 26, 1942.

Air Force premiered three months later on February 3, 1943, at New York City's Radio City Music Hall. Critics applauded the film as one of Hollywood's finest screen achievements – inspiring and authentic. The Academy of Motion Picture Arts and Sciences awarded George Amy the Oscar for Best Film Editing of 1943 and nominated the film for Best Original Screenplay (Dudley Nichols), Best Cinematography (James Wong Howe, Elmer Dyer, Charles A. Marshall) and Best Special Effects (Hans Koenekamp, Rex Wimpy, Nathan Levinson).

Repairs on the "Mary Ann" are about complete when Japanese aircraft appear overhead. John Garfield covers his crewmates as George Tobias, Charles Drake, and Harry Carey rush to finish their work.

NEW YORK TIMES

"On the natural assumption that Army fliers can do almost anything that requires grit, determination, high competence and just plain Yankee luck, the Warner Brothers have turned out a film about an Army bomber crew which matches in sheer incredibility some of the certified yarns that pop up every week. 'Air Force' is its title . . . a continuously fascinating, frequently thrilling and occasionally exalting show which leaves you limp and triumphant at the end of its two hour ordeal. For what the Warners have put together – with the help of Dudley Nichols, who wrote the script, and Howard Hawks, who directed a uniformly excellent cast – is a high-flying epic compounded from most, if not all, the ringing tales of the Air Forces' heroism in the far Pacific during the first months of this war. Inspired by the brilliant record which our Army fliers hung up, the boys gave way completely to their boundless enthusiasm and awe and ripped out a picture which tingles with the passion of spirits aglow . . ."

Bosley Crowther
February 4, 1943

Japanese snipers reach the edge of Clark Field as the "Mary Ann" prepares to takeoff. American soldiers desperately try to hold them off till the bomber gets into the air.

AERIAL GUNNER

Paramount

— 1943 —

CAST

Foxy Pattis: CHESTER MORRIS; Ben Davis: RICHARD ARLEN; Peggy Lunt: LITA WARD; Sandy Lunt: JIMMY LYDON; Gadget Blaine: DICK PURCELL; Sergeant Jones: KEITH RICHARDS; Private Laswell: BILL BENEDICT; Barclay: RALPH SANFORD

CREDITS

Director: WILLIAM PINE; Producer: WILLIAM PINE, WILLIAM THOMAS; Screenplay: MAXWELL SHANE; Original Story: MAXWELL SHANE; Cinematographer: FRED JACKMAN, JR.; Art Direction: F. PAUL SYLOS; Film Editor: WILLIAM ZEIGLER; Musical Score: DANIEL AMFITHEATROF; Sound Technician: CHARLES ALTHOUSE

Hollywood continued to draw on the military for its topics, as headlines monitored the progress of America's fighting men at the front. Paramount Studios examined the training of the Army Air Force's aerial gunners in a 1943 action feature entitled *Aerial Gunner.*

The Maxwell Shane script has Lt. Ben Davis (Richard Arlen) assigned to a USAAF gunnery school, under the tutelage of instructor Sgt. Foxy Pattis (Chester Morris).

Pattis resents Davis' cocky attitude and tries his best to wash him out of the school. Despite his efforts, the young lieutenant passes the training requirements with flying colors. Following graduation, Davis is ordered to a bomber squadron in the Pacific, only to find his old instructor assigned as a gunner on board his airplane. With their first taste of action, the crew consolidates into a fine working team. Gradually the two adversaries learn to respect each other's courage. Pattis ultimately makes the greatest sacrifice of all and is killed protecting his crewmates as they escape from a Japanese-held island.

Aerial Gunner's chief asset lay in the fact that most of it was shot on location at the U.S. Army Air Force Aerial Gunnery School in Harlingen, Texas. Paramount's Pine-Thomas Production Company spent nearly two weeks at the school shooting scenes for the film as AAF recruits progressed through the various phases of air and ground

Chester Morris makes a pointed remark to gunnery student Richard Arlen as the rest of the class looks on.

Richard Arlen and Dick Purcell learn to handle .30 caliber machine guns along with the actual AAF trainees that were used in the film.

A nervous Jimmy Lydon is ordered aloft by instructor Chester Morris as Richard Arlen, Dick Purcell, and Billy Benedict look on.

training. Besides defraying a substantial part of the production's cost, it lent an air of authenticity to the picture and made up for some rather obvious flaws in the script.

Aerial Gunner had its world premier at the U.S. Army Air Force Gunnery School in Harlingen, Texas on May 10, 1943, with military and studio officials in attendance.

NEW YORK DAILY NEWS

"Paramount producers William Pine and William Thomas have been making a series of quick-action films, with Chester Morris and Richard Arlen as a co-starring team, that have been quite successful as "B" class films. Their latest production, 'Aerial Gunner', is the most ambitious picture they have turned out to date, and is packed with enough aerial action to satisfy any motion picture fan . . ."

Kate Cameron
June 25, 1943

Most of "Aerial Gunner" was shot on location at the U.S. Army Air Force Gunnery School in Harlingen, Texas. Here a flight of AT–6's roar past the main gate for the benefit of the cameras.

BOMBARDIER

R.K.O.

— 1943 —

CAST

Major Chick Davis: PAT O'BRIEN; Captain Buck Oliver: RANDOLPH SCOTT; Burt Hughes: ANNE SHIRLEY; Tom Hughes: EDDIE ALBERT; Jim Carter: WALTER REED; Joe Connors: ROBERT RYAN; Sergeant Dixon: BARTON MAC LANE; Japanese Officer: LEONARD STRONG; Chito Rafferty: RICHARD MARTIN; Paul Harris: RUSSELL WADE; Captain Rand: JAMES NEWILL; Chaplain Craig: JOHN MILJAN; Instructor: CHARLES RUSSELL

CREDITS

Director: RICHARD WALLACE; Producer: ROBERT FELLOWS; Screenplay: JOHN TWIST; Original Story: JOHN TWIST, MARTIN RACKIN; Cinematographer: NICHOLAS MUSURACA; Art Direction: ALBERT D'AGOSTINO, AL HERMAN; Set Decoration: DARRELL SILVERA, CLAUDE CARPENTER; Special Effects: ROY GRANVILLE, VERNON WALKER; Film Editor: ROBERT WISE; Musical Score: ROY WEBB; Sound Technician: BAILEY FESLER; Wardrobe: RENIE

Following the lead set by other motion picture studios, RKO decided to examine the rigorous training received by the men behind the Norden Bombsight in their 1943 production entitled *Bombardier,* starring Pat O'Brien and Randolph Scott.

The screenplay, by John Twist, is loosely based on actual events surrounding the establishment of the first U.S. Army Air Force School for bombardiers. Major Chick Davis (Pat O'Brien) is the chief proponent of high altitude bombardment with the Norden Bombsight. Despite the efforts of dive-bombing advocate Captain Buck Oliver (Randolph Scott), Davis convinces his superiors of the importance of his ideas and persuades them to set up a school to teach recruits to use the sight. His foresight

Walter Reed prepares to salvo a bomb load as his instructor looks on.

proves invaluable. The attack on Pearl Harbor finds the first class of bombardiers prepared and ready for duty. Davis leads the squadron to the South Pacific for a night bombing raid on Tokyo's largest aircraft plant. His former rival, Captain Oliver, agrees to fly ahead and mark the target with incendiaries. Shot down over enemy territory, he eludes capture and sets fire to the plant. Guided by the flames, the squadron finds its objective, and bombs rain down to destroy the enemy installation.

Although heavily propagandized, *Bombardier* contained a good deal of authentic footage shot on location at Kirtland Field's Bombardier Training School in Albuquerque, New Mexico. Director Richard Wallace and his crew spent six weeks at the facility filming the daily training routine of the bombardier cadets as they learned the intricacies of their Norden Bombsights. Many of the cadets appeared as extras in the film.

Released in July of 1943, *Bombardier* received generally favorable reviews from the critics and an Academy Award Nomination for Best Special Effects (Vernon Walker, James Stewart, Roy Granville).

Pat O'Brien and Randolph Scott supervise the loading of 100 lb practice bombs on board one of the school's B-17's. Most of the film was shot on location at Kirtland Field in Albuquerque, New Mexico.

VARIETY

'Bombardier' weaves commercial film values into its story of Army Air Forces' bomb sight experts and registers as entertainment on both counts. Details of training and eventual purpose of the bombardiers use up majority of the footage but picture winds up with a story wallop guaranteed to satisfy any American – the destruction of a Jap aircraft plant. Seldom has such thrilling battle footage reached the screen in Hollywood-made features and its seeming authenticity is a major credit to the technical forces marshalled by Robert Fellows in guiding the production . . . "

July 10, 1943

Pilots and crews from the 19th B.G. flew the B-17 formation scenes used in the latter part of "Bombardier." The group had only recently returned from combat in the Pacific and were temporarily based at Kirtland Field awaiting orders.

Searchlights pinpoint Randolph Scott's B-17 as he approaches Tokyo in the film's climactic bombing mission.

A GUY NAMED JOE

Metro-Goldwyn-Mayer

— 1943 —

CAST

Pete Sandidge: SPENCER TRACY; Dorinda Durston: IRENE DUNNE; Ted Randall: VAN JOHNSON; Al Yackey: WARD BOND; Nails Kilpatrick: JAMES GLEASON; The General: LIONEL BARRYMORE; Dick Rumney: BARRY NELSON; Ellen Bright: ESTHER WILLIAMS; Colonel Sykes: HENRY O'NEILL; James Rourke: DON DE FORE; Sanderson: CHARLES SMITH

CREDITS

Director: VICTOR FLEMING; Producer: EVERETT RISKIN; Screenplay: DALTON TRUMBO; Original Story: CHANDLER SPRAGUE, DAVID BOEHM; Cinematographers: KARL FREUND, GEORGE FOLSEY; Air Operations: PAUL MANTZ; Art Direction: CEDRIC GIBBONS, LYLE WHEELER; Set Decoration: EDWIN B. WILLIS; Special Effects: A. ARNOLD GILLESPIE, DONALD JAHRAUS, WARREN NEWCOMBE; Film Editor: FRANK SULLIVAN; Musical Score: HERBERT STOTHART; Sound Technician: DOUGLAS SHEARER; Wardrobe: IRENE

Released during Christmas of 1943, Metro-Goldwyn-Mayer's wartime fantasy *A Guy Named Joe* reflected, perhaps, Hollywood's reaction to the stress and violence of an all-too-real-war. Based in part on Everett Riskin's film *Here Comes Mister Jordan,* the Dalton Trumbo screenplay tells of a dead flier who returns to earth to aid the allied war effort.

The opening scene of the picture has hot-shot Army flier Major Pete Sandidge (Spencer Tracy) returning to England in his flak-riddled B-25. Belly-landing the bomber, Sandidge cooly climbs from the cockpit only to be greeted by Squadron Commanding Officer Lt. Colonel "Nails" Kilpatrick (James Gleason). Kilpatrick respects Pete's abilities as a pilot, but is fed up with his recklessness, and transfers him to Scotland on reconnaissance duty. Pete's luck finally runs out while single-handedly attacking a German convoy. Finding himself in the hereafter, he reports for duty to his new Commanding Officer (Lionel Barrymore). His orders are to go back to earth and help flying cadet Ted Randall (Van Johnson) win his wings. Invisible to all, Pete's presence guides the young student through the rigors of flight training. When Randall finally graduates, Pete accompanies him to a base in the South Pacific, where, in combat, the young flier will need all the skills his ghostly mentor has bestowed on him. After seeing him through a number of dangerous missions, Pete realizes it is time for him to return to heaven, content that his spiritual duties have been completed.

To a nation torn by war and destruction, *A Guy Named Joe* was a most welcome sight. The melange of fantasy, combat action, and open sentimentality appealed to both audiences and critics alike, making it one of the most successful motion pictures of the year. Work on the film began in February of 1943, under the direction of Victor Fleming (*Test Pilot*). Since budget restrictions prohibited the production company from going on location, all of the

"Gosh, what's it like up there, Pete?" . . . "Well when you're up there . . . everything's kinda still, and you've got a feeling you're half-way to heaven . . ."

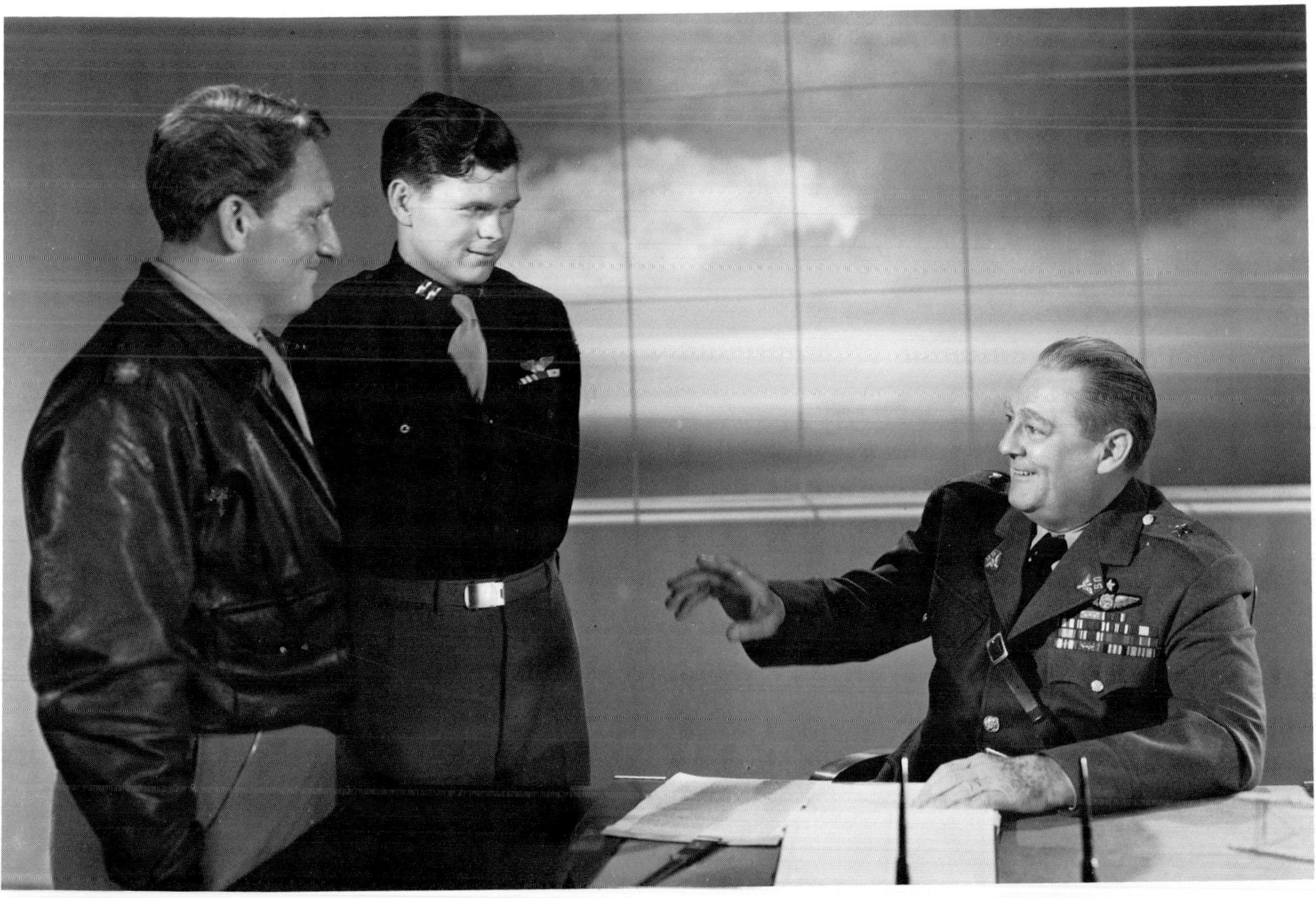

Dead fliers Spencer Tracy and Barry Nelson report for duty with their new Commanding General, Lionel Barrymore.

Producer Everett Riskin, Spencer Tracy, Irene Dunne, and director Victor Fleming relax for a moment on the set of "A Guy Named Joe." This was Tracy's fifth and final film with the noted director ("Captains Courageous," "Test Pilot," "Dr. Jekyll and Mr. Hyde," "Tortilla Flat").

Spencer Tracy gives some ghostly advice to student pilot Van Johnson. All of the flying scenes in the film were shot at the MGM Studios using process footage gathered at AAF bases around the country. Johnson's BT-13 trainer was on loan to the studio from Luke Field, Arizona.

flying scenes were shot at the MGM Studios using stock process footage gathered at various Army Air Force bases around the country. Metro's second unit spent nearly six months filming air and ground scenes at Luke Field, Arizona; Randolph Field, Texas; Columbia Field, South Carolina; and Drew and MacDill Fields in Florida, for use on the backlot.

Assisting Fleming with the technical aspects of the production was AAF advisor Major Edward G. Hillery. Assigned TDY (temporary duty) to the studio, Hillery was intimately familiar with air operations in the South Pacific. In 1941 he was Commanding Officer of the 36th Fighter Group, flying the then-new Curtiss P-40's. When war broke out, he took command of the first P-39 unit (8th Fighter Group) operating out of Port Moresby, New Guinea, and later became Operations Officer of the newly-formed Fifth Air Force. A severe bout with dysentery forced his early return to the States. He later recalled some of his experiences in Hollywood:

"As I was an early returnee from the Pacific and had combat experience in New Guinea, Army Air Force Headquarters in Washington chose me for the job at MGM. All of my time was spent on the set since most of the picture was filmed at the studios in Culver City. I met with Dalton Trumbo, the writer, every morning to assure that the day's shooting would be military in words and action. Director Vic Fleming was a meticulous man – reshooting each scene until he was satisfied with its content. He was very popular and we constantly had visitors on the set, including General "Hap" Arnold, Jimmy Stewart, and Clark Gable."[2]

Hillery recalls that Fleming relied heavily upon MGM's special effects department to recreate the aerial combat scenes needed for the film. "We were at a disadvantage in that no combat film footage was available. So A. Arnold "Buddy" Gillespie, head of the Special Effects Department, was forced to do [among others] the scene, in which the carrier is attacked by Tracy's B-25, in miniature on the studio's backlot. He was considered to be the best in the business."[3]

It was midway through the shooting schedule that the shocking news of Van Johnson's near fatal motorcycle accident reached the studio. Pulling through with a fractured skull and numerous facial injuries, it was estimated that Johnson's recovery would take months. MGM officials felt that shooting around the young actor would cost too much money and began looking for a replacement. Ironically, his scenes thus far were very good, and it was Spencer Tracy, among others, who insisted (in no uncertain terms) that he be given the chance to finish the picture. As a result, production of the film did not end until late September 1943.

A Guy Named Joe premiered three months later on December 23, 1943, at the Astor Theater in New York City. The Academy of Motion Picture Arts and Sciences later nominated the film for one Academy Award for Best Original Story of 1943 (David Boehm, Chandler Sprague).

Pete's former girlfriend – ferry pilot Irene Dunne – finds many of his endearing qualities in Van Johnson and soon finds herself falling in love.

LIFE MAGAZINE

"Taking its title from General Claire Chennault's thumbnail sketch of all pilots, MGM's 'A Guy Named Joe' manages to remain strong and exciting despite such weaknesses as verbosity and a climax that is pure 'Perils of Pauline.' Its strength lies in the restraint of its acting, the realism of its flying sequences and the absence of pilots that clench their teeth and grimly announce, "This is it" on practically every occasion . . . More effectively than any other recent movie, it succeeds in giving its audience the feel of what it is like to be in the cockpit of a combat plane . . ."

December 27, 1943

Mechanics inspect Irene Dunne's P-38 following her attack on a Japanese ammo dump. This scene was filmed entirely on one of MGM's soundstages using exterior process footage shot at Drew Field, Florida. Dunne's P-38E was equipped with electric motors to turn the props and was obtained from an air depot in Omaha, where it had been used for ground instruction.

MEMPHIS BELLE

U.S. Army Air Force

— 1944 —

CREDITS

Director: LT. COLONEL WILLIAM WYLER; Producer: U.S. ARMY AIR FORCE; Narrative: CAPTAIN EDWIN GILBERT, T/SGT. LESTER KOENIG; Cinematographers: MAJOR WILLIAM CLOTHIER, LT. COLONEL WILLIAM WYLER, LT. HAROLD TANNENBAUM; Film Editor: SGT. LYNN HARRISON; Musical Score: CPL. GAIL KUBIK; Narrators: CPL. JOHN BEAL, EUGENE KERN.

Major William Wyler's memorable wartime documentary *Memphis Belle* represents a stark contrast to the motion pictures being made in Hollywood at the time. Released in April of 1944, the film follows a typical 8th Air Force Bomber Group into combat over Europe, culminating in the twenty-fifth and final mission of the B-17 "Memphis Belle."

The picture begins with glimpses of the peaceful English countryside, of quaint churches, rustic buildings, and waving fields of grain. Amid this tranquility, lie the airfields, where bombers are being readied for their next mission. "This is a battlefront," cautions the narrator, "a battlefront like no other in the long history of mankind's wars." Bombs are brought to the aircraft; fuses inserted and screwed tight, guns armed, engines checked. Meanwhile the crews are briefed: target for the day, flak concentrations, fighters, weather, and headings. Afterward they attend religious services, then pile into Jeeps for the trip to the revetments.

Prior to take-off we meet the crew of the "Memphis Belle": Captain Robert Morgan, pilot, age 24, from Asheville, N.C.; Captain James Verinis, co-pilot, age 25, from New Haven, Conn.; Captain Vince Evans, bombardier, age 23, from Fort Worth, Texas; Captain Charles Leighton, navigator, age 24, from East Lansing, Mich.;

Tech. Sgt. Harold Loch, flight engineer, age 23, from Green Bay, Wisc.; Tech. Sgt. Robert Hanson, radioman, age 23, from Spokane, Wash.; Staff Sgt. John Quinlan, gunner, age 24, from Yonkers, N.Y.; Staff Sgt. Casimer Nastal, gunner, age 19, from Detroit, Mich.; Staff Sgt. Cecil Scott, gunner, age 27, from Rahway, N.J.; Staff Sgt. Clarence Winchell, gunner, age 26, from Chicago, Ill. Coming from various walks of life and different parts of the country, they are representative of thousands of American airmen fighting in the skies over Europe.

One by one, the heavily-laden bombers lift into the early morning mist, heading east across the Channel. Climbing to altitude, the crew don their oxygen masks as ice forms on the windows and vapor-trails stream behind the planes. Deadly bursts of flak appear in the sky as the formation approaches the target. The bombers lurch upward as they unload their lethal cargo. Turning for home, the "Belle's" crew spot the first Luftwaffe fighters sweeping in for the kill. Machine guns chatter as they call out positions around

The "Memphis Belle" takes off from 91st Bomb Group headquarters in Bassingbourne-Cambridgeshire, England. Assigned to the 324th Bomb Squadron, she became the first 8th Air Force bomber to complete twenty-five missions over Europe.

The crew of the B-17 "Memphis Belle" (L to R) Tech. Sgt. Harold Loch, Staff Sgt. Cecil Scott, Tech. Sgt. Robert Hanson, Captain James Verinis, Captain Robert Morgan, Captain Charles Leighton, Staff Sgt. John Quinlan, Staff Sgt. Casimer Nastal, Captain Vincent Evans, Staff Sgt. Clarence Winchell. The "Belle" was named in honor of Captain Morgan's fiancee, Miss Margaret Polk of Memphis, Tennessee.

An 8th Air Force bombardier, garbed in high altitude flight gear, prepares to salvo his load.

A 91st Bomb Group B-17 unloads 100 pound incendiaries on a target in France.

the clock: "Pick 'em up . . . four of them coming in at 9 o'clock . . . they're breaking at 11 o'clock . . . get 'em! get 'em!" Moments later, a stricken Fortress falls into a deadly spin, smoke billowing behind her: "Come on you guys . . . get out of that plane . . . there go three chutes . . . there go two more."

At the base, ground crews anxiously watch the sky, looking for the first sign of the bombers. At last their vigil is over. The drone of engines fill the air as the group limps home. Some planes fire flares to indicate wounded aboard; ambulances race toward them as the aircraft come to a screeching halt. We see the strained faces and hear the weary voices of crewmen who've been lucky enough to make it back. Many don't. "Memphis Belle" is one of the lucky ones. Before landing, she buzzes the field in triumph. Having completed twenty-five missions, she and her crew have earned the right to go home. For them, the death and destruction has come to an end.

Wyler's *Memphis Belle* remains to this day, one of the finest documentaries to be produced during the war. Shot in Technicolor, the film's graphic portrayal of a typical 8th Air Force bombing mission conveyed, in simple terms, the realities of everyday life for bomber crews during the early part of the war. Taking nearly fourteen months to complete, Wyler and fellow AAF cameramen Major William Clothier and Lt. Harold Tannenbaum shot the entire film while assigned to the 8th Air Force's 91st Bomb Group, based in Bassingbourne-Cambridgeshire, England.

Using hand-held 16mm cameras, Wyler and his crew accompanied the 91st on thirteen combat missions over such strategic targets as the submarine pens at Lorient, France, the aircraft works at Bremen, Germany, and the rail yards at Rouen, France. During this period (October 1942 – May 1943) they shot over 16,000 feet of film.

Although intended as a composite picture of all 8th Air Force bomber operations, Wyler decided to use the last mission of the B-17 "Memphis Belle" – the May 17, 1943 raid on Wilhelmshaven – as the focus for his documentary. At a time when the Luftwaffe still had a commanding superiority in the air, the "Belle" had managed to bring her ten-man crew home, unscathed, through twenty-five missions over France, Germany, and Belgium. This was not without sacrifice on her part though, as she had been riddled by machine gun and cannon fire, damaged by flak, and on five separate occasions had an engine shot out. On June 6, 1943, she and her crew were retired from active combat duty and returned to the United States for a well-earned rest.

Flares indicate wounded aboard as corpsmen await the group's return.

A jubilant crew emerges from the "Belle" following their last mission – May 17, 1943. During their seven-month combat tour, they accounted for eight enemy aircraft shot down, another five probables, and at least a dozen badly damaged.

Released in April 1944, through the auspices of the AAF's First Motion Picture Unit (commanded by Major Paul Mantz), *Memphis Belle* drew immediate and unending praise from critics across the country. For his directorial efforts, Major Wyler was awarded the Distinguished Service Medal and a promotion to the rank of Lt. Colonel. Together with John Huston's *San Pietro,* John Ford's *Battle of Midway*, and Louis de Rochemont's *The Fighting Lady, Memphis Belle* was responsible for bringing the real war to life for people on the homefront and became one of the most famous combat films to emerge from World War II.

The "Memphis Belle" and its crew are honored during a ceremony at the Combat Crew Replacement Center prior to returning to the United States, June 9, 1943. Each of the crew members received the Distinguished Flying Cross, the Air Medal, and three Oak Leaf Clusters.

NEW YORK TIMES

"A thorough and vivid comprehension of what a daylight bombing raid is actually like for the young men who wing our heavy bombers from English bases into the heart of Germany is magnificently provided in a forty-one minute fact film, recorded by Air Force photographers and entitled 'The Memphis Belle.' Here, in this Technicolored picture, is visioned the whole course of a bombing mission in all its real and exciting detail . . . essentially it tells the story of all the fliers in the Eighth Bomber Command and of all the ground crews who shove them skyward. It is a story that every American should know . . ."

Bosley Crowther
April 14, 1944

LADIES COURAGEOUS

Universal

— 1944 —

CAST

Roberta Harper: LORETTA YOUNG; Virgie Alford: GERALDINE FITZGERALD; Colonel Brennan: RICHARD FRASER; Jerry Vail: ANNE GWYNNE; Nadine Shannon: DIANA BARRYMORE; Wilhelmina Van Kronk: EVELYN ANKERS; Frank Garrison: DAVID BRUCE; Mary Frances: JUNE VINCENT; Jill Romilly: LOIS COLLIER; Tommy Harper: PHILLIP TERRY; Brig. General Wade: SAMUEL S. HINDS; Lt. Snapper Walgreen: FRANK JENKS; Lt. Alex Anderson: KANE RICHMOND; Genevieve: MARIE HARMON; Bea Jay: JANET SHAW

CREDITS

Director: JOHN RAWLINS; Producer: WALTER WANGER; Screenplay: NORMAN REILLY RAINE, DORIS GILBERT; Original Story: VIRGINIA COWLES; Cinematographer: HAL MOHR; Art Direction: JOHN B. GOODMAN; Set Decoration: R.A. GAUSMAN, A.J. GILMORE; Special Effects: JOHN P. FULTON; Film Editor: PHILLIP CAHN; Musical Score: DIMITRI TIOMKIN; Wardrobe: VERA WEST

The lady fliers of the Women's Auxiliary Ferry Service (WAFS) became the subject of a 1944 Universal release entitled *Ladies Courageous.* The film, which starred Loretta Young, Geraldine Fitzgerald, and Diana Barrymore, was based on the story behind the WAFS establishment in 1942 and their early struggle for recognition within the AAF's Air Transport Command.

The Norman Reilly Raine-Doris Gilbert screenplay has Roberta Harper (Loretta Young) fighting "the brass" to establish an all-women ferry squadron to relieve men for combat duty overseas. Her wishes finally realized, she takes command of twenty-five pilots and begins the task of organizing them into a smoothly running unit. Realizing they have to prove themselves, the ladies pitch in on cross-

Sisters Loretta Young and Geraldine Fitzgerald have differing points of view on how the WAFS should be run.

country delivery flights, flying searchlight missions, towing targets, and in general, volunteering for any duties previously done by men. Personal rivalries and conflicts temporarily delay the group's progress along the way, but in the end they receive the recognition and respect they so justly deserve.

Although sanctioned by the Army Air Force as the official motion picture story of the WAFS, *Ladies Courageous* proved to be little more than an embarrassment to the members of this earnest group of pilots. Aside from some interesting flying sequences, the Walter Wanger production offered little in the way of reality and gave audiences the unfortunate impression that the WAFS were flying soap-opera queens.

Universal did receive a great deal of AAF cooperation in putting their production together, even though it was not be apparent from the film. All of the flying sequences were shot on location at the Long Beach Army Air Force Base in California. Director John Rawlins and a company of 115 actors and technicians spent three weeks at the base filming air operations at the Air Transport Command's 6th Ferry Group. WAFS Squadron Commander Barbara "BJ" London and five of her pilots rendered technical assistance and flew in many scenes of the film while not performing normal duties at the field.

Ladies Courageous opened in April 1944, to the general disappointment of all those involved.

A group of WAFS race to their planes before a cross-country ferry flight.

Actual WAFS Evelyn Sharp (center) and Barbara "BJ" London (right) relax with Loretta Young between scenes at Long Beach Army Air Base.

VARIETY

"Exploits of the WAFS (Women's Auxiliary Ferrying Squadron) provide the basis for this over-theatricalized drama of the early femme ferry pilots who argued to be taken into regular Army service. Wandering, and at times confusing, continuity fails to generate much punch for audience attention . . . Over-dialogued script hops aimlessly between girl's quarters at the airfield, take-offs and landings, and several flashbacks to give onlookers an idea of previous events that projected several of the girls into the service . . . Picture has been given adequate production mounting around the airfield but director John Rawlins has been handicapped by the loosely knit and over-dialogued script . . ."

April 22, 1944

Richard Fraser briefs the WAFS on which ferry routes to fly on their mission.

The WAFS prepare to take off on a mass ferry flight. The line-up includes a P-47, two P-40's, two P-51's, and a B-24.

WING AND A PRAYER

Twentieth Century-Fox

— 1944 —

CAST

Bing Harper: DON AMECHE; Moulton: DANA ANDREWS; Oscar Scott: WILLIAM EYTHE; Beezy Bessemer: RICHARD JAECKEL; Captain Waddell: CHARLES BICKFORD; Admiral: SIR CEDRIC HARDWICK; Cookie Cunningham: KEVIN O'SHEA; Malcolm Brainard: HENRY MORGAN; Ensign Gus Chisholm: RICHARD CRANE; Executive Officer: GLEN LANGAN; Ensign Cliff Hale: RENNY MC EVOY; Paducah Holloway: ROBERT BAILEY; Commander O'Donnell: REED HADLEY; Dooley: GEORGE MATHEWS; Flat Top: B.S. PULLY; Hans Jacobson: DAVE WILLOCK; Benny O'Neill: MURRAY ALPER; Ensign Chuck White: CHARLES LANG; Ensign "Lovebug" Markham: JOHN MILES

CREDITS

Director: HENRY HATHAWAY; Producer: WALTER MOROSCO, WILLIAM BACHER; Screenplay: JEROME CADY; Original Story: JEROME CADY; Cinematographer: GLEN MAC WILLIAMS; Art Direction: LEWIS CREBER, LYLE WHELLER; Set Decoration: THOMAS LITTLE, FRED RODE; Special Effects: FRED SERSEN; Film Editor: J. WATSON WEBB; Musical Score: HUGO FRIEDHOFER

Influenced by the many fine documentaries that were emerging from the armed forces, Hollywood's filmmakers began to move away from mere "flag-waving" exercises, and develop film themes of a more realistic nature. Twentieth Century-Fox's *Wing and A Prayer*, released in August of 1944, gave American movie audiences their first convincing view of carrier warfare in the Pacific.

The story, by Jerome Cady, revolves around the men of VT-5, a crack torpedo plane squadron. Lt. Commander Ed Moulton (Dana Andrews) and the unit arrive aboard ship soon after the devastating attack on Pearl Harbor.

Squadron Commander Dana Andrews is welcomed aboard ship by fellow officer Reed Hadley.

William Eyethe briefs the crew of his TBF torpedo plane, Richard Jaeckel and Murray Alper. This particular scene was filmed on Sound Stage 9 at the Fox Studios in Hollywood.

Anxious for a fight, the men are ordered by Air Group Commander Bing Harper (Don Ameche) to avoid combat at all costs. Unbeknown to them, their carrier is to act as a decoy in a plan to draw the Imperial Fleet into a trap off Midway Island. Frustrated by the orders, the fliers are forced to run from every engagement with the enemy. Finally, in early June 1942, the Japanese fleet steams into position. The air groups are ordered to seize the offensive, as the pilots of VT-5 take-off for what will become the historic Battle of Midway.

Although filmed for the most part on Hollywood soundstages, Fox's *Wing and A Prayer* recreated the look and feel of the Pacific air war with a degree of authenticity uncommon in films of the period. Work on the picture began in early 1943, under the supervision of producers Walter Morosco and William Bacher. In agreeing to provide assistance on the film, the Navy Department insisted that the story be based on fact. Accordingly, the script was fashioned around the official combat records of the air groups that participated in the Battle of Midway action. Since it would be impossible (due to wartime demands) to tie up an entire aircraft carrier for use in a Hollywood motion picture, it was decided to shoot all of the film on Fox's backlot, using exterior process footage filmed aboard an actual aircraft carrier as background.

Arrangements were made with the Navy Department for director Henry Hathaway to photograph these sequences on the newly commissioned USS *Yorktown* II (CV-10). "We did all the long shots aboard the *Yorktown* during her shakedown cruise in the Gulf of Paria, somewhere between Trinidad and Venezuela," recalls Hathaway. "We were only allowed to take five people along: myself, three cameramen, and a grip. For seven weeks we captured everything on film: take-offs, landings, crashes, pilots getting in and out of their planes . . . everything. When I returned to the studio and was ready to shoot the close-ups, I had process plates made of these shots and simply put the actors in front of them."[4]

The complex task of building an entire aircraft carrier on the studio's backlot fell to Fox's talented set designer, Lew Creber. Working from drawings and photographs supplied by the Navy Department, Creber supervised the construction of no less than thirty-six sets, including replicas of the pilot's ready room, flight deck, crew quarters, combat information center, and captain's bridge. Additionally, a concrete and wood flight deck was constructed for use in the exterior scenes. Roughly 400 feet long, it was an exact replica of the *Yorktown's* flight deck, complete with 40mm gun sponsons, catwalks, arresting gear, and landing area.

Overseeing the technical aspects of the project was Navy Lt. Robert L. Middleton, a veteran of nearly two years of combat in the Pacific. Now a retired Lt. Commander, Middleton recalls some of the details of his assignment:

"I had just returned from the combat zone, in December of 1943, when I was ordered to Twentieth Century-Fox to begin work on *Wing and A Prayer.* The sound stages had already been set-up with mockups of ready rooms, ship's bridge, flight deck, etc., but lacked all the furnishings and equipment normally found on board ship. Before filming could commence, these items would have to be obtained. We [Middleton and a group of studio employees] spent nearly two weeks at the Oakland Supply Depot requisitioning all the equipment that was needed. As I remember, it took three freight cars to move the load to the studio. I then flew to NAS North Island, in San Diego, to inquire about combat airplanes for use in the film. I was told by the [disinterested] Chief of Staff there that there were none. A few days later, a terse dispatch from Washington made a dozen carrier planes available. The group consisted of a mixed number of F6F's, TBF's and SB2C's. The planes were flown up to Clover Field in Santa Monica, then taxied along Pico Boulevard [complete with a police motorcycle escort] and directly onto the studio's back lot. The aircraft were then placed on the concrete flight deck, where they were used for the duration of filming."[5]

Formal production of the picture began on February 7, 1944. Five separate sound stages were employed during the three months it took to complete the film. Many of the

A flight of SB2C Helldivers form-up over the USS Yorktown II (CV-10) during her shakedown cruise in the Gulf of Paria.

Director Henry Hathaway (left) joins Admiral J.J. "Jocko" Clark (right) on the bridge of the "Yorktown" during her shakedown cruise. Hathaway and a crew of three cameramen shot nearly 50,000 feet of film during their seven week stay aboard the carrier.

An F6F Hellcat (VF-5) roars off the deck of the "Yorktown" during its shakedown cruise. Background scenes such as these provided much of the atmosphere in "Wing and A Prayer."

B.S. Pully tends an injured pilot in this scene shot aboard the studio's flight deck. The F6F in the background is one of a dozen operational carrier planes acquired for use on Fox's backlot.

scenes were shot on Sound Stage 9 (one of the largest on the lot) which contained a replica of the *Yorktown's* flight deck, complete with captain's bridge, flight control tower, and a fully operational TBF Avenger torpedo plane. It was on this set that Hathaway staged all of the close-up or process scenes of his pilots flying their TBF's into combat.

From a technical standpoint, one of the more interesting scenes to be filmed at this time, involved the climactic attack on the Japanese fleet. Much of the sequence was staged by Fox's Special Effects coordinator, Fred Sersen. Lt. Commander Middleton recalls the details:

"Scale models of the carrier task force had been constructed and placed in the studio's lake on the backlot. All the ships were radio-controlled and fitted with explosive devices to simulate bomb hits. A torpedo pilot's eye-view of the attack was obtained by hoisting a camera platform twenty-five feet above the lake and gradually lowering it to the surface of the water as the platform moved forward. The camera was equipped with a zoom lens, which gave the effect of a high speed dive on the enemy ships. This was done for several takes as the task force was being maneuvered. AA [anti-aircraft] bursts were filmed separately by photographing exploding black powder charges that were tossed into the air. Combining the shots on a process screen, used as a backdrop for the TBF mockup, resulted in a very realistic scene showing the plane under fire as it made its attack on the Japanese fleet."[6]

TBF turret gunner Richard Jaeckel scans the sky for Japanese fighter planes during a patrol mission.

By early May, the last of the sound stage and backlot sequences had been completed. *Wing and A Prayer* premiered in August of 1944 and won the acclaim of critics nationwide, who praised the picture as "a first rate piece of film-making" . . . "one of Hollywood's most noteworthy tries at matter-of-fact realism." The film later won an Academy Award nomination for Best Original Story of 1944 (Jerome Cady).

Japanese fighters strafe Richard Crane and his turret gunner after ditching their TBF in the ocean. The Navy provided the studio with two TBF hulks for use in crash scenes such as these. This scene was shot in the twenty-seven acre lake on the studio's backlot.

NEW YORK TIMES

"A fighting salute to the intrepid Navy airmen who did so much to cripple the Jap fleet off Midway Island has come from the Twentieth Century-Fox Studio in 'Wing and a Prayer.' It is at once a sobering reminder of the perilous conditions under which the American Navy sailed the vast Pacific in the months immediately following Pearl Harbor and a first-rate piece of movie-making to boot. The facts may not always be represented in exact proportion, but Director Henry Hathaway has so skillfully woven documentary film footage into the story that it is difficult at times to spot the ending of an incident out of history and the beginning of an episode fashioned on the typewriter of scenarist Jerome Cady . . ."

Thomas Pryor
August 31, 1944

THIRTY SECONDS OVER TOKYO

Metro-Goldwyn-Mayer

— 1944 —

CAST

Lt. Colonel James Doolittle: SPENCER TRACY; Ted Lawson: VAN JOHNSON; David Thatcher: ROBERT WALKER; Ellen Lawson: PHYLLIS THAXTER; Dean Davenport: TIM MURDOCK; Davey Jones: SCOTT MC KAY; Bob Cleaver: GORDON MC DONALD; Charles Mc Clure: DON DE FORE; Bob Gray: ROBERT MITCHUM; Shorty Manch: JOHN R. REILLY; "Doc" White: HORACE MC NALLY; Lt. Randall: DONALD CURTIS; Lt. Miller: LOUIS JEAN HEYDT; Don Smith: WILLIAM PHILLIPS; Brick Holstrom: DOUGLAS COWAN; Captain York: PAUL LANGTON; Lt. Jurika: LEON AMES

CREDITS

Director: MERVYN LE ROY; Producer: SAM ZIMBALIST; Screenplay: DALTON TRUMBO; Original Story: TED W. LAWSON, ROBERT CONSIDINE; Cinematographers: ROBERT SURTEES, HAROLD ROSSON; Art Direction: CEDRIC GIBBONS, PAUL GROESSE; Set Decoration: EDWIN WILLIS, RALPH HURST; Special Effects: A. ARNOLD GILLESPIE, DONALD JAHRAUS, WARREN NEWCOMBE; Film Editor: FRANK SULLIVAN; Musical Score: HERBERT STOTHART; Sound Technician: DOUGLAS SHEARER; Wardrobe: IRENE

Few Hollywood films of the war era approximated the documentary form as well as Metro-Goldwyn-Mayer's aerial epic *Thirty Seconds Over Tokyo,* released in November of 1944. Based on the best-selling book by Lt. Ted W. Lawson, the film is a vivid account of the preparation, execution, and aftermath of the first U.S. bombing raid on Tokyo on April 16, 1942.

The story begins in early February 1942, as Lt. Ted Lawson (Van Johnson) and his crew, co-pilot Lt. Dean Davenport (Tim Murdock), navigator Lt. Charles McClure (Don DeFore), bombardier Lt. Bob Cleaver (Gordon McDonald), and gunner Cpl. David Thatcher (Robert Walker), join twenty-three other hand-picked B-25 flight

Van Johnson and Jack Reilly speculate about their target after arriving aboard the carrier "Hornet." This scene was shot on a 135 foot section of the "Hornet's" flight deck built in Sound Stage 15 at the MGM studios.

crews at Eglin Field, Florida, to prepare for the upcoming raid. For three arduous weeks, the men concentrate on perfecting their low-level flying skills and short field take-offs. Commanding Officer Lt. Colonel Jimmy Doolittle (Spencer Tracy), cautions the fliers that secrecy is of the utmost importance and to refrain from even guessing about their target. From Eglin Field, the group proceeds to Alameda, California, where their B-25's are loaded on board the aircraft carrier USS *Hornet*. Once at sea, Doolittle gathers the crews together and announces that their primary target is Tokyo, with secondaries at Yokohoma, Nagoya, Kobe, and Osaka. A few days later, an unexpected encounter with an enemy picket boat forces the premature take-off of the bombers. Led by Doolittle, the sixteen B-25's roar off the *Hornet's* deck and point their noses toward the heart of Japan. Sweeping inland from the sea, Lawson and his crew successfully bomb their target from 1500 feet and head for the safety of the Chinese mainland. A storm forces their crash-landing on the coast, where friendly guerillas find the five injured crewmen huddled in shock. A desperate race now begins, as the Chinese patriots carry the men inland ahead of advancing Japanese troops. During the pain-filled trek, Lawson's shattered leg must be amputated. At length, the crew reaches Free China, where they board a C-47 for the flight back home. Reunited with their families, Lt. Lawson and his men are decorated for heroism above and beyond the call of duty.

MGM's production of *Thirty Seconds Over Tokyo* achieved a realism unprecedented in a wartime studio production. Nominated for two Academy Awards, the film took audiences aboard Lawson's ill-fated B-25, "The Ruptured Duck," as she roared off the deck of the *Hornet* to strike the first American blow of the war.

Much of the credit for the film's integrity must go to producer Sam Zimbalist, who worked closely with scenarist Dalton Trumbo in transferring Lt. Lawson's first-hand account of the mission into a screenplay. The task of preparing the script took nearly four months and involved numerous interviews with Lawson and other participants of the raid.

Van Johnson and Robert Walker enjoy a moment of relaxation with director Mervyn LeRoy (center) and technical advisor Major Dean Davenport (right) while on location at Hurlburt Field, Florida.

While at sea, Spencer Tracy informs his fliers that their primary target is Tokyo, with secondaries of Yokohama, Kobe, Osaka, and Nagoya.

Major Ted Lawson (right) discusses some minor production details with director Mervyn LeRoy (left) and producer Sam Zimbalist (center) during a visit to the MGM Studios.

During this time, written permission had to be obtained from all those crewmen involved, in order to use their actual names in the film.

Arrangements were made to photograph the opening sequences of the picture at Eglin Field's Auxiliary Airfield No. 9 (Hurlburt Field) near Pensacola, Florida – the original airfield used by Doolittle's men for their training. Surrounded as it was by a large hunting preserve, the field's isolated location would prove ideal for filming all of the training sequences and short field take-offs that were required for the picture.

One of the three Mather Field B-25's used at the studio is run-up on the "Hornet" set. North American Aviation mechanics pre-flighted the aircraft each day to make sure they operated satisfactorily during filming of the picture. A painted backdrop of additional B-25's appears in the rear.

In early February 1944, director Mervyn LeRoy and a production company of ninety-three actors and technicians left Los Angeles for the 2800 mile location trip to Florida. Upon arrival at Hurlburt Field, the cast and crew set up operations in a number of GI barracks adjacent to the airfield.

With Metro's crew settled in from Hollywood, the aircraft and flight crews that had been promised to the studio began arriving at the field. Approximately twelve B-25C's and D's were drawn from Mather Field's 336th and 952nd Twin Engine Flight Training Squadrons for use in the film. Externally, these aircraft closely resembled the original B-25B's used by Doolittle, and would provide perfect stand-ins for the screen version of the raid.

Actual filming began on February 12, 1944. For nearly six weeks, Hurlburt Field echoed to the roar of the B-25's, as LeRoy and his crew re-enacted the secret training exercises required for the mission. Assisting him with the technical aspects of the story was Major Dean Davenport, who had served as Lawson's co-pilot on the original raid. Assigned temporarily to the studio, his many responsibilities included coordinating all of the flying sequences for the picture and interfacing with the numerous military personnel working on the project.

Among the most important scenes shot at Hurlburt, were the short field carrier take-offs that Doolittle's men were required to perfect. Mather Field flight instructor Lt. Winston Green of St. Louis, Missouri, was on location at the time and later recalled the details:

"The entire length of the airfield had been outlined with the flight deck markings of the USS *Hornet*, with flags placed along the runway at 200, 300, and 500 foot increments. For the actual raid, the bombers had to take-off in

Spencer Tracy supervises the loading of bombs, as his squadron prepares to launch their planes. Tracy's bomber is actually a B-25D with lower turret still in place; Doolittle's B-25B's had theirs removed to lighten the aircraft and make room for additional fuel tanks.

less than 500 feet at approximately 50 miles per hour [a B-25 normally takes-off in 1500 feet at 90 miles per hour]. Since our ships were much heavier than the original aircraft, we stretched that out to 700 feet. When the director gave me the signal to go, I taxied onto the runway, locked my brakes, set full flaps and proceeded to rev the engines at full throttle. At the same time, I began pushing the control yoke back and forth, setting the plane into a rocking motion. When the nose was as high as I could get it, I released the brakes, said a prayer, and took-off. Without fail, the nosewheel would lift so high that the tail skid hit the runway, sending sparks all over the place. As I remember it all looked very real on the screen and luckily no one got hurt. Now that I think back on it, if an engine would have quit or even sputtered, with the ship just above stall speed – it would have been all over. I guess at nineteen, you don't think of such things, you just do them."[7]

By March, the last of the Eglin Field scenes had been completed and the crew returned to California to begin work on the interiors. Paramount among these, were the launching scenes shot aboard the USS *Hornet*. Since the Navy found it impossible to provide the studio with an

Director Mervyn LeRoy and his cameraman move in for a close-up of actor Van Johnson, as a wind machine creates a gale on the "Hornet" set.

The "Ruptured Duck" prepares to take-off from the "Hornet." Revving the engines from the co-pilot's seat is technical advisor Major Dean Davenport, who served as Lawson's co-pilot on the original mission.

A limited amount of newsreel footage of Doolittle's take-off from the USS Hornet was integrated with the sound stage and miniature scenes filmed at the MGM studios to give the illusion of the real thing.

actual aircraft carrier, all of the sequences had to be shot on a 135 foot replica of the *Hornet's* flight deck constructed inside MGM's Sound Stage 15, the largest stage on the lot. Spotted along the *Hornet* set, were three of the Mather Field B-25's that had been used in Florida. As the actors manned their aircraft and prepared to take-off, the engines on each of the bombers were run-up to give the illusion of the real thing.

The actual take-offs themselves were a clever blend of newsreel footage and some excellent miniature scenes staged by Metro's special effects coordinator A. Arnold Gillespie. Gillespie later described his work on the film in Mike Steen's book *Hollywood Speaks*:

"I guess the most intricate miniatures I've ever done were Jimmy Doolittle's B-25 bombers taking off from the carrier *Hornet* in *Thirty Seconds Over Tokyo*. We used a scale of one inch to a foot, and built sixteen radio-controlled planes [wing span 66", length 52"] and a detailed miniature of the *Hornet*. The flight deck of the ship was over sixty feet long, which shows that miniatures are not necessarily little. The airplanes and the miniature of the *Hornet* were set in our three-hundred-foot square water tank on Lot 3. A miniature that big in a tank that small had to be kept stationary. So we devised a method of making it appear the

MGM's take-offs were effected with large scale miniatures built by the special effects department. Here one of the radio-controlled bombers takes to the air, while actors stand in front of a process screen.

ship was moving by making it rise, pitch and roll hydraulically, while moving water past it with pumps and wave machines. At the right moment, the bombers were launched, one by one, along a piano wire attached to an overhead trolley controlled with small synchronous motors. The resulting footage was then projected on a process screen, with actors standing in front of it, for the desired effect."[8]

While the main production company completed the interiors at the studio, a second unit was hard at work in the San Francisco-Oakland Bay area, recreating the raiders low-level approach to the Japanese mainland. On loan to them were a number of B-25's from Mather Field and a B-24 camera ship flown in from Kirtland Field's Bombardier Training School near Albuquerque, New Mexico. Special mounts had been installed in each of the Liberator's gun turrets to provide flexible camera stations for Metro's cinematographers to shoot from. Using Oakland's Estuary as a double for Japan's Yoshita River, the filming sorties were flown at altitudes of from ten to twenty feet above the water, leaving little room for error by plane or pilot. As a result, it became standard practice, especially if the ocean was the least bit rough, to flush down the aircraft with fresh water after every flight.

A fire in the city of Oakland provided a good deal of the background footage for the Tokyo bombing scenes. Here one of Mather Field's B-25's sweeps past a natural gas storage tank on the east side of the city.

MGM cameraman Jack Smith catches one of Mather Field's B-25's as it skims over the Pacific Ocean during air-to-air filming near Oakland, California. In many instances, the filming sorties were flown at altitudes of from ten to twenty feet, leaving little room for error by plane or pilot.

By the end of April, the last of the location scenes had been completed and MGM's camera crews returned to the studio. One final incident occurred during the production of the film which proved of interest. USAF Major James Davis (Retired) of Sacramento, California, recalls the details:

A badly injured Van Johnson and the crew of the "Ruptured Duck" crawl up on the beach following their crash landing off the Chinese coast.

"We received an urgent call from the studio one day, asking if we could fly a couple of our [Mather Field] B-25's down to a fire in East Oakland. They wanted to use the footage as background for the bombing of Tokyo. Using 16mm hand-held cameras, we filmed the scenes from the nose and waist section of my ship, as the other B-25 [repainted as Lawson's "Ruptured Duck"] flew in and around the fire. It got pretty 'hairy' at times as we were flying at very low altitudes and had to watch out for telephone lines and any other obstructions that got in our way. Everything worked out OK though, and we returned to base unscathed after our 'mission' over Oakland."[9]

Production of the film officially ended on June 28, 1944. *Thirty Seconds Over Tokyo* had its War Bond Premiere five months later on November 15, 1944, at the Capitol Theatre in New York City. Although overly long (two hours, 18 minutes), critics praised the film as one of the finest and most genuine pictures to emerge from the war. The Academy of Motion Picture Arts and Sciences nominated the film for Best Cinematography (Robert Surtees, Harold Rosson) and awarded it the Oscar for Best Special Effects of 1944. (A. Arnold Gillespie, Donald Jahraus, Warren Newcombe).

Chinese patriots carry Johnson inland away from advancing Japanese troops. Although the film stressed the cooperation that existed between the United States and its Chinese allies, it never mentioned that the civilians who aided Lawson were actually Communist guerillas opposed to Chiang Kai Chek's regime.

NEW YORK TIMES

"The true and tremendous story of Capt. Ted W. Lawson and his Army bomber crew which took part in our first sensational air raid on Japan in April 1942 is told with magnificent integrity and dramatic eloquence in Metro's film from Captain Lawson's diary, 'Thirty Seconds Over Tokyo' . . . There is cause for gratification that Metro took great pains with this film and that it handled the thrilling material with restraint and in a realistic style. For the facts were so much wilder than most fiction and the evidence of courage so plain that a less-discrete treatment might have made this a stupendously distasteful film. And that would have been most unfortunate considering the importance of the deed . . . It is not in the least surprising that this film was permitted to use the actual names of the principal participants in the "Doolittle raid," for it is a fitting tribute to all of them. And it is certainly a most stimulating and emotionally satisfying film."

Bosley Crowther
November 16, 1944

Benson Fong and Dr. Kung Chuan Chi bid Van Johnson goodbye following the amputation of his leg. "Thirty Seconds Over Tokyo" gave substantial parts to many Chinese actors, some of whom had never acted on the screen before.

WINGED VICTORY

Twentiety Century-Fox

— 1944 —

CAST

Frankie Davis: PRIVATE LON MC CALLISTER; Helen: JEANNE CRAIN; Irving Miller: SERGEANT EDMOND O'BRIEN; Jane Preston: JANE BALL; Alan Ross: SERGEANT MARK DANIELS; Dorothy Ross: JO-CARROLL DENNISON; Danny Scariano: CORPORAL DON TAYLOR; Ruth Miller: JUDY HOLLIDAY; Doctor: CORPORAL LEE J. COBB; O'Brian: T/SERGEANT PETER LIND HAYES; Major Halper: CORPORAL ALAN BAXTER; Mrs. Ross: GERALDINE WALL; Whitey: CORPORAL RED BUTTONS; Bobby Grills: CORPORAL BARRY NELSON; Dave Anderson: SERGEANT RUNE HULTMAN; Captain Mc Intyre: CORPORAL GARY MERRILL; Lt. Thompson: SERGEANT GEORGE REEVES; Barker: PFC. GEORGE PETRIE; Milhauser: PFC. ALFRED RYDER; Adams: CORPORAL KARL MALDEN; Gleason: PFC. MARTIN RITT; Cadet Peter Clark: CORPORAL HARRY LEWIS; Flight Surgeon: CORPORAL HENRY ROWLAND; Carmen Miranda: S/SERGEANT SASCHA BRASTOFF; Master of Ceremonies: CORPORAL ARCHIE ROBBINS; Andrews Sisters: CORPORAL JACK SLATE, CORPORAL RED BUTTONS, PFC. HENRY SLATE

CREDITS

Director: GEORGE CUKOR; Producer: DARRYL F. ZANUCK; Original Screenplay: MOSS HART; Cinematographer: GLEN MAC WILLIAMS; Art Direction: LYLE WHEELER, LEWIS CREBER; Set Decoration: THOMAS LITTLE, AL ORENBACH; Special Effects: FRED SERSEN; Film Editor: BARBARA MC LEAN; Musical Score: SERGEANT DAVID ROSE; Sound Technician: EUGENE GROSSMAN, ROGER HEMAN; Wardrobe: KAY NELSON

Released in December 1944, *Winged Victory* was Darryl F. Zanuck's cinematic tribute to the men of the United States Army Air Force. Based on the successful Broadway stage musical by Moss Hart, the film follows a group of American airmen from induction, through flight training, and on to combat in the South Pacific.

The story opens quietly in the small, typically American town of Mapleton, Ohio. Three of Mapleton's residents, Frankie Davis (Lon McCallister), Alan Ross (Mark Daniels), and Danny Scariano (Don Taylor) have received their notices that they've been accepted into the Army Air Force. The trio report for duty at the basic training center, where they meet three equally excited recruits, Brooklynite Irving Miller (Edmond O'Brien), Oregon farmboy Bobby Grills (Barry Nelson), and Texan Dave Anderson (Rune Hultman). The six recruits agree to stick together through all of their training. The strain and sweat of "basic" is mild compared to the two weeks of classification tests that "wash out" many of the cadets. Danny is the first to fail and elects to go to gunnery school. The rest pass the exams and report for primary flight training. On his first solo night flight, Frankie loses control of his training plane and crashes to his death. The four remaining boys go on to graduate and are awarded their long-awaited wings. Taking delivery of a new B-24 bomber, Irv and Alan find Danny assigned to their crew as a gunner. The three men pause briefly to reminisce about old times, before christening their bomber "Winged Victory," and taking off for duty in the South Pacific.

Although over-sentimentalized and a bit corny, Moss Hart's screenplay does capture, between regular bouts of marching and singing, the feel of what it took to become an AAF pilot. The cast, with the exception of the female roles, was composed entirely of enlisted members of the Army Air Force. GI talent scouts interviewed thousands of applicants before selecting the 300 airmen that would star in the film. Each had had prior experience in show business.

Lon McCallister graduates from basic training. The scene was shot at the Preflight Training Center at Santa Ana Army Air Force Base in Santa Ana, California.

Kevin McCarthy entertains fellow airmen Don Taylor, Mark Daniels, and Edmond O'Brien during a break at basic training camp.

Barry Nelson taxies into position for a night training flight. All 300 members of the cast were enlisted AAF personnel.

The AAF cadets are awarded their wings in this scene shot at the AAFB at Stockton, California. The aircraft in the background are Cessna AT-17 training planes.

Formal production of the picture began in July 1944, under the direction of George Cukor. During the filming, the AAF sent no less than fourteen technical advisors to the studio. Among them were experts on physical training, graduation exercises, flight training, a chaplain, flight surgeon, and several pilots with combat experience. Seven different military bases were used during this time with the majority of scenes being shot at the preflight training center at Santa Ana Army Air Force Base, Gardner Field in Taft, California, and Camp Pendleton Marine Corps Base near Oceanside, California. Nearly 100 military aircraft, ranging from BT-13 trainers to B-24 bombers, were placed at Cukor's disposal during the three months of shooting.

Winged Victory had its gala premiere on December 20, 1944, at Grauman's Chinese Theater in Hollywood. Critics hailed the film as a notable achievement in transforming a stage play into the medium of motion pictures. It proved to be one of the most successful pictures of the year with all profits being donated to Army Relief.

Edmond O'Brien, Mark Daniels, and their crew take delivery of their new B-24 bomber "Winged Victory."

NEW YORK TIMES

"The Army Air Force show, 'Winged Victory,' which was a big and deserving hit upon the stage, has now been transposed into the medium which was most appropriate to it all the time – the large-scale and swiftly fluid medium of the motion picture screen . . . it gives every promise of being one of the most successful films about this war . . . Darryl F. Zanuck, who produced it as a film for Twentieth Century-Fox, has put into it all the spectacle that the original (play) so narrowly implied. He and the Air Forces' bigwigs who, after all, are the "angels," as it were, have given it a stunning production, with real planes and training fields and men. They have photographed in vivid actuality all the outdoor scenes that were limited on the stage and they have pictured, from the earth-bound looker's viewpoint, all the wonder that the "wild blue yonder" holds..."

Bosley Crowther
December 21, 1944

THIS MAN'S NAVY

Metro-Goldwyn-Mayer

— 1945 —

CAST

Ned Trumpet: WALLACE BEERY; Jess Weaver: TOM DRAKE; Jimmy Shannon: JAMES GLEASON; Cathey Cortland: JAN CLAYTON; Maude Weaver: SELENA ROYLE; Joe Hodum: NOAH BEERY, SR.; Lt. Commander Roger Graystone: HENRY O'NEILL; Tim Shannon: STEVE BRODIE; Bert Bland: GEORGE CHANDLER; Operations Officer: DONALD CURTIS; Cadet Rayshek: ARTHUR WALSH; David: WILL FOWLER; Sparks: RICHARD CROCKETT

CREDITS

Director: WILLIAM A. WELLMAN; Producer: SAMUEL MARX; Original Screenplay: BORDEN CHASE; Cinematographer: SIDNEY WAGNER; Art Direction: CEDRIC GIBBONS, HOWARD CAMPBELL; Set Decoration: EDWIN B. WILLIS, GLEN BARNER; Special Effects: A. ARNOLD GILLESPIE, DONALD JAHRAUS; Film Editor: IRVINE WARBURTON; Musical Score: NATHANIEL SHILKRET; Sound Technician: DOUGLAS SHEARER; Wardrobe: IRENE

Following the attack on Pearl Harbor, the Lighter-Than-Air (LTA) Branch of the Navy was expanded to meet the rapidly increasing demands of the war. The first motion picture to deal with this little-known service was a low budget air epic entitled *This Man's Navy.* Released in January of 1945, the picture starred MGM stalwarts Wallace Beery, Tom Drake, and Jimmy Gleason.

The story, by Borden Chase, concerns a veteran airship pilot Ned Trumpet (Wallace Beery), who likes nothing better than to tell tall sea-tales and boast of his exploits to his fellow shipmates. Although unmarried, Trumpet brags of an imaginary son, until challenged by long-time pal Jimmy Shannon (James Gleason). Temporarily at a loss, Trumpet ultimately produces Jess Weaver (Tom Drake), a crippled

Striking a familiar pose, Wallace Beery spins one of his famous yarns for long-time pal Jimmy Gleason. The scene was shot at NAS Santa Ana, California.

Free ballooning was part of the curriculum of all airship trainees during the war. This particular scene was shot on location at NAS Lakehurst in New Jersey.

youth he has befriended. Cured through Trumpet's financial help, Tom goes along with the story and joins the LTA service as a pilot-trainee. Following Jess' graduation, the "father-son" team of Air Squadron Four depart on their first coastal patrol mission together. During the flight they attack and sink a German U-boat, and Jess is decorated for heroism. The story ultimately leads the pair to the CBI (China-Burma-India Theater of War), where Trumpet triumphantly flies his airship to the rescue of his son and the passengers of a Navy transport plane, which has crashed in the jungles of Burma.

Borden Chase's screenplay, based on a story by USN Commander Herman E. Halland (Retired), clings more or less to the formula developed for military pictures before the war. Competently directed by WWI air ace William Wellman, the film's detailed look at LTA air operations proved absorbing and a subject, up till that time, untouched by Hollywood's screen-writers.

Filmed during the summer of 1944, Wellman's production company shot most of the picture on location at Naval Air Stations in New Jersey and California. The cast and crew spent nearly eight weeks at NAS Lakehurst, NAS Santa Ana, NAS Del Mar, and NAS Moffett Field filming air

A Goodyear ZPK patrol ship lifts off from NAS Lakehurst. Powered by two R1340 engines, these airships carried a crew of three officers and nine enlisted men.

operations and battle sequences at the base's LTA facilities. Over a half-dozen LTA Squadrons and one HTA (heavier-than-air) Training Squadron were involved during the three months it took to complete the film.

This Man's Navy premiered in January 1945 and drew generally good response from critics and audiences who were, by then, tiring of Hollywood's war films.

MOTION PICTURE HERALD

"Wallace Beery has the benefit here of a story far better than he's had in a long while and of a role that retains the best of his mannerisms while dispensing with the others. Unlike some he's had, this is a vehicle that has merit of its own, a well written and excellently directed presentation of the part lighter-than-air craft plays in the war, a relatively little known and genuinely exciting subject . . ."

January 6, 1945

Technical advisor, Lt. Commander Clyde Schetter, USNR (seated left) offers a suggestion to director William Wellman (seated right) while on location at NAS Lakehurst.

THE FIGHTING LADY

United States Navy

Twentieth Century-Fox

— 1945 —

CREDITS

Directors: CAPTAIN EDWARD J. STEICHEN, LT. COMMANDER DWIGHT LONG, LT. COMMANDER R.L. MIDDLETON, PHILLIPPE DE LACY; Producer: LOUIS DE ROCHEMONT; Narrative: JOHN STUART MARTIN, EUGENE LING; Cinematographers: CAPTAIN EDWARD J. STEICHEN, LT. COMMANDER DWIGHT LONG; Film Editor: ROBERT FRITCH; Musical Score: DAVID BUTTOLPH, ALFRED NEWMAN; Sound Technicians: GEORGE LEVERETT, ROGER HEMAN; Narrator: LT. ROBERT TAYLOR

Equalling the success of William Wyler's wartime documentary, *Memphis Belle,* was Louis de Rochemont's 1945 Academy Award winner, *The Fighting Lady.* Jointly produced by the U.S. Navy and Twentieth Century-Fox Studios, the film chronicles life aboard the aircraft carrier USS *Yorktown* II (CV-10), from the time of its commissioning in April 1943, through numerous battles in the Pacific, ending ultimately in the decisive Battle of the Philippine Sea in June 1944.

The *Yorktown's* story begins quietly and unpretentiously in late 1941, at the Newport News Shipbuilding and Drydock Company in Virginia. After thirteen months of construction, she slides down the launching ways into the chilled waters of Chesapeake Bay. Capable of speeds up to 32.7 knots and of operating up to 110 aircraft, she is the second Essex Class carrier built – a new class of ship that will form the backbone of the Navy's fast-carrier strike force in the Pacific.

During the long shakedown cruise, the *Yorktown's* crew is introduced: the aircraft mechanics, the ship's cooks, the hospital corpsmen, the royally-treated pilots. The very survival of this ship, as well as the fulfillment of its mission, will depend upon all of these men working together in unison.

In mid-July 1943, the *Yorktown* passes through the Panama Canal on its way to Pearl Harbor and the Pacific Fleet. At length, the crew learns of its first target – the tiny atoll of Marcus Island. The night before the mission is filled

The USS Yorktown steams out of Chesapeake Bay on her maiden voyage, April 15, 1943.

with writing letters home, prayers and Communion, last-minute repairs on the aircraft, and just plain waiting, wondering what the future will hold.

In the early morning hours of August 31, 1943, the waiting comes to an end. Air Group Five roars off the deck of the *Yorktown* to join aircraft from the carriers USS *Essex* (CV-9) and USS *Independence* (CVL-22) in six successive attacks on Marcus Island. The raid leaves enemy air installations on the island in rubble.

The months ahead are filled with triumph and tragedy for the crew of the "Fighting Lady," as she and her sister ships thrust deeper into Japanese-held territory. Launching air strikes on Tarawa and Makin in the Gilbert Islands, Truk and Palau in the Carolines, and Roi and Kwajalein in the Marshalls, her pilots wreck havoc on Japanese air and sea forces, and win the Presidential Unit Citation for exceptionally meritorious service in combat.

In early June 1944, the *Yorktown* and the ships of Task Force 58 move into position off the Mariana Islands for the invasion of Saipan, Guam, and Tinian. This constitutes the largest assemblage of carriers and carrier-based

The crew of the "Yorktown" attends religious services prior to their first combat mission. The F6F Hellcats in the background belong to Air Group Five.

Commander James Flatley, Commanding Officer of CVG-5, leads air groups from the "Yorktown" and "Essex" on a raid on Marcus Island, August 31, 1943.

aircraft in history: seven CV's and eight CVL's with a combined complement of over 900 aircraft. Anticipating the American move, the Japanese Navy musters nine carriers and nearly 500 aircraft to engage TF-58 in what will become the largest carrier action of the war – The Battle of the Philippine Sea.

Armorers prepare .50 caliber ammunition belts for the USS Yorktown's air group.

The true face of war emerges in this last climactic battle. As the call to general quarters is sounded, the *Yorktown* comes alive to the scramble of pilot's feet, the shouts of sweating sailors, to ordnance rolling across the deck, and most of all, to the roar of engines, as the aircraft take off to meet the enemy.

We follow the pilots of Air Group One as they engage in air-to-air combat, as they attack the Japanese fleet, and for some, as they limp home to crash on the *Yorktown's* flight deck. By battle's end, the Imperial Navy's fleet lay annihilated – over 450 aircraft destroyed, three carriers sunk, and one carrier badly damaged. So complete is the destruction, that Japanese carrier aviation will never again be a factor in the war. For the men of the "Fighting Lady," it is time to reflect and give thanks for being alive. With five major campaigns behind them, they've been ordered home. For them, the ordeal is over.

Typical of the many feature-length documentaries made during the war, *The Fighting Lady* detailed, in simple fashion, the business of waging war, with few of the frills found in studio-made productions. Taking nearly eighteen months to complete, the film was shot by a crew of U.S. Navy combat cameramen under the supervision of Lt. Dwight Long, Captain Edward Steichen, Commander

The "Fighting Lady" awaits the return of her pilots. Cameramen spent over fourteen months on board ship filming the documentary.

Robert Middleton, and Fox production assistant Phillippe de Lacy. Supplementing the scenes shot on board ship, was a great deal of combat footage filmed from gun cameras mounted on the carrier's F6F fighters, TBF torpedo planes, and SBD dive bombers. Although intended as a screen biography of the USS *Yorktown,* much of the film was shot on board the *Yorktown's* sister ships USS *Essex* (CV-9), USS *Hornet* (CV-12), USS *Lexington* (CV-16), USS *Wasp* (CV-18), USS *Bunker Hill* (CV-17), and USS *Ticonderoga* (CV-14). In all, over 60,000 feet of 16mm color film was exposed during the production of the picture.

The Fighting Lady premiered in January 1945 to wide acclaim by the film critics. It won the Academy Award for Best Documentary Film of 1945, with all profits from the picture donated to the Navy Relief Society.

NEW YORK TIMES

"The story of the men who sail our aircraft carriers and the pilots who rise from these floating airdromes to obliterate the enemy in the Pacific is shown in vivid, bold pictorial strokes in the Technicolor film 'The Fighting Lady.' This Navy-photographed documentary feature, contains some of the most spectacular aerial combat pictures yet made in this war . . . a picture every American should see that he may better know and appreciate what our Navy is doing in the Pacific."

Thomas Pryor
January 18, 1945

The Landing Signal Officer (LSO) indicates right wing low as one of the "Lady's" aircraft return to the ship.

GOD IS MY CO-PILOT

Warner Brothers

— 1945 —

CAST

Colonel Scott: DENNIS MORGAN; Johnny Petach: DANE CLARK; General Chennault: RAYMOND MASSEY; Big Mike: ALAN HALE; Catherine: ANDREA KING; Tex Hill: JOHN RIDGELY; Colonel Cooper: STANLEY RIDGES; Ed Rector: CRAIG STEVENS; Bob Neal: WARREN DOUGLAS; Sergeant Baldridge: STEPHEN RICHARDS; Private Motley: CHARLES SMITH; Colonel Haynes: MINOR WATSON; Tokyo Joe: RICHARD LOO

CREDITS

Director: ROBERT FLOREY; Producer: ROBERT BUCKNER; Screenplay: PETER MILNE, ABEM FINKEL; Original Story: COLONEL ROBERT L. SCOTT, JR.; Cinematographer: SID HICKOX; Aerial Cinematographer: CHARLES A. MARSHALL; Air Operations: CAPTAIN FRANK "SPEED" NOLTA, MAJOR FRANK CLARKE; Art Direction: JOHN HUGHES; Set Decoration: JACK MC DONAGHY; Special Effects: ROY DAVIDSON, ROBERT MARKS, EDWIN DU PAR; Film Editor: FOLMER BLANGSTED; Musical Score: FRANZ WAXMAN; Sound Technician: OLIVER GARRETSON; Wardrobe: LEAK RHODES

The Spring of 1945 saw the release of the last aviation epic of the war, Warner Brothers' *God Is My Co-Pilot.* Adapted from the best-selling book by Colonel Robert Lee Scott, the film recounts the true story of a thirty-four year old fighter pilot who defied efforts to ground him because of age and went on to become a leading ace with General Claire Chennault's legendary "Flying Tigers."

As a boy growing up in Georgia, Scott (Dennis Morgan) dreams of someday becoming an airplane pilot. Persistence rewarded, he wins his Army wings at Randolph Field,

Texas, and is assigned to fly airmail routes for the military. The outbreak of war later finds him in command of an Air Corps flying school in California. Anxious to get into the fight, Scott is told he is too old. He finally succeeds in getting transferred to active duty by volunteering to fly supplies over the "Hump" to China. During this time, he talks General Chennault (Raymond Massey) into loaning him a P-40 for the protection of the unarmed cargo planes in his group. This leads to strafing missions along the Burma Road and ultimately to Scott's assignment to the "Flying Tigers." Through the many months of combat, he becomes known as "a one-man air force," downing a total of thirteen Japanese fighter planes over China. Combat fatigue eventually grounds the now thirty-five year old flier, but not before he's won numerous decorations for bravery and become one of the highest scoring aces in the CBI (China-Burma-India Theater of War).

Although Warner's adaptation of Colonel Scott's biography started out with a sincere grasp on reality, the scenario soon gave way to the imagination of screenwriters Peter Milne and Abem Finkel. The introduction of fictitious characters and overstressed religious messages (Hollywood-style) detract from the overall credibility of the story and result in a well-meaning but predictable formula film whose only redeeming value lay in some of its spectacular flying scenes.

Work on the picture began in July of 1944. Arrangements were made to film the exteriors at the Army Air Force training facility at Luke Field, Arizona. Located outside of Phoenix, the base would serve as the main site for

Raymond Massey addresses his men at the AVG headquarters in Kunming. This set was constructed on Warner Brothers Ranch near Calabasas, California. The aircraft in the foreground was one of two actual P-40E's salvaged from an AAF reclamation depot for use in the film.

Chinese coolies repair the runway after a Japanese bombing raid. Luke's Auxiliary Airfield No. 7 doubled for Kunming in this scene.

Chennault's men take to the air during a Japanese attack. The P-40's were supplied by the 6th OTU at Luke Field, Arizona.

Captain James Brown and Captain Cliff Peterman, of the 6th OTU, roar past the cameras for a scene in the film.

Dane Clark realizes his number is up as Japanese Zero's lace his P-40 with machine gun fire.

staging all of the take-off, landing, and mass formation scenes in the picture. As many as sixty AAF aircraft were scheduled to appear in the aerial sequences, making *God Is My Co-Pilot* one of the most ambitious film projects of the war.

On loan to the studio were approximately twenty-five P-40E's and F's from Luke's 6th Operational Training Unit. Commanded by Captain Clifford S. Peterman, the unit functioned as a P-40 transition training group for American and Chinese fighter pilots being sent overseas. Likewise, Luke's 3028th Army Air Base Unit provided the eighteen

Raymond Massey briefs his AVG pilots on the Hong Kong bombing mission.

AT-6 training planes to double as Japanese Zero's in the film. Add twenty B-25C's, D's, and G's from Mather Field's 952nd Twin Engine Training Squadron, and Warners had at its command one of the largest complements of military aircraft ever assembled for use in a single motion picture.

In addition to the aircraft from Luke and Mather, the Army Air Force's First Motion Picture Unit had agreed to provide an A-25, A-29, and AT-11 for use as camera ships during the scheduled air-to-air filming sessions. Former movie stunt pilots Captain Frank "Speed" Nolta and Major Frank Clarke were called in to coordinate all of the aerial sequences while the unit was on location.

Filming officially began on August 1, 1944. For two months Warner's production crew struggled in the intense Arizona heat to complete their scenes on time. It was during these first few weeks of filming that the only fatal accident of the production occurred. While shooting one of the more involved scenes in the film – the climactic bombing raid on Hong Kong – a mid-air collision took place between one of Mather's B-25's and an opposing AT-6 "Zero" from Luke. USAF Colonel James Brown (Retired) of Burbank, California, was deputy commander of the 6th Operational Training Unit (6th OTU) at the time and vividly recalls the incident:

"The accident occurred very early in the filming schedule. We'd been asked to make a series of head-on strafing passes on a formation of B-25's for a scene in the film. The sequence involved quite a few aircraft [twelve B-25's, seven P-40's and eighteen AT-6's] and was sufficient for us to go beyond the fourteen OTU pilots that had been working on

"OK you Yankee Doodle Dandies, come up and get a load of that scrap metal you sold us" sneers Japanese air ace Richard Loo.

Mechanics re-arm the AVG P-40's prior to a mission. These enlisted men were among the dozens of Luke Field personnel who acted in the film.

the film and borrow some instructors from the regular AT-6 training groups at Luke. We sent word down that we only wanted those instructors who were very capable formation pilots. In the course of filming the sequence, the pilots had been briefed on what the director wanted and we'd talked to one another about making these passes, the rate of closure, etc., and decided it was better to turn and get out of the way early, than to break too late. The 'Zero's' were to attack in a three-ship 'V' formation with an OTU pilot leading each flight. The weather was good that day – no problems. One of the [6th OTU] pilots was leading his flight in an attack on the bomber formation. He had told this young second lieutenant, that was on his left wing, to hang in there tight and not to be daydreaming, as this was going to be pretty close. As they approached the formation and made their pass, the flight leader broke and rolled off to his right. His left wing man started to turn, but didn't break soon enough and flew right into one of the B-25's. The collision sheared the wings off the bomber and it went into a downward spiral – nobody bailed out. Nobody got out of the AT-6 either. Five men were killed – three in the B-25 and two in the AT-6. Had this young instructor turned with his flight leader, like he was supposed to, he would have been OK. But he didn't. He lagged just a few seconds behind, just long enough to cause the collision. It put a damper on things for quite a while, and you can be sure we were all very cautious after that."[10]

While Warner's second unit completed their scenes in Arizona, director Robert Florey and his crew were hard at work at the studio, filming the soundstage and backlot sequences for the picture. Much of their time was spent at the Warner Brothers Ranch near Calabasas, California, where a complete replica of Chennault's AVG Headquarters had been constructed. Fleshing out the background of the Kunming set, were the six wooden P-40 replicas from Republic's *Flying Tigers* and two actual P-40E's that had been salvaged from an AAF Reclamation Depot near San Francisco. The latter two aircraft would also be used extensively in the close-up scenes and interior process shots of Dennis Morgan, Dane Clark, et. al., battling their Japanese adversaries in the skies over China.

Three of Mather's B-25's take-off with an escort of P-40's. Nearly sixty aircraft participated in the picture, making it one of the most ambitious film projects of the war.

Colonel Scott idles his P-40 during filming at Luke Field, Arizona. The China ace found time to fly in a number of scenes for the film between his regular duties as the production's technical advisor.

Raymond Massey and Dennis Morgan discuss some technical details with Colonel Robert Scott (center) between takes at the Warner Ranch near Calabasas, California.

Assisting Florey with the technical aspects of the production was Colonel Robert L. Scott, who had been assigned to the studio for the duration of the filming schedule. Dividing his time between Luke Field and the Warner Brothers Studios in Burbank, Scott found time to do much of his own flying in the picture. One of the more important scenes involved AVG pilot Johnny Petach, who is shot down over Kunming. Viewing the "rushes" with studio head Jack Warner, Scott later recalled his disappointment with the phony miniature work in the scene, and his offer to re-shoot it using his own P-40:

"The special effects people had used this $7500 scale model, attached to a piano wire, to stage the crash; then cut to a real P-40 with Petach [Dane Clark] being lifted from the wreck. I told Warner I didn't like the toy plane sliding down the wire and offered to re-shoot the scene using my own aircraft. We filmed it at the Warner Ranch, out west of Encino [Calabasas]. I came flying in over a small ridge with the flaps down and my landing gear up. I had them cover the crash site with a layer of Fuller's Earth, so that as I approached the ground, the dust would be sucked up in the vortex created by the aircraft. This effectively blotted the plane from the cameras, and made it appear that it was bellying-in. We then 'faded' to the wreck of Petach's P-40 on the ground. It looked fine in the 'dailies' and I was heartily congratulated by Jack [Warner] for a job well done. Lo and behold – when the picture came out, they still had

Japanese troops scurry for cover as Scott strafes their Burma Road convoy. This scene was shot along a fire break in the Santa Monica Mountains, some thirty miles from the studio. Colonel Scott piloted his own aircraft in the scene.

used that little old model on the piano wire – which looked phony, not only to me, but to every little kid in America. Why had they used it? Well, as Mr. Warner explained it 'that model and all the process work had cost the studio $400,000' and besides the union would not permit him to substitute the scene with something that a non-union worker, like myself, had done!"[11]

The last of the soundstage interiors and retakes for the film were completed on October 23, 1944. *God Is My Co-Pilot* premiered four months later in Colonel Scott's hometown of Macon, Georgia. Running a lean ninety minutes, the film became a popular, if not a critical, success and remains to this day a classic for its impressively staged aerial sequences.

Warners' second unit poses with some of the fliers of the 6th Operational Training Unit following location filming at Luke Field, Arizona, September 1944.

NEW YORK TIMES

". . . obviously Warner Brothers took the title of Colonel Robert L. Scott's war book 'God Is My Co-Pilot' much more literally than the author did. For their rip-roaring film based on that chronicle, is heavily and often embarrassingly larded with piety . . . This injection of the spiritual in an otherwise noisy action film is patently ostentatious and results in a maudlin effect on the whole affair . . ."

Bosley Crowther
March 25, 1945

Chapter Three

Post War Reflections: 1946-1949

For Hollywood, as for the rest of America, the immediate post war years were a time of transition, filled with reordered priorities and new attitudes. The war had largely changed the motion picture from a medium of mass entertainment to a powerful medium of national policy. With rare exceptions, propaganda had been the order of the day, and few had cared to question the content of the "cinematic flag-wavers" that flooded the silver screen. It was only after the war had ended that filmmakers began to take a closer, more intelligent, look at the conflict and its effects on the individuals caught up in it.

One of the first, and perhaps one of the finest, of these was Samuel Goldwyn's film, *The Best Years of Our Lives*, released in 1946. Directed by retired AAF Colonel William Wyler, the story tells of three veterans – an Army infantry sergeant, an Air Force bombardier, and a crippled Navy seaman – who return home to middle America to face the traumas of everyday life in the new post war world. It was, as some have called it, a drama borne out of its time, poignantly capturing the quiet sufferings of those who fought to win the war, and who now had to fight to make a new start in a society that promised them no special favors for the sacrifices they had made.

As the nation settled into a peacetime routine, and the wounds of war began to heal, motion picture executives once again considered the production of films with wartime backgrounds. MGM became the first studio to test the post war movie market with two films released in 1947 – *The Beginning or the End* and *High Barbaree*. The former was a semi-documentary account of the development and dropping of the first atomic bomb on Japan; the latter revolved around the surviving crewmen of a PBY patrol plane that had been forced down in the Pacific. While both of these motion pictures deserve credit for beginning the post war trend in war-related films, their quality was of marginal value, and box-office results clearly indicated that the American public just wasn't ready to be reminded of the conflict yet.

It was not until the winter of 1948 that the first major combat film of the post war era was released. Warner Brother's *Fighter Squadron* followed the fictional exploits of the "hot-shot" fliers of the 17th Fighter Group as they battled their Luftwaffe counterparts in the skies over Europe. Although the picture was basically a throw-back to the gung-ho "flag-wavers" that were made during the early forties, it proved popular with movie audiences, and paved the way for a handful of later, more credible, films about the war.

The best of these concentrated on the moral plight of wartime commanders whose duty it was to commit men to battle, and for some, to death. Notable among these was MGM's *Command Decision*, which examined one officer's fight to continue long-range daylight bombing raids over Germany despite prohibitive losses and opposition from his superiors; Warner Brother's *Task Force*, which traced the development of carrier warfare through the eyes of a singularly dedicated Naval air officer; and Twentieth Century-Fox's *Twelve O'Clock High*, which focused on the struggles of a young 8th Air Force general who is brought in to shape-up a demoralized, battle-weary bomber group during the early days of the war. It was in films of this caliber that Hollywood redeemed itself as a veracious telling medium. Free of all wartime restrictions, they offered American movie audiences an intense, realistic vision of men in combat, without the mock heroics that had become so much a part of this genre.

As had been the case after the First World War, it had taken Hollywood years before it could look at the war and its participants with the open frankness that the passage of time allowed. The films of the post war era, whether good or bad, offered American movie-goers an all too brief retrospective of one of this nation's most momentous periods – a look back that would soon become impossible when the advent of the Korean War and the era of the Cold War made self-criticism unpatriotic.

THE BEST YEARS OF OUR LIVES

R.K.O.

— 1946 —

CAST

Milly Stephenson: MYRNA LOY; Al Stephenson: FREDRIC MARCH; Peggy Stephenson: TERESA WRIGHT; Fred Derry: DANA ANDREWS; Marie Derry: VIRGINIA MAYO; Wilma Cameron: CATHY O'DONNELL; Butch Engle: HOAGY CARMICHAEL; Homer Parrish: HAROLD RUSSELL; Hortense Derry: GLADYS GEORGE; Pat Derry: ROMAN BOHNEN; Mr. Milton: RAY COLLINS; Cliff: STEVE COCHRAN; Mrs. Parrish: MINNA GOMBELL; Mr. Parrish: WALTER BALDWIN; Mrs. Cameron: DOROTHY ADAMS; Mr. Cameron: DON BEDDOE; Bullard: ERSKINE SANFORD; Luella Parrish: MARLENE AAMES; Rob Stephenson: MICHAEL HALL

CREDITS

Director: WILLIAM WYLER; Producer: SAMUEL GOLDWYN; Screenplay: ROBERT SHERWOOD; Original Story: MACKINLAY KANTOR; Cinematographer: GREGG TOLAND; Air Operations: PAUL MANTZ; Art Direction: PERRY FERGUSON, GEORGE JENKINS; Set Decoration: JULIA HERON; Film Editor: DANIEL MANDELL; Musical Score: HUGO FRIEDHOFER; Sound Technician: RICHARD DE WEESE; Wardrobe: SHARAFF

Acclaimed as a masterpiece of the American cinema, Samuel Goldwyn's 1946 Academy Award winning production of *The Best Years of Our Lives*, captured the mood and spirit of post-war America as no other film of its time. Adapted from a novel by war correspondent Mac Kinlay Kantor, and directed by former AAF Colonel William Wyler (*Memphis Belle*), the film follows the experiences of three ex-servicemen who return home to America to face the traumatic realities of life in the post-war world.

Their story begins on board a B–17 enroute to the small mid-west town of Boone City (patterned after Cincinnati, Ohio), USA. Huddled behind the plexiglas nose of

Huddled behind the plexiglas nose of their B-17, Fredric March, Harold Russell, and Dana Andrews share some thoughts of home and family as they wing their way back to Boone City. The dramatic aerial footage in these opening segments of the film was shot from Paul Mantz's B-25 camera ship.

the bomber, the three men: 8th Air Force Captain Fred Derry (Dana Andrews), Army Sergeant Al Stephenson (Fredric March), and Navy Machinist Mate Homer Parrish (Harold Russell), share their reminiscences of home and family and their uneasy hopes for the uncertain future. Their homecomings prove to be as different as their divergent backgrounds. Fred returns to his family, who are shiftless and impoverished as always, and quickly realizes he has little in common with his blond garish war-bride. He also finds the deflation from decorated war hero to soda jerk (a job he held before the war) painfully unbearable. Al finds that his family has matured in his absence and that he'll have to get to know them all over again. Homer, who has lost both his hands in a fire at sea, fears the pity of his fiancee, family and friends, and finds their well-meaning but clumsy gestures embarrassing and demeaning. Caught between the painful memories of a war just past and the bitter realities of life in the present, the three veterans ultimately resolve to make a new start in a world that promises them no special favors for the sacrifices they've made.

Few films of the post-war era dramatized the plight of

Navy veteran Harold Russell is welcomed home by fiancee Cathy O'Donnell, as the rest of his family look on. An actual double-amputee, Russell went on to win the Oscar for his fine performance in the film.

Racked by wartime nightmares, a shaken Dana Andrews awakens to an understanding Teresa Wright.

our veterans returning home from the war as effectively as *The Best Years of Our Lives.* Released in the winter of 1946, the story of the three homeward-bound veterans had a universal appeal to film audiences, who closely identified with the readjustment problems of friends and loved ones who had seen action overseas. The film's immense popularity was reflected in its seven (out of eight nominations) Academy Awards, including Fredric March for Best Actor in a Major Role, Harold Russell for Best Supporting Actor, William Wyler for Best Director and Robert Sherwood for Best Screenplay.

Feeling no pain, Army veteran Fredric March is determined to dance the night away with his patient, but foot-weary, wife Myrna Loy. Harold Russell looks on from the sidelines.

From the outset, the production of *The Best Years of Our Lives* had taken on a special meaning for director William Wyler, who had himself seen action overseas, and returned home with a number of readjustment problems of his own. Wanting to portray the story as honestly and realistically as possible, Wyler hit upon the idea of shooting the entire film in a deep-focus style of cinematography similar to that used in his documentaries. Additionally, all of his actors were instructed to purchase their own clothes for use on the screen and to use little or no makeup for the duration of the shooting schedule. To give the sets that "lived-in look," studio technicians were ordered to construct all of the Boone City homes to life-size dimensions, rather than slightly larger to accommodate camera equipment.

Among his leading stars, Wyler decided to cast an actual double-amputee, Harold Russell, to play the role of Navy veteran Homer Parrish. Russell, who lost both his hands in a wartime training exercise, had previously acted (as himself) in an Army-made documentary entitled *Diary of A Sergeant.* This would be his first appearance in a major Hollywood production.

Filming of the picture began on April 15, 1946, following the completion of Robert Sherwood's screenplay. During the three months of production, Wyler staged the majority of his scenes at the Samuel Goldwyn Studios in Hollywood. By the time the picture was finished, over 400 reels of film had been shot (subsequently edited down to sixteen) at an investment of over $2.1 million dollars.

One of the most memorable sequences in the film has former bombardier Dana Andrews reliving some of his wartime experiences as he walks through a graveyard of junked warplanes. Wyler filmed the sequence on location at Ontario Army Air Field in Chino, California, about twenty-five miles east of Los Angeles. A former Fourth Air Force training facility, the base had been converted into a scrap yard for nearly 2000 military airplanes soon after the war ended. Wyler later described the poignant scene in which Andrews climbs into an abandoned B-17 in a rare piece of magazine writing published in 1947:

". . . we wanted to have Fred Derry relive one of his war experiences, and as a consequence have him realize that in order to win his personal battles as a civilian, it was necessary to apply the same courage and strength of character that he and twelve million others applied to win the war . . . We did nothing to the interior of the B-17 except show Fred seated and staring out through the dusty plexiglas. Then we went to a long exterior shot of the plane, in which we could see the engine nacelles, stripped of engines and propellers. We then panned from nacelle to nacelle, as though there really were engines in them, and the engines were starting up for takeoff. Then we made another long shot, on a dolly, and also head-on. We started moving the dolly in toward the nose of the B-17, through which we could see Fred seated at the bombardier's post. This shot moved in, from a low angle, and as it moved in, it created the illusion of the plane coming toward the camera, as if for a takeoff. To these shots we planned to add sound effects of engines starting, and then let the musical score suggest flight. We then cut inside to a shot of Fred's back, and as we moved in, we saw his hand reach for the bomb release. We continued moving in until we reached an effective close-up of Fred, framed against the plexiglas nose of the bomber . . . as a result of reliving this experience, Fred decides to take a job as a laborer, which isn't well paid, but may lead to a future in the building industry. . ."[1]

This scene, among others, was to go straight into the cinema history books. *The Best Years of Our Lives* opened at New York's Astor Theatre on November 21, 1946. It immediately became a phenomenal success with audiences and critics alike. The New York Film Critics voted it Best Picture of the Year and chose Wyler as Best Director. The Academy of Motion Picture Arts and Sciences awarded the film Best Picture of 1946, Best Director (William Wyler), Best Actor (Fredric March), Best Supporting Actor (Harold Russell), Best Screenplay (Robert Sherwood), Best Musical Score (Hugo Friedhofer), and Best Editing (Daniel Mandell). In addition, Samuel Goldwyn was given the Academy's Irving Thalberg Award and Harold Russell received a special award "for bringing hope and courage to his fellow veterans through his appearance in *The Best Years of Our Lives,*" thus becoming the only actor in film history to receive two Oscars for a single performance.

Climbing into the nose of a discarded B-17, Andrews relives a wartime mission in one of the film's most memorable moments. The scene, was shot in an aircraft graveyard adjacent to Ontario Army Air Field, about twenty-five miles east of Los Angeles.

NEW YORK TIMES

"It is seldom that there comes a motion picture which can be wholly and enthusiastically endorsed not only as superlative entertainment but as food for quiet and humanizing thought . . . 'Best Years of Our Lives' catches the drama of veterans returning home from war as no film – or play or novel that we've yet heard of – has managed to do. In telling the stories of three veterans who come back to the same home town – one a middle aged sergeant, one an air force officer and one a sailor who has lost both hands – it fully reflects the delicate tensions, the deep anxieties and the knowing despairs that surely have been experienced by most such fellows who have been through the same routine . . . this one is plainly a labor not only of understanding but of love from three men who put their hearts into it . . ."

Bosley Crowther
November 22, 1946

Director William Wyler and cinematographer Greg Toland (on boom) film a segment of the aircraft graveyard scene as Dana Andrews walks among rows of stripped P-39 Aircobras.

THE BEGINNING OR THE END

Metro-Goldwyn-Mayer

— 1947 —

CAST

Major General Leslie Groves: BRIAN DONLEVY; Colonel Jeff Nixon: ROBERT WALKER; Matt Cochran: TOM DRAKE; Anne Cochran: BEVERLY TYLER; Jean O'Leary: AUDREY TOTTER; Dr. J. Robert Oppenheimer: HUME CRONYN; Dr. John Wyatt: HURD HATFIELD; Dr. Enrico Fermi: JOSEPH CALLEIA; President Roosevelt: GODFREY TEARLE; Dr. Marre: VICTOR FRANCEN; Dr. Chisholm: RICHARD HAYDN; Dr. VannevarBush: JONATHAN HALE; K.T. Keller: JOHN LITEL; General Thomas Farrell: HENRY O'NEILL; Captain William S. Parsons: WARNER ANDERSON; Colonel Paul Tibbets: BARRY NELSON; President Truman: ART BAKER; Dr. Albert Einstein: LUDWIG STOSSEL; Dr. Harold C. Urey: JOHN HAMILTON; Dr. James B. Conant: FRANK FERGUSON; Dr. E.P. Wigner: TOM STEVENSON; Dr. Lee Szilard: JOHN GALLAUDET; Grace Tully: NELLA WALKER; Charles G. Ross: EDWARD EARLE; Dr. Arthur H. Compton: MORONI OLSEN; Dr. Troyonski: NORMAN LLOYD; Pilot: JIM DAVIS; Walter S. Carpenter, Jr., CHARLES TROWBRIDGE; Dr. W.H. Zinn: FRANK WILCOX; General Brehon Somervell: HENRY HALL; Lt. General W.D. Styer: PAUL HARVEY; Quaker Scientist: LARRY JOHNS; Dr. Rand: ROBERT KEANE; Dr. Ernest O. Lawrence: JAMES BUSH

CREDITS

Director: NORMAN TAUROG; Producer: SAMUEL MARX; Screenplay: FRANK WEAD; Original Story: ROBERT CONSIDINE; Cinematographer: RAY JUNE; Air Operations: PAUL MANTZ; Art Direction: CEDRIC GIBBONS; Set Decoration: EDWIN B. WILLIS; Special Effects: A. ARNOLD GILLESPIE, WARREN NEWCOMBE, DONALD JAHRAUS; Film Editor: GEORGE BOEMLER; Musical Score: DANIELE AMFITHEATROF; Sound Technician: DOUGLAS SHEARER; Wardrobe: IRENE

Scientists watch in awe as an eerie mushroom cloud rises above the New Mexico desert following the first atom bomb test, July 16, 1945.

Metro-Goldwyn-Mayer's 1947 release *The Beginning or the End* became the first Hollywood film to tell the story behind the development and dropping of the first atomic bomb. Based on an original story by war correspondent Bob Considine (*Thirty Seconds Over Tokyo*), the film loosely recounts the events which led to the bombing of Hiroshima on August 6, 1945.

The origins of what ultimately became known as the "Manhattan Project" began in 1939, when physicists at Columbia University succeeded in splitting the uranium atom, with the possible consequent release of unimaginably large amounts of energy. When Professor Albert Einstein (Ludwig Stossel) points out the military implications of the experiment to President Roosevelt (Godfrey Tearle), it sets into motion a six-year, two billion dollar effort to build the first atom bomb. The project ultimately involves more than twenty-five universities, upwards of thirty-seven industrial enterprises and more than 120,000 people in nineteen states and Canada. On July 16, 1945, the first bomb is successfully tested in a remote New Mexico desert tract known as "Jornada del Muerta" or "Journey of Death." The event marks the beginning of the end of the Second World War. Three weeks later Hiroshima disappears in a seering atomic blast, which kills more than 65,000 people, and brings to a close the most devastating war in the history of mankind.

Although MGM's production deserves recognition for being the first film to deal with the development of the bomb, *The Beginning or the End* proved to be little more than an exercise in over-dramatized histrionics. The re-enactment of the first sustained nuclear chain reaction at the University of Chicago was authentic and well-staged, as

Noted atomic physicist Dr. J. Robert Oppenheimer visits his Hollywood counterpart Hume Cronyn during a break in filming at the MGM Studios. Oppenheimer supervised the development and testing of the first atomic bomb at Los Alamos, New Mexico.

A curious Jim Davis questions "Enola Gay" crewmen Robert Walker and Barry Nelson about the secrecy of their upcoming mission.

was the critical bomb test at Los Alamos, New Mexico, and the final bomb drop on Hiroshima. Unfortunately, the dramatic concessions deemed necessary by the studio's scriptwriters (i.e., the introduction of fictional characters and romantic involvements) detracted from the overall credibility of such scenes and resulted in a typical Hollywood version of what could have been an impressive story.

Work on the film began in May 1946, under the direction of Norman Taurog. Since government security regulations prevented the production company from going on location, studio executives decided to shoot the entire picture on Metro's backlot, using background process footage filmed at such key story locations as the Pentagon Building in Washington, D.C., Columbia University's Pupin Physics Laboratory in New York, and the Los Alamos Atomic Research Laboratories in New Mexico.

One of the more interesting and complex sequences to be filmed during this time was the climactic bombing of Hiroshima. The interior shots of Colonel Paul Tibbetts' "Enola Gay" bomber were staged in an actual B-29 obtained from the Army Air Force's First Motion Picture Unit in Culver City, California. The aircraft had previously been sectionalized for use in AAF training films and proved perfect for the studio's purposes.

Since no film record of the actual bomb drop existed, the special effects department was forced to duplicate the blinding flash of the bomb's explosion with a battery of some 130 arc lamps. The ominous mushroom cloud that followed was created by filming, in slow motion, a cloud of colored dye released in a tank of water and glycerine. The shot was then superimposed over a background aerial scene for the desired effect. The completed sequence so impressed officials at the Pentagon that it was later used in a number of Air Force training films.

The Beginning or the End premiered at the Capitol Theater in New York City on February 21, 1947. The film met with mixed reviews from the critics, and box-office results clearly indicated that the American public was not quite ready to see films about the war just yet.

Robert Walker and Warner Anderson wait patiently as the "Enola Gay" wings its way toward Japan and the city of Hiroshima. These scenes were filmed in an actual B-29 obtained from the Army Air Force's First Motion Picture Unit in Culver City, California.

NEW YORK TIMES

". . . for the most part, the re-enactments [in 'The Beginning or the End'] are commendably graphic and tense, and they are competently strung together in an impressive dramatic line . . . unfortunately, in making this picture, Metro has seemed to confuse the humbleness of its achievement with the magnitude of atomic power. And it is questionable, really and truly, whether the producers are more impressed with the story which they are telling or with their mission to put it on the screen . . . despite its generally able re-enactments, this film is so laced with sentiment of the silliest and most theatrical nature that much of its impressiveness is marred. This sentiment derives from two romances . . . so hackneyed in treatment, so completely inappropriate to them and so mawkishly employed at the finish . . . that only the most romantic patrons are likely to take them without extreme distress . . ."

Bosley Crowther
February 22, 1947

HIGH BARBAREE

Metro-Goldwyn-Mayer

— 1947 —

CAST

Alec Brooke: VAN JOHNSON; Nancy Fraser: JUNE ALLYSON; Captain Thad Vail: THOMAS MITCHELL; Diana Case: MARILYN MAXWELL; Lt. Moore: CAMERON MITCHELL; Alec: CLAUDE JARMAN, JR.; Dr. Brooke: HENRY HULL; Mrs. Brooke: GERALDINE WALL; Della Parkson: BARBARA BROWN; Mr. Case: PAUL HARVEY

CREDITS

Director: JACK CONWAY; Producer: EVERETT RISKIN; Screenplay: ANNE CHAPIN, WHITFIELD COOK, CYRIL HUME; Original Story: CHARLES NORDHOFF, JAMES HALL; Cinematographer: SIDNEY WAGNER; Air Operations: PAUL MANTZ, LT. JOHN MUOIO; Art Direction: CEDRIC GIBBONS, GABRIEL SCOGNAMILLO; Set Decoration: EDWIN B. WILLIS, RALPH S. HURST; Special Effects: A. ARNOLD GILLESPIE; Film Editor: CONRAD A. NERVIG; Musical Score: HERBERT STOTHART; Sound Technician: DOUGLAS SHEARER; Wardrobe: IRENE

Metro-Goldwyn-Mayer offered movie audiences a rather romanticized view of the air war in the Pacific in their 1947 release entitled *High Barbaree*. Based on an original story by Charles Nordhoff and James Norman Hall (*Mutiny on the Bounty*), the film concerns the surviving crewmen of a PBY patrol plane which has been forced down in enemy-controlled waters.

During a routine patrol mission, Navy Lt. Alec Brooke (Van Johnson) and the crew of his PBY patrol plane attack and sink a Japanese submarine off the island of Tulagi. The encounter leaves the flying boat severely damaged, with one engine on fire, the co-pilot dead and the radio transmitter inoperable. Struggling to regain control of the battle-

PBY pilot Van Johnson and navigator Cameron Mitchell scan the horizon for enemy aircraft during a routine patrol mission.

Van Johnson and Cameron Mitchell pose with some of the Naval personnel involved in the production of the film. All of the air and ground sequences were filmed near North Island Naval Air Station in San Diego. Combat veteran, Lt. John Muoio (far right), served as the film's technical advisor and chief pilot for all of the aerial sequences involving the Catalina flying boats.

damaged aircraft, Brooke is forced to make an emergency landing in enemy waters. The young pilot soon discovers that the rest of his crew, with the exception of navigator Lt. Joe Moore (Cameron Mitchell), have been killed. Adrift for days before being rescued, the thirst crazed Lt. Brooke reminisces to Moore about his boyhood days in a small midwest town and the girl (June Allyson) he left behind.

Directed by MGM veteran, Jack Conway, *High Barbaree* proved to be an interesting film when it concentrated on the Naval aspects of the Nordhoff-Hall story. A pair of PBY Catalina flying boats were taken out of mothballs and recommissioned specifically for the filming of these scenes, which were shot on location at Naval Air Station North Island near San Diego, California, and in the coastal waters off of Coronado Island. Unfortunately, these scenes were far outnumbered by the long sugary flashback sequences depicting the deathless love between Van Johnson and his boyhood sweetheart June Allyson, which quickly turned the whole affair into a rather boring grade "B" love story.

High Barbaree had its world premier at the Egyptian Theater in Los Angeles on May 17, 1947. Reviews of the film were mixed.

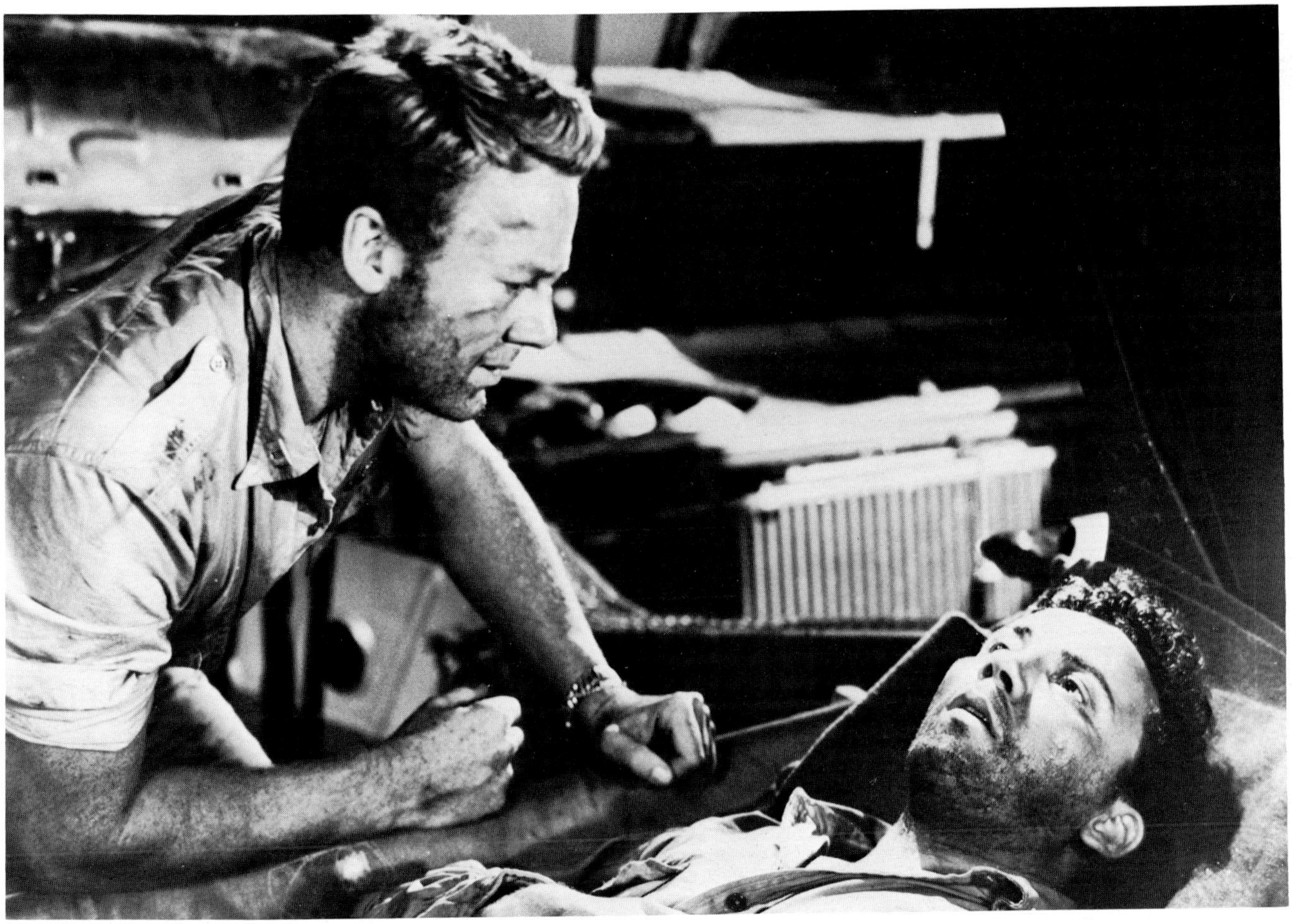

After ditching, Johnson realizes that all of his crew, with the exception of Cameron Mitchell, has been killed.

NEW YORK TIMES

"At the end of a long flashback story which ship-wrecked Van Johnson tells in 'High Barbaree' the shipmate to whom he tells it turns up his toes and dies. We don't like to treat such things lightly, but we suspect that he was just plain bored to death. For the story which Mr. Johnson spins at interminable length while he and his wartime companion drift about the Pacific in a crippled plane is a pretty mono tonous narration of a storybook childhood, of a criss-crossed romance with an old playmate, and of dreams of the mythical isle of High Barbaree . . ."

Bosley Crowther
June 6, 1947

June Allyson provided the love interest for Van Johnson in this story by Charles Nordhoff and James Norman Hall. Their aircraft is a Ryan STA sport plane.

THUNDERBOLT

U.S. Army Air Force

Monogram Pictures

— 1947 —

CREDITS

Director: LT. COLONEL WILLIAM WYLER; Producer: U.S. ARMY AIR FORCE; Narrative: T/SGT. LESTER KOENIG; Cinematographers: LT. COLONEL WILLIAM WYLER, CAPTAIN JOHN STURGES; Film Editor: CAPTAIN JOHN STURGES; Musical Score: CPL. GAIL KUBIK; Narrators: JAMES STEWART, EUGENE KERN, LLOYD BRIDGES

Released to the general public in June of 1947, *Thunderbolt* is a graphic documentary account of aerial warfare in the Mediterranean Theater of Operations during World War II. Directed by Lt. Colonel William Wyler (*Memphis Belle*) and Captain John Sturges (*The Great Escape*), the film revolves around the planes and pilots of the 57th Fighter Group (specifically the 65th Fighter Squadron) during ground support operations over Italy in the spring of 1944.

The picture begins shortly after the 57th Fighter Group arrives at Alto Air Base, on the Island of Corsica, to support the allied invasion of Rome. Flying their new P-47 Thunderbolts, the group soon embarks on one of the most important ground support mission of the war – "Operation Strangle." Fierce resistance by German troops and the worst Italian winter in decades had the U.S. Fifth and British Eighth Armies bottled-up near the town of Cassino. Casualties were mounting at an alarming rate. "Strangle" was devised to break the five-month stalemate by reducing the enemy's flow of supplies to a level which would make it impractical for him to maintain and operate his forces in central Italy. It gave first priority to the destruction of enemy marshalling yards and repair facilities and charged the bomber and fighter-bomber units of the U.S. 12th and 15th Air Forces with carrying out the mission.

On March 19, 1944 combat orders come down from 57th Fighter Group Headquarters. Twenty-seven year old Lt. Colonel Gilbert O. Wymond gathers the men of the

Lt. Colonel Gilbert Wymond chats with his crew chief as "Thunderbolt" co-director Captain John Sturges (far right) captures the action on film.

65th Fighter Squadron together to brief them on their mission. Targets for the day include bridges, rail lines, tunnels, and motor vehicles. Any means by which the enemy can move men and supplies to the front are to be destroyed. As pilots receive last-minute instructions, ground crews ready the P-47's that line the field. Machine guns are loaded with ammunition, 500 pound bombs hung in place, and rocket launchers mounted under each wing.

One by one, the heavily-laden fighters lift off the runway and climb into the cold Italian sky. As the planes approach the target, they break formation and swoop down to release their deadly cargo. In a series of devastating low-level attacks, the squadron destroys six bridges, an enemy tank column, and blow-up a number of key rail lines. On the way back to base, the pilots forage for quarry, as they strafe a troop train and destroy an ammunition dump. Mission completed, the men breath easier as they touch down on terra firma, weary but happy to be home.

"Operation Strangle" lasts for nearly two months. During this time, enemy shipments of fuel, food, and ammunition fall off to such an extent, that by the 11th of May, it is estimated that the Germans have barely enough supplies to last them two weeks. At this point, the Allied ground forces launch an offensive which effectively breaks the stalemate at Cassino and ends ultimately in the capture of Rome. For its participation in this campaign, the 57th Fighter Group is awarded its third Presidential Unit Citation.

Like its 8th Air Force counterpart *Memphis Belle*,

P-47's from the 57th Fighter Group wreck havoc on an enemy truck convoy during the Allied invasion of Rome. The 57th F.G. received its third Presidential Unit Citation for its participation in the campaign.

Wyler's cameramen capture a 65th Fighter Squadron P-47 as it begins a strafing run on an enemy objective.

Thunderbolt ranks as one of the best documentaries to emerge from World War II. Taking nearly eight months to complete, the film was unique in that much of it was shot from remote 16mm cameras mounted under the wings, on the tails and in the cockpits of various 57th Fighter Group P-47's. Start and stop buttons were mounted on the aircraft's instrument panel, allowing the fighter pilots to operate the cameras at will during ground attack missions over Southern Italy. Additional air-to-air footage of the group's "Jugs" was filmed from a B-25 camera ship assigned to Wyler's unit.

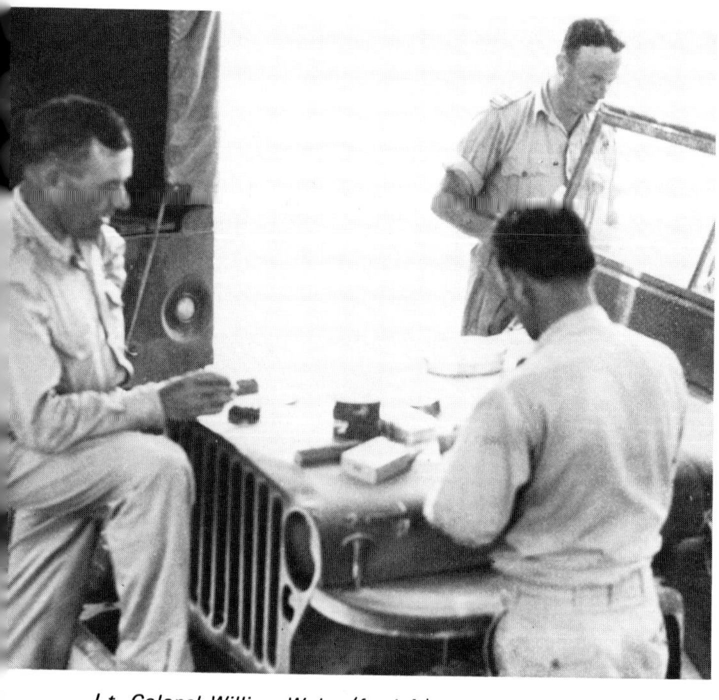

Lt. Colonel William Wyler (far left) holds a story conference with some of his co-workers on the film.

Although completed in October of 1945, *Thunderbolt* did not see general release until 1947, when it was distributed to theaters by special arrangement with Monogram Pictures Corporation and the Department of the Air Force.

NEW YORK TIMES

"The employment of tactical air power in support of ground troops is thrillingly demonstrated in 'Thunderbolt' a forty-three minute Army Air Force film in Technicolor . . . The film revolves around the 57th Fighter Group, based on Corsica in the early stages of the Italian campaign, whose planes were equipped with automatic cameras that recorded on 16mm color film the operation against enemy targets . . . [the film] graphically describes this use of air power while giving a vivid portrayal of how fighter pilots lived, fought and died . . ."

Bosley Crowther
October 27, 1945

FIGHTER SQUADRON

Warner Brothers

— 1948 —

CAST

Major Ed Hardin: EDMOND O'BRIEN; Captain Stu Hamilton: ROBERT STACK; Colonel Bill Brickley: JOHN RODNEY; Sergeant Dolan: TOM D'ANDREA; Brig. General Mc Cready: HENRY HULL; "Tennessee": JAMES HOLDEN; Captain Duke Chappell: WALTER REED; Brig. General Gilbert: SHEPPERD STRUDWICK; Major Sanford: ARTHUR SPACE; Shorty: JACK LARSON; Wilbur: WILLIAM MC LEAN; Jacobs: MICKEY MC CARDLE

CREDITS

Director: RAOUL WALSH; Producer: SETON I. MILLER; Original Screenplay: SETON I. MILLER; Cinematographers: SID HICKOX, WILFRED M. CLINE; Air Operations: PAUL MANTZ, STAN REAVER, F.H. NOLTA; Art Direction: TED SMITH; Set Decoration: LYLE REIFSNIDER; Special Effects: ROY DAVIDSON, H.F. KOENEKAMP; Film Editor: CHRISTIAN NYBY; Musical Score: MAX STEINER; Sound Technician: LESLIE G. HEWITT

Having become a leader in the production of wartime propaganda films, Warner Brothers Studios surprised no one when they released in 1948 the first major air combat film of the post-war era. Produced and written by Seton I. Miller (*Dawn Patrol*), *Fighter Squadron* follows the exploits of the "hot-shot" pilots of the 17th Fighter Group as they battle the Luftwaffe in the skies over Europe.

The opening scene of the film has the men of the 17th F.G. returning to base after a bomber escort mission over France. Former "Flying Tiger" ace Major Ed Hardin (Edmund O'Brien) has radioed the tower that he's coming in with battle damage. Ground crews race to his rescue as Hardin brings the bullet-riddled P-47 in for a belly-landing. His luck intact, the cocky fighter pilot cooly climbs from the

Walter Reed and Robert Stack rush to the aid of Edmund O'Brien following his crash landing. This particular P-47D, used in numerous crash scenes, was acquired from Wright-Patterson AAFB, Ohio.

Director Raoul Walsh (center) and technical advisor Major Joseph Perry (3rd from left) discuss a scene with actors Jack Larson, Robert Stack, Edmund O'Brien, and Walter Reed.

cockpit with three more kills to his credit. A rebel at heart, Hardin is shocked to find that he is soon to become the squadron's new commanding officer. Reluctantly accepting the position, he makes it clear to longtime pal Captain Stu Hamilton (Robert Stack) and the rest of the squadron that anyone found disobeying orders will be transferred out of the group. When he learns that he has an ally in General Mike McCready (Henry Hull), Hardin presses his case for the employment of new fighter tactics. McCready approves his

Georgia's 128th Fighter Bomber Squadron was one of four Air National Guard units selected to provide planes and pilots for use in "Fighter Squadron."

request to drop belly-tanks when attacked by German fighters and later OK's the use of the P-47's in ground attack missions. Tragically, Hardin is shot down during the D-Day invasion, but his memory sustains the men of the 17th Fighter Group as they go on to become one of the highest scoring units in the ETO (European Theater of Operations).

Competently directed by veteran filmmaker Raoul Walsh (*Desperate Journey*), *Fighter Squadron's* only flaw is the lack of an adequate and believable script. The locales and action sequences, taken individually, are quite impressive, but the over-abundance of Hollywood heroics (the good guys versus the bad guys) ultimately takes its toll in one's ability to accept the cliche-ridden narrative.

Work on the film first began in early 1947. Since *Dawn Patrol* proved to be a box-office goldmine for the studio, Warner's decided to put screenwriter Seton Miller to work on a contemporary version of his famous World War I epic. In updating the story, Miller drew heavily on the combat exploits of the 8th Air Force's 4th and 56th Fighter Groups, two of the highest scoring fighter units in the ETO. Included in the script was a scene based on the heroic rescue of 4th Fighter Group ace Major Pierce McKennon by Lt. George Green, who landed his single-seat P-51 in a German field to pick up the downed pilot during a mission to Berlin on March 18, 1945.

In order to minimize the expenses inherent in a project of this scope, the cost-conscious Warner executives decided to utilize stock footage from the Army Air Force's Technicolor documentary *Thunderbolt* in all of the film's combat

Robert Stack prepares for leave, as "Flying Tiger" hot-shot, Edmund O'Brien, warns him about the perils of being a married man.

sequences. It was this decision that prompted the studio to select Republic's rugged P-47 as the star of its new epic. Since all of the active stateside Army Air Force units had already retired their venerable "Jugs," the Air National Guard (ANG) agreed to provide the planes and pilots needed for the studio's production. A sixteen-plane, eighteen-pilot contingent was drawn from ANG units in Georgia (128th and 158th Fighter Bomber Squadrons), North Carolina (156th Fighter Bomber Squadron), and Tennessee (105th Fighter Bomber Squadron) for use in the picture.

On May 26, 1948, director Raoul Walsh and a production company of 115 actors and technicians arrived at Michigan's Oscoda Army Air Force Base to begin the first phase of filming. Located on the shores of Lake Huron, the dormant base, with its remote location, English-like countryside, and excellent weather, proved to be a perfect location site for shooting the picture.

With the arrival of the sixteen ANG P-47's and the ground crews and support equipment from nearby Selfridge Air Force Base, Oscoda soon took on a look reminiscent of a wartime English fighter base. In order to blend in with the combat footage from *Thunderbolt,* each of the ANG "Jugs" were temporarily repainted in the wartime markings of the 12th Air Force's 57th Fighter Group.

Assisting with the technical and historical aspects of the production was Major Joseph Perry of the 56th Fighter Group and Major Leroy Gover, a former 4th Fighter Group ace attached to the N.C. ANG's 156th Fighter Bomber

Hollywood ace Robert Stack gets some last minute instructions from Major Joseph Perry before the cameras start rolling. Perry was normally assigned to the 56th Fighter Group at nearby Selfridge AFB, Michigan.

Edmund O'Brien and Robert Stack find the cockpit accommodations a bit crowded in this scene based on the real life rescue of 4th Fighter Group ace Major Pierce McKennon.

Warner Brother's cameramen catch fifteen P-47 Thunderbolts as they sweep over Oscoda Army Air Force Base during location filming in Michigan, May 1948.

Squadron. Both men had been assigned to the studio for the duration of the shooting schedule and would play an important part in staging all of the picture's air and ground sequences.

Actual filming got underway on May 28, 1948. For two weeks, the Michigan field resounded to the throaty roar of the Thunderbolts, as the air guard pilots recreated history for Walsh's cameras. Oscoda would be used for all of the dogfighting, ground attack and mass formation scenes in the picture.

The eighteen ANG pilots who participated in the filming of "Fighter Squadron" pose with their Hollywood counterparts at Oscoda Army Air Force Base.

Veteran stunt pilot Paul Mantz handled all of the air-to-air filming from his highly modified B-25 camera ship while the company was on location. Acquired in a surplus sale after the war, the Mitchell bomber was equipped with five different camera stations to enable the cinematographers to cover the action from any angle. Most of the filming at Oscoda was done from the bombardier's compartment, where a section of the canopy had been removed for an unobstructed view.

It was while Walsh and his crew were on location in Michigan that the only fatal accident of the production occurred. During a lull in the shooting schedule, the P-47's had taken off for a close formation training session over Lake Huron (which doubled for the English Channel in the film). During the execution of a loop with three other aircraft, Lt. Louis Mikell's P-47 began to disintegrate. Entering a spin, Mikell safely exited the aircraft and deployed his parachute. Unfortunately, he was not wearing a "Mae West" at the time and soon drowned in the icy waters of Lake Huron before he could be rescued.

With the shooting schedule completed at Oscoda, the cast and crew returned to California for another four weeks of filming. For the West Coast sequences, the studio had acquired the services of the California ANG's 195th Fighter Squadron, based at the San Fernando Metropolitan Airport (now Van Nuys Airport) near Los Angeles. At the time, the unit was flying the P-51 Mustang, an aircraft which bore a remarkable resemblance to the German Messerschmitt fighter plane of World War II fame. With a quick coat of black watercolor paint, a few swastikas, and the appropriate iron crosses, Walsh had all the ME-109's he needed for the

Aloft and on the prowl, P-51 "Messerschmitts" from the California ANG's 195th Fighter Squadron form-up over the San Fernando Valley for a dogfight sequence.

The planes of the 17th Fighter Group taxi out for the film's climactic D-Day mission. Seventeen P-47's were obtained for use in the scenes shot at Oscoda AAFB, Michigan.

aerial combat scenes that still had to be shot.

Filming resumed on June 16, 1948. Joining the 195th F.S. Mustangs at Metropolitan Airport were four of the ANG P-47's used at Oscoda and a war surplus B-17G leased from Paul Mantz for the opening sequences of the picture. Among the many scenes shot at this time was a remake of the aerial attack on the German airfield from *Dawn Patrol.* Leading the low-level attack was technical advisor Major Leroy Gover, who was nearly killed when a ground charge was prematurely set off by a studio technician. Luckily neither Gover nor his P-47 were injured and the sequence later became one of the highlights of the picture.

Formal production of the film ended on August 5, 1948 following completion of the sound stage interiors and process shots. *Fighter Squadron* premiered three months later at the Strand Theater in Atlanta, Georgia. Defeated in part by the outdated script and mock heroics, the picture met with only fair response from the critics. Movie audiences in general loved the film though and box-office receipts quickly made it one of the biggest money-makers of the year.

NEW YORK TIMES

"All (or most all) of the cliches that one has ever heard (or seen in the movies) about the brave fellows who zoomed and strafed in the boundless blue and then spent their evenings drinking, are in this ['Fighter Squadron'] rowdy film, which is, rather significantly, the first of a new crop of war films . . . Some of the flying scenes are inserts of old actuality shots made by automatic gun cameras in Thunderbolt fighters – and they are good. Also the shots of the fighter planes roaring off the field and coming in are thrillingly beautiful and absorbing. But 'Fighter Squadron,' as a whole, is a "hot rock" film. The kids and the comics' fans may love it, but the old boys will find it a big laugh."

Bosley Crowther
November 20, 1948

California ANG pilots Major Robert DeHaven, Major Bob Foy, Lt. Nate Spitzer, Lt. Dick Harris, Lt. Bob Massey and Captain Larry Powell (right) discuss some upcoming combat scenes with Lt. Colonel Raymond Gallagher and stunt flier Paul Mantz (left).

COMMAND DECISION

Metro-Goldwyn-Mayer

— 1948 —

CAST

Brig. General K.C. Dennis: CLARK GABLE; Major General Roland Kane: WALTER PIDGEON; T/Sgt. Immanuel Evans: VAN JOHNSON; Brig. General Clifton Garnet: BRIAN DONLEVY; Elmer Brockhurst: CHARLES BICKFORD; Colonel Edward Martin: JOHN HODIAK; Congressman Arthur Malcolm: EDWARD ARNOLD; Captain George Washington Lee: MARSHALL THOMPSON; Major George Rockton: RICHARD QUINE; Lt. Ansel Goldberg: CAMERON MITCHELL; Major Homer Prescott: CLINTON SUNDBERG; Major Desmond Lansing: RAY COLLINS; Colonel Earnest Haley: WARNER ANDERSON; Major Belding Davis: JOHN MC INTYRE; Congressman Stone: MORONI OLSEN; James Carwood: JOHN RIDGELY; Captain Lucius Jenks: MICHAEL STEELE; Congressman Watson: EDWARD EARLE; Lt. Colonel Virgil Jackson: MACK WILLIAMS; Major Garrett Davenport: JAMES MILLICAN

CREDITS

Director: SAM WOOD; Producer: SIDNEY FRANKLIN; Screenplay: WILLIAM R. LAIDLAW, GEORGE FROESCHEL; Original Story: WILLIAM WISTER HAINES; Cinematographer: HAROLD ROSSON; Air Operations: PAUL MANTZ; Art Direction: CEDRIC GIBBONS; URIE MC CLEARY; Set Decoration: EDWIN B. WILLIS, JACK D. MOORE; Special Effects: A. ARNOLD GILLESPIE, WARREN NEWCOMBE; Film Editor: HAROLD F. KRESS; Musical Score: MIKLOS ROZSA; Sound Technician: DOUGLAS SHEARER

As the war years receded, audiences began to see the release of motion pictures that examined the war and its participants with an open frankness that would have been impossible a few years before. One of the better of these films was Metro-Goldwyn-Mayer's *Command*

Squadron leader John Hodiak confers with his C.O. Clark Gable and aide Van Johnson following a rough mission over Germany.

Decision, a penetrating study of military ethics – at the highest levels of command – which questioned the loss of combat crewmen resulting from the 8th Air Force's long-range daylight bombing campaign against Germany.

Based on the successful Broadway play by former 8th Air Force officer, William Wister Haines, the story takes place at an American airbase in England during the latter part of the war. Brig. General K.C. Dennis (Clark Gable) has ordered "Operation Stitch" into effect in an effort to knock out the three German manufacturing centers known to be producing a new jet fighter plane for the Luftwaffe. The raid will be costly, but the loss in lives and aircraft must be weighed against the eventual loss of many more if the German aircraft gets into operation. For two days the bomb groups put up a "maximum effort." The staggering losses that result bring Dennis into conflict with his superior, Maj. General Kane (Walter Pidgeon), who demands justification for the prohibitive losses. Visiting Congressional investigator, Arthur Malcomb (Edward Arnold), also wants to know why "our boys are needlessly being sent to their slaughter." Dennis argues that the target must be des-

For Gable, the role of an 8th Air Force officer was a natural, having served with the "Mighty Eighth's" 351st Bomb Group during the war. Captain Gable is shown here following a wartime bombing raid on the seaport town of Nantes, France.

All of the combat footage in "Command Decision" was extracted from an AAF documentary entitled "Target for Today." This scene shows B-17's from the 94th Bomb Group heading for Berlin.

troyed – that if the Lantz-Wolf One gets into the sky, it could eventually effect the outcome of the war. Unfortunately, his far-sighted logic falls on deaf ears, and Dennis is relieved of his command. Ultimately, he is vindicated when his successor, Brig. General Garnet (Brian Donlevy), finds the courage to continue the bombing missions and complete "Operation Stitch" as Dennis had planned.

Command Decision became the first in a long line of command-oriented films to examine the moral plight of the desk-bound officers who fought the air war from the ground and made the decisions that committed men to battle and for some to death. In addition to an intelligent script and excellent performances by the entire cast, the film was remarkable in capturing the background realities of how a modern war machine is run. Although largely fictional, the terse screenplay was based in part on two of the bloodiest and most savagely fought air battles of the war – the August 17 and October 14, 1943, Regensburg-Schweinfurt bombing missions, which cost the 8th Air Force a total of 120 B-17's lost and over 1200 crewmen missing in action.

Gable and Congressional visitors Edward Arnold and Moroni Olsen watch from the tower as a crippled bomber attempts an emergency landing. This scene was written specifically for the screen version of the Broadway play.

In transferring Haines' story to the screen, Metro's executives wisely displayed a good deal of restraint in not embellishing the film with an over-abundance of battle scenes. Aside from the addition of some stock 8th Air Force combat footage and a sequence in which General Dennis talks down a crippled bomber, the screen version of the story remained faithful to its Broadway counterpart.

For Gable, the role of Brig. General K.C. Dennis came close to perfect typecasting. As a combat officer with the 8th Air Force's 351st Bomb Group, he spent seven months in the ETO, filming heavy bomber operations over France and Germany. His arrival in England prompted Luftwaffe Reichsmarshall Hermann Goering to offer a reward and promotion to any fighter pilot who brought the actor down – dead or alive. At the end of Gable's tour of duty, he was awarded the Air Medal "for exceptionally meritorious achievement" while participating in five separate bombing missions over enemy territory.

Gable plots the next mission to Sweinhafen. "Command Decision" was based in part on the tragic Regensburg-Schweinfurt bombing raids, which cost the 8th Air Force a total of 120 B-17's lost and over 1200 crewmen missing in action.

Formal production on *Command Decision* began on April 24, 1948, under the direction of Hollywood veteran Sam Wood. With most of the action confined to Dennis' headquarters, the majority of scenes were staged at the MGM Studios in Culver City, California. Assisting Wood with the technical details of the story was Lt. Colonel Charles A. Birdsall, an 8th Air Force veteran who had flown twenty-eight combat missions over Europe with the 94th Bomb Group.

All of the air and ground sequences involving actual B-17's, as well as the combat aircrew briefing scenes depicted in the film, were extracted from an official wartime AAF documentary entitled *Target for Today.* Additionally, Wood and his company of actors spent a number of days on location at the nearby San Fernando Metropolitan Airport, filming scenes around a pair of B-17's leased to the studio by Paul Mantz.

The last of the sound stage interiors and retakes were completed on July 23, 1948. *Command Decision* premiered five months later on December 26, 1948, at the Egyptian Theater in Los Angeles. It drew the attention of critics nation-wide who praised it as a first-rate job of filmmaking and the first realistic war drama of the post-war period.

NEW YORK TIMES

"This corner is not prepared to warrant that 'Command Decision' is the best of all conceivable films on World War II. It covers a limited area – this picture which Metro has made from the excellent play and novel by William Wister Haines. And it faithfully shuns the old temptation to pull in action outside its natural frame. But within its field of observation of the behavior of Air Force personnel on the "brass" or command-decision level, it gives us a most impressive sense of real heroism in high places behind the battle scenes . . ."

Bosley Crowther
January 20, 1949

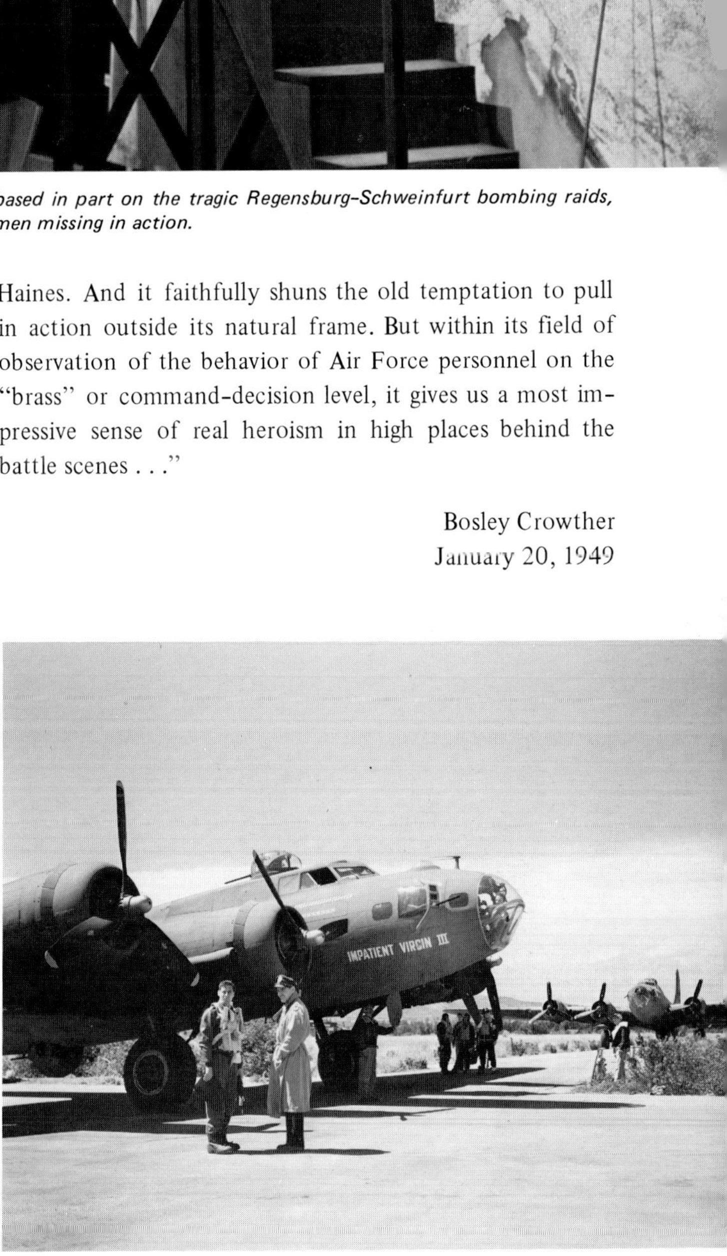

John Hodiak and Clark Gable await the signal to start filming from director Sam Wood. The B-17's were leased from stunt pilot Paul Mantz, and used in ground scenes involving the principal actors.

TASK FORCE

Warner Brothers

— 1949 —

CAST

Jonathan L. Scott: GARY COOPER; Mary Morgan: JANE WYATT; McKinney: WAYNE MORRIS; Pete Richard: WALTER BRENNAN; Barbara McKinney: JULIE LONDON; McCluskey: BRUCE BENNETT; Reeves: JACK HOLT; Bentley: STANLEY RIDGES; Dixie Rankin: JOHN RIDGELY; Jack Southern: RICHARD ROBER; Senator Vincent: ART BAKER; Ames: MARONI OLSEN; Pilot: RAY MONTGOMERY; Timmy: HARLAN WARDE; Tom Cooper: JAMES HOLDEN; Jerry Morgan: RORY MALLINSON; Jennings: JOHN GALLAUDET; Winston: WARREN DOUGLAS

CREDITS

Director: DELMER DAVES; Producer: JERRY WALD; Original Screenplay: DELMER DAVES; Cinematographers: ROBERT BURKS, WILFRED M. CLINE; Air Operations: PAUL MANTZ; Art Direction: LEO K. KUTER; Set Decoration: GEORGE J. HOPKINS; Special Effects: ROY DAVIDSON, EDWIN DU PAR; Film Editor: ALAN CROSLAND, JR.; Musical Score: FRANZ WAXMAN; Sound Technician: CHARLES LANG; Wardrobe: LEAH RHODES

In an effort to capitalize on the box-office success of its Technicolor air epic *Fighter Squadron*, Warner Brothers decided to dramatize the story of Naval Aviation's part in the recent war in their 1949 production entitled *Task Force*. Written and directed by Delmer Daves *(Destination Tokyo)*, the film follows the career of Naval aviator Jonathan Scott from the time of his assignment aboard the first American aircraft carrier *Langley*, to his final wartime command aboard the Essex Class carrier *Franklin*.

Director Delmer Daves and his film crew prepare to shoot a scene aboard the USS Antietam, November 5, 1948. Although modified to resemble a two seat Curtiss F8C-2 Helldiver, the aircraft is actually a Boeing Model 100, owned by stunt pilot Paul Mantz.

As Scott (Gary Cooper) stands on the bridge of his ship, awaiting the motor launch that will take him to shore and retirement, he reflects on a career that has seen carrier aviation grow from a mere curiosity to a potent instrument of war. It seems like only yesterday when, as a young Lieutenant (j.g.) he became one of the first Naval aviators to land on the tiny sixty-five foot deck of the *Langley*. Those early years were filled with triumph and tragedy, as Scott and his far-sighted comrades fought to gain recognition for carrier aviation in the halls of Congress, and with the old-school officers, who believed only in the invinceability of their battleships.

At the time of the Japanese raid on Pearl Harbor, Scott is at sea aboard the aircraft carrier *Enterprise.* The surprise attack has left the Pacific Fleet crippled with only a handful of destroyers and aircraft carriers to carry on the war effort. The importance of the carriers is fully realized in the Battle of Midway, as Scott and members of his air group help defeat the Japanese in what eventually becomes the pivotal battle of the Pacific.

The USS Antietam (CV-36) doubled for several different carriers in the film including the USS Saratoga, Yorktown, Hornet and Franklin.

Wayne Morris and the men of his air group rush to their planes prior to taking off for the Battle of Midway. The F4F Wildcat in the background was one of a handful of vintage types used for close-up scenes aboard the USS Antietam.

For actor Wayne Morris, his role in "Task Force" was a familiar one, having spent six years in the service as a Naval aviator. During his wartime assignment with VF-15 (aboard the USS Essex), Morris was credited with seven kills and awarded the Distinguished Flying Cross and two Air Medals. He is shown here in his F6F Hellcat.

Promoted to the rank of Captain, he is given command of the carrier *Franklin* as she joins the ships of Task Force 58 in the invasion of Okinawa. During this climactic battle, a Kamakazi attack turns the *Franklin* into a flaming inferno. Despite the explosions that rack her hull, Scott and his crew refuse to abandon their crippled ship. Gutted by flames, listing badly, and suffering over 1000 casualties, the *Franklin* gallantly steams back to New York Harbor under her own power, a symbol of America's determination to win the war against Japan.

Released in September 1949, *Task Force* remains one of the finest aviation films produced during the post-war period. Using the fictional story of Admiral Jonathan Scott to document the history of Naval Aviation, the picture is at its best when it concentrates on the exploits of the Navy fliers and leaves the tedious romance between Jane Wyatt and Gary Cooper behind. Originally scheduled to go before the cameras in August 1945, *Task Force* had a long and varied history before finally reaching movie audiences in the late forties.

With the arrival of V-J Day on September 2, 1945, Warner's decided to temporarily shelve the picture until such time as they felt the public was ready to see war films again. In the meantime, producer Jerry Wald and writer-director Delmer Daves continued to research the history of Naval

The USS Yorktown (CV-5) under attack during the Battle of Midway. This was typical of the numerous combat scenes that were intercut with the studio dramatizations in the film.

Aviation and develop a script which they felt would be acceptable to studio executives.

In early 1948, the filmmakers were finally given permission to move ahead with their project. From the outset, Daves had intended to build much of his picture around the 4,000,000 feet of documentary film he had gleaned from official Navy archives. Accordingly, all of the early segments of the story were filmed in black and white, to blend in with the historic newsreel footage shot of the *Langley*, and the later World War II segments filmed in color, to blend in with the 16mm combat footage shot aboard various wartime carriers. Arrangements had also been made with the Navy Department to shoot all of the studio's shipboard exteriors on board two actual aircraft carriers, the USS *Antietam* (CV-36) and USS *Bairoko* (CVE-115), based at NAS North Island in San Diego, California.

On October 23, 1948, Daves and a production company of one hundred seventeen actors and technicians arrived in San Diego to begin the first phase of location filming. The following day, the entire crew boarded the 27,000 ton Essex Class carrier USS *Antietam* to start work on the exteriors. Built too late to see action during World War II, the *Antietam* was scheduled to double for several different carriers in the film, including the *Saratoga, Yorktown, Hornet,* and *Franklin,* which figured so prominently in the story.

For three weeks the ship echoed to the sounds of battle, as Warners' crew turned the clock backwards for the benefit of their motion picture cameras. Over ninety-five tons of equipment, from lights and cable to period furniture, had to be brought aboard the carrier to support the

In one of the many combat scenes filmed aboard the "Antietam," rescue crews rush to aid the crew of a crashed SBD Dauntless dive bomber.

Walter Brennan maps out his strategy for the invasion of Okinawa as the commanders of Task Force 58 look on.

filming operations. Since the *Antietam* was under strict orders to operate according to schedule, much of the shooting had to be done during seaborne training maneuvers off the coast of California between San Diego and Alameda.

During this time Carrier Air Group Fourteen (CAG-14) provided ample numbers of F6F's, F8F's and TBM's for the take-off and landing sequences that were later used in the

During the climactic battle of Okinawa, Cooper's ship, the USS Franklin, is severely damaged by Kamakazi fighter planes.

sound stage process scenes. In addition to these aircraft the studio had also brought aboard an F8C-2 Helldiver (actually a highly-modified Boeing Model 100), F4F Wildcat, and SBD Dauntless for use in the flight deck close-ups involving the principal actors. By the end of the shooting schedule, over 1,000 of the *Antietam's* officers and enlisted men had appeared in the picture, performing their normal shipboard duties in scenes with the Warner stars.

With the filming of carrier scenes aboard the *Antietam* complete, director Daves and his production crew transferred operations to the USS *Bairoko* to begin work on the early flight training sequences that appear at the beginning of the picture. The diminutive *Bairoko,* a World War II vintage escort carrier, doubled as the USS *Langley* during the three days it took to complete these shipboard sequences (the original *Langley* had been sunk by the Japanese shortly after the outbreak of war).

Among the many scenes filmed aboard the *Bairoko* was a re-enactment of the first U.S. Navy carrier take-off by Lt. Commander V.C. Griffin on October 22, 1922. Veteran stunt pilot Paul Mantz staged the sequence using a DeHavilland DH-4 biplane, modified to resemble the Vought VE-7SF that Griffin had used. Mantz's flight sequences were later intercut with actual newsreel footage of the event, resulting in a very effective representation of the historic *Langley* take-off.

Gary Cooper sweats out a battle in the "Franklin's" Combat Intelligence Center (CIC).

Location filming at NAS North Island was wrapped-up by the end of November, with Warners' production crew returning to the Burbank studios to complete the remaining sound stage interiors and process shots. Production officially ended on January 5, 1949.

Task Force premiered eight months later in a special two-ocean screening held aboard the USS *Midway* (CVB-41) in the Atlantic, and the USS *Valley Forge* (CV-45) in the Pacific. Critics greeted the film enthusiastically. "A classic of its kind," said one reviewer, "one of the most authentic war pictures ever made." Audiences were equally enthusiastic, and the film ultimately became one of the largest grossing pictures of the post-war era.

NEW YORK TIMES

"Now that sufficient interval has passed since the end of World War II for the public to look back on its torments with reflection and sentiment, Warner Brothers has come forth with a sizzling and sentimental film which traces the painful expansion of the Navy's air arm and its great use in the war. 'Task Force' is the title of this long semi-historic job which is part fiction, part documentary . . . when the film finally comes to showing real carrier activity out at sea and the actual aspects of recent warfare, it springs into vivid, thrilling life . . . scenes of aircraft launchings and recoveries on the windy decks, of ready-room waiting, flag-plot sweating and business in the C.I.C. (Combat Intelligence Center) down in the bowels of the ship are full of exciting fascination and superlative imagery . . ."

Bosley Crowther
October 1, 1949

Cameramen catch a CAG-14 TBM as it makes an arrested carrier landing aboard the USS Antietam, November 1948. Footage, such as this, was later used in the sound stage process scenes filmed at the Warner Brother's Studios in Burbank.

TWELVE O'CLOCK HIGH

Twentieth Century-Fox

— 1949 —

CAST

General Frank Savage: GREGORY PECK; Lt. Colonel Ben Gately: HUGH MARLOWE; Colonel Keith Davenport: GARY MERRILL; General Pritchard: MILLARD MITCHELL; Major Harvey Stovall: DEAN JAGGER; Sgt. Mc Illhenny: ROBERT ARTHUR; Captain "Doc" Kaiser: PAUL STEWART; Major Cobb: JOHN KELLOGG; Lt. Bishop: BOB PATTEN; Lt. Wilson: DON HICKS; Lt. Zimmerman: LEE MAC GREGOR: Birdwell: SAM EDWARDS; Interrogation Officer: ROGER ANDERSON; Sgt. Ernie: JOHN ZILLY; Lt. Pettinghill: WILLIAM SHORT; Lt. McKessen: RICHARD ANDERSON; Captain Twombley: LAWRENCE DOBKIN; Sentry: KENNETH TOBEY; Nurse: JOYCE MAC KENZIE

CREDITS

Director: HENRY KING; Producer: DARRYL F. ZANUCK; Screenplay: SY BARTLETT, BEIRNE LAY, JR.; Original Story: SY BARTLETT, BEIRNE LAY, JR.; Cinematographer: LEON SHAMROY; Air Operations: PAUL MANTZ; Art Direction: LYLE WHEELER, MAURICE RANSFORD; Set Decoration: THOMAS LITTLE, BRUCE MAC DONALD; Special Effects: FRED SERSEN; Film Editor: BARBARA MC LEAN; Musical Score: ALFRED NEWMAN; Sound Technicians: W.D. FLICK, ROGER HEMAN

The year 1950 saw the premiere of what was perhaps the finest cinematic study of aerial combat ever achieved by a Hollywood studio. Nominated for four Academy Awards, Twentieth Century-Fox's production of *Twelve O'Clock High* poignantly captured the heroism, human sacrifice, and grim reality of the air war over Nazi-occupied Europe as no other film, before or since, has managed to do. Borne out of the efforts of two screenwriters who had been there, the story focuses on a young 8th Air Force general who is brought in to shape-up a demoralized, battle-weary bomber group during the early days of the war.

The opening scene of the film has former AAF Major Harvey Stovall (Dean Jagger) making a nostalgic return visit to the abandoned air base at Archbury, England, where he had been stationed during the war. As Stovall stands at the edge of the runway, now rutted and overgrown, his mind wanders back to a desperate time in 1942 when his unit, the 918th Bomb Group, was fighting for its survival in the skies over Europe.

As part of the infant 8th Air Force, the 918th is involved in the first daylight precision bombing raids against Germany. Murderous opposition by the Luftwaffe has resulted in heavy losses and a gradual decline in the group's morale. The aircrews are exhausted and resentful, and the situation is only worsened by Commanding Officer Colonel Keith Davenport's (Gary Merrill) strong tendency to over-identify with his men. Bomber Command orders General Frank Savage (Gregory Peck) to replace the battle-weary Davenport and rebuild his "hard luck group" into an efficient combat unit.

Savage immediately establishes a "make-or-break" policy at the base – ineffective subordinates are demoted, privileges are cancelled, and the aircrews are ordered on countless training missions to bring them back to fighting efficiency. Savage drives the men hard – some to their breaking point. Resentful at first, they gradually come to respect his relentless methods. The group's bombing performance begins to improve, casualties drop, and morale picks up. Ultimately, Savage comes to respect the efforts of his men and begins to see them as friends, not just combat crews. In the end it proves to be his downfall, as the all-too-human commander cracks under the strain of sending his comrades out to fight and die.

The discovery of the 918th B.G.'s Toby Mug in a post-war London arcade prompts Dean Jagger to make a nostalgic return visit to his old base at Archbury.

Released on the eve of the Korean War, *Twelve O' Clock High* was one of those timeless dramas destined to become an American film classic. Outstanding acting, an excellent screenplay, the technical accomplishments of its production staff, and the generous cooperation of the United States Air Force, resulted in an intense, unsentimentalized vision of men in combat, free of the mock heroics that had become so much a part of this genre.

Six of the twelve B-17's acquired for "Twelve O'Clock High" break formation over the Archbury set at Eglin Field, Florida, April 1949.

Technical advisor Colonel John deRussy prepares to land his B-17 in the opening scene of the film. All of the landing and take-off sequences were shot at Ozark Field, Alabama, now the site of the Ft. Rucker Army Aviation Training Complex.

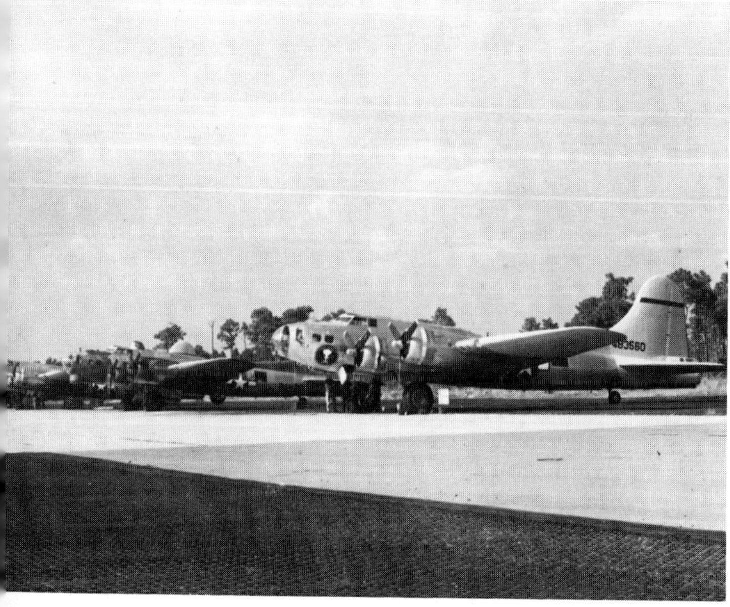

A line-up of B-17's from the 3205th Drone Group await their temporary wartime markings for "Twelve O'Clock High." Although all of the aircraft used in the film were "G" models, most had been radically modified to QB-17 pilotless drone or DB-17 drone controller configuration.

Much of the film's credibility can be attributed directly to the screen-writing efforts of former Army Air Force officers Sy Bartlett and Beirne Lay, Jr. Both men had been intimately involved in 8th Air Force bomber operations during the war and later decided to use real-life wartime incidents to form the basis for their novel and screenplay. The character of General Frank Savage, for example, closely paralleled that of Colonel Frank Armstrong, Jr., commander of the first 8th Air Force bomber group based in England. It was Armstrong who was ordered, in early 1943, to take command of and rebuild the battered 306th Bomb Group based in Thurleigh. In three months of bomber operations over Europe, the unit had suffered some of the highest losses in the ETO. The group later became the model for the ficticious 918th Bomber Group.

Pre-production planning for the film began in January 1949, under the direction of veteran filmmaker Henry King. One of the first chores facing the long time director-aviator (King earned his pilot's license in 1919) was to find a suitable stateside location site to represent the midlands area of England. After an 11,000 mile scouting trip and numerous conferences with Air Force officials in Washing-

Paul Mantz's belly-landing at Ozark Field remains one of the most spectacular scenes in any aviation film.

ton, King settled on two airbases in the southeast to shoot all of the exteriors for the film.

At Eglin Field, Florida, the production crew acquired the use of an isolated satellite field (one of nine on the 800,000 acre complex) for the duration of their six-week shooting schedule. Here studio technicians erected a detailed replica of an 8th Air Force bomber base, complete with Quonset huts, briefing rooms, and a period English control tower. Since the field's white concrete runways did not lend themselves to filming an 8th Air Force epic (war-time English airfields were black to make them less visible to enemy bombers), all of the take-off and landing sequences had to be shot some ninety miles to the north at Ozark Field, Alabama (now known as Ft. Rucker Army Air Field).

Assisting King with the myriad technical details of the production was USAF Colonel John H. deRussy, the film's military advisor. An experienced B-17 pilot, deRussy had served as operations officer of the 8th Air Force's 305th Bomb Group during the war. His many responsibilities on the film included the acquisition of sufficient aircrews for the proposed air and ground sequences. "All of the pilots that flew in the film were selected from officer volunteers

Mantz's B-17 finally comes to rest some 1200 feet from the point of touchdown.

Paul Stewart oversees the rescue of wounded crewmen from "Eager Beaver."

John Kellogg gives the cold shoulder to the newly-arrived commanding officer of the 918th Bomb Group, Gregory Peck.

stationed at Eglin Field," remembers deRussy. "Some had considerable flying experience in the B-17, others had very little. So we checked out and trained those who needed it and then trained the entire group in B-17 formation flying."[2] As ranking officer on the film, deRussy would personally lead all of the B-17 flights in the picture.

As many as twelve B-17's were acquired for use in the film's aerial sequences. At least six of these came from Eglin's 3205th Drone Group, which had been using the obsolete bombers in ditching tests and as targets for newly-developed missiles. The balance of Fox's "bomb group" was drawn from Air Force storage depots in Alabama and New Mexico. A number of the latter aircraft had been used as radio-controlled drones in the 1946 Bikini Atoll atom bomb tests, and were only safe for short periods of use. The aircraft still showed radioactive side-effects from the blast, and periodically had to be checked with geiger counters for safety reasons.

To match the stock combat footage that would later be edited into the film, studio technicians repainted each of the bombers in the olive drab and grey camouflage markings of the 8th Air Force's 91st Bomb Group – circa 1943. Since most of the B-17's had been reconfigured for various post-war uses, the majority required the installation of original gun turrets and .50 caliber machine guns before they would be ready for their temporary war time roles before the cameras.

On April 17, 1949, King and his company of seventy-two actors and technicians arrived in Florida to begin work on the exteriors. During the six weeks of filming, the crew split most of their time equally between the two location sites (Ozark and Eglin), travelling aboard a chartered Delta Airlines DC-6 that the studio had leased for the occasion.

Among the first scenes to be filmed at Ozark Field, Alabama, was Dean Jagger's nostalgic return to the abandoned airbase at Archbury, which appears at the beginning of the picture. Closed shortly after World War II, Ozark's derelict appearance and overgrown runways proved ideal for the purpose. Once the scene had been shot, the field was mowed flat and made to appear operational for the balance of the shooting schedule.

It was while the company was on location at Ozark that one of the most dramatic scenes in the film took place. The script called for a battle-damaged B-17 to belly-land

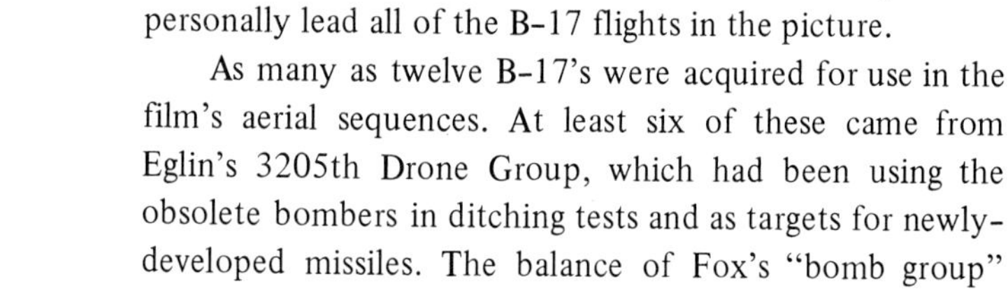

Paul Mantz (far right), mechanic Bob King (next to Mantz) and a group of Hollywood cameramen pose before Mantz's specially-equipped B-25 camera ship.

"Consider yourselves dead," Peck tells the men of the 918th during their first meeting. With only about twenty actors brought from Hollywood, director King relied heavily on Eglin Field personnel to flesh-out scenes such as these.

off the runway and smash through a line of tents, before grinding to a halt. Since Air Force regulations prohibited any military pilots from being involved in the scene, Fox contracted stunt pilot Paul Mantz to do the crash (according to director Henry King, Mantz agreed to do the scene for $2500).

The B-17 used in the sequence was one of the radiation-contaminated drones from the Bikini Atoll tests. Mantz's chief mechanic, Bob King, remembers that every possible precaution was taken to ensure the safety of the stunt:

"The Air Force had given us one of these war-weary drones, which they considered expendable, to use in the crash scene," recalls King. "The first thing I did was to remove the ball-turret that protruded from the belly of the aircraft. Then I rigged a welded rod across all four throttles and another across the master cut-off switches so the 'old man' could yank them all off at once while strapped securely in his seat."[3] Normally a two-man job, Mantz did not have the benefit of a co-pilot on the flight because studio executives refused to pay the additional $1500 Bob King had requested to go along.

On the morning of May 12th, all was in readiness, as crash trucks and ambulances moved into position near the crash site. Prior to take-off, director Henry King briefed Mantz on what he expected. The veteran flier was instructed to set the Fortress down within the range of four remote cameras and slide through the tent city that had been prepared for the scene. King also requested that the props be left in fine pitch: "I want all the noise we can get in this scene."

After making a low practice pass over the crash site, Mantz came barreling in over the fence at 110 knots. As he cut the power and settled on the dry grass field, the veteran flier realized he had little control over the wildly skidding 38,000 pound bomber. Luckily, enough of the main wheels remained exposed below the engine nacelles that he was able to regain some directional control through judicial use of the brakes. Ripping through the tents as planned, the bomber finally came to rest some 1200 feet from the touchdown point.

Director Henry King (left) explains an upcoming scene to Gregory Peck as Dean Jagger and Lawrence Dobkin look on. The high altitude flying gear worn by the actors was at times unbearably hot in the sunny Florida weather.

Hugh Marlow addresses the gold-bricking crew of the "Leper Colony," a B-17 reserved for misfits.

Bob King later pointed out that Mantz was nearly killed when a metal pole that supported one of the tents narrowly missed hitting the windshield of the bomber. "I heard a loud pop when the prop caught it," recalls King,

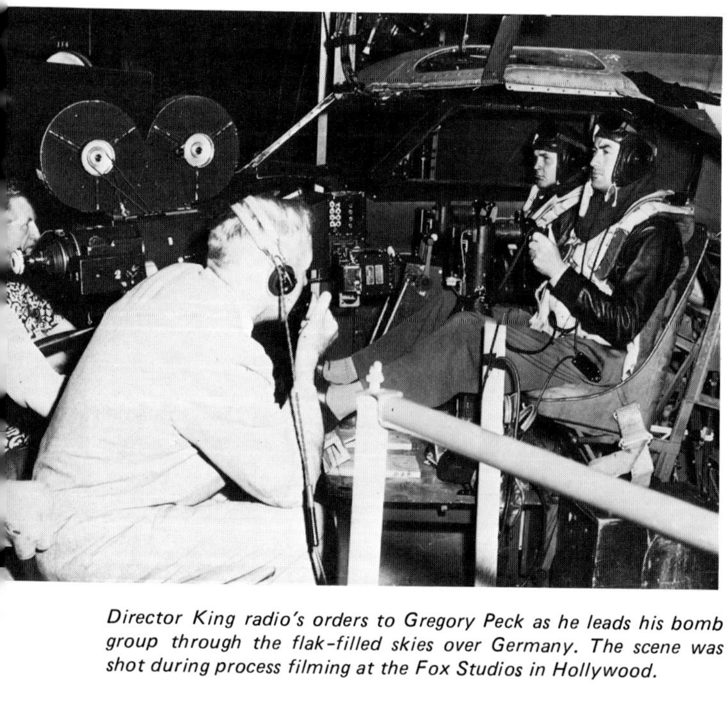

Director King radio's orders to Gregory Peck as he leads his bomb group through the flak-filled skies over Germany. The scene was shot during process filming at the Fox Studios in Hollywood.

"then saw the pole fly past the aircraft and into the air with the rest of the debris from the tents."[4] Unbeknown to Mantz or King, one of the tents had blown down the night before the crash and its wooden pole inadvertently replaced with a steel counterpart.

At Eglin Field, the production company concentrated on completing the exterior scenes shot in and around the Archbury sets built by Fox's construction crews. With only twenty actors brought from Hollywood, King relied heavily on base personnel to flesh-out these scenes. It was also from Eglin that the mass formation flights for the film originated. All of the air-to-air photography was handled from Paul Mantz's specially equipped B-25 camera ship. The majority of these sequences would later be used in the sound stage process scenes shot at the Fox Studios in Hollywood.

By the end of May, the last of the Eglin scenes had been completed and the crew returned to California to begin work on the interiors. For the greater part of five weeks, actor Gregory Peck and his comrades fought their way through the flak-filled skies of Germany aboard a sectionalized B-17G sitting on Fox's Sound Stage 9. An electrically driven replica of one of the Fortress' R-1820 engines had been installed on the aircraft's number two engine nacelle to complete the effect for the cameras.

Peck ultimately cracks under the strain of sending his men out to fight and die. Dean Jagger, Gary Merrill, and Hugh Marlowe carry the young general off the field.

Production of the film officially ended on July 1, 1949. *Twelve O'Clock High* premiered seven months later on January 26, 1950, at the Roxy Theater in New York City. Critics praised the film for its honesty and integrity, "one of the finest studies of men in combat ever accomplished by the Hollywood high command." And indeed it was. The film brought Henry King his best critical notices in years and was immensely popular with movie audiences across the nation. It went on to win the New York Film Critics Award for Best Actor of 1949 (Gregory Peck), the Academy of Motion Picture Arts and Sciences Award for Best Supporting Actor (Dean Jagger) and Best Sound Recording (Thomas Moulton), and two additional Oscar nominations for Best Picture of the Year and Best Actor (Gregory Peck).

NEW YORK TIMES

"There hasn't yet been one film from Hollywood which could compare in rugged realism and punch to 'Twelve O'Clock High' . . . this tremendously vivid fictional story of a young general who toward the end of 1942, takes command of a bomber group operating from a base in England and elevates it from bleak depression to a peak of aggressiveness and pride, has conspicuous dramatic integrity, genuine emotional appeal and a sense of the moods of an air base that absorb and amuse the mind . . ."

Bosley Crowther
January 28, 1950

Actors recreate an aerial combat scene inside Fox's Sound Stage 9. The aerial footage appearing on the process screen in the background was earlier filmed over Eglin Field during two days of mass formation flights.

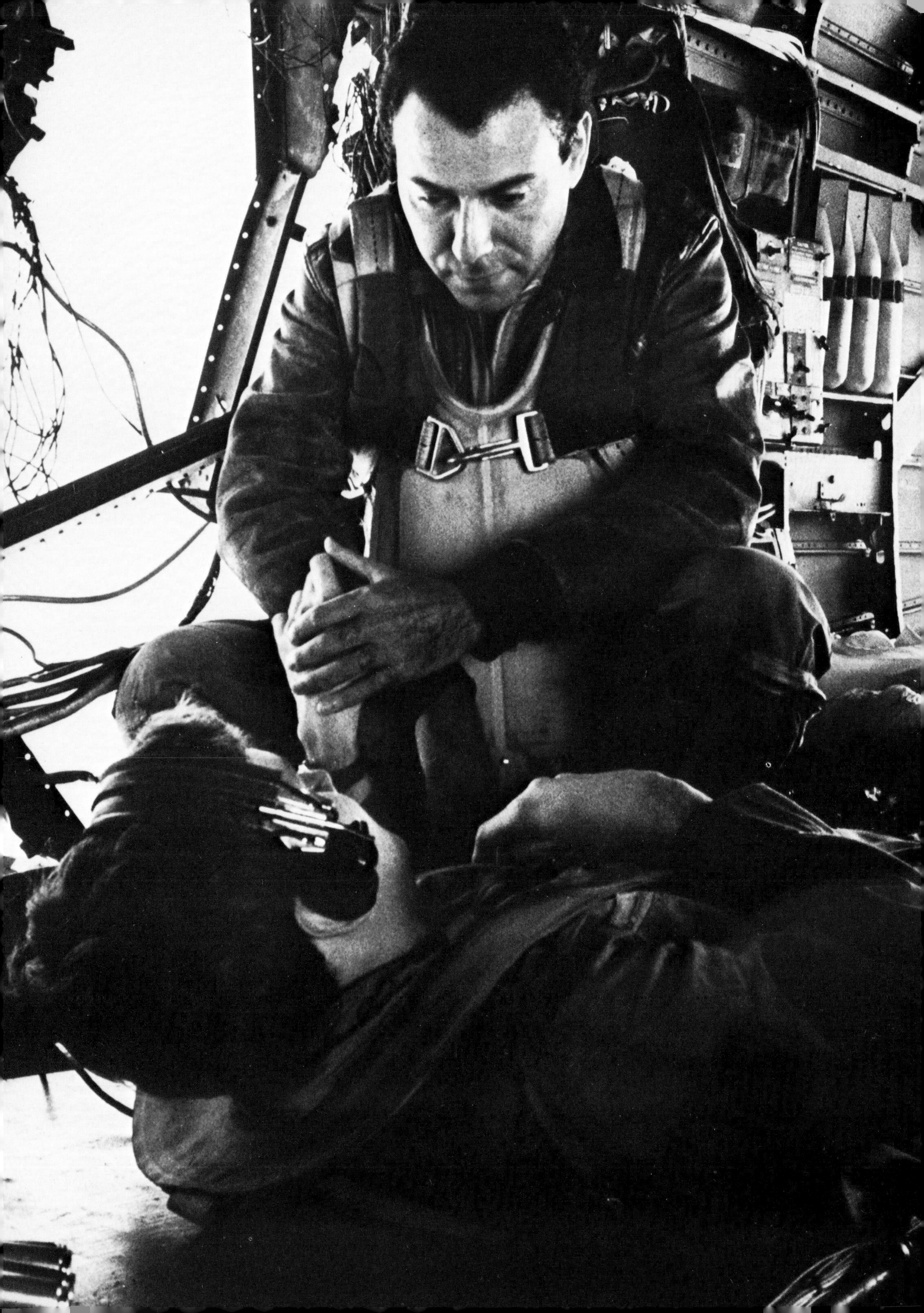

Chapter Four

Changing Perspectives: 1950-1980

Hollywood's brief flirtation with realism in its post-war combat films came to an abrupt but inevitable end with the advent of the Cold War against Communism, and the declaration of war in Korea in June of 1950. From this point forward, America's films about World War II would be transformed and transfigured to reflect the rapidly changing attitudes of a nation in transition.

Shaped in great part by the fighting in Korea, the air combat films of the early fifties proved for the most part to be heavy-handed variations of the old wartime melodramas of the 1940's. Long on battle action and short on theme, they included RKO's production of *Flying Leathernecks*, which traced the development of Marine air power in the Pacific; Republic's *Wild Blue Yonder*, a wartime account of the men who manned America's super weapon, the B-29 Superfortress; and the Monogram and Columbia productions of *Flat Top* and *Battle Stations*, which depicted life aboard the aircraft carriers *Princeton* and *Franklin* during the last crucial months of war in the Pacific.

It was not until the late fifties and sixties that American filmmakers began to look beyond the combat aspects of the air war to explore the deeper and darker psychological motivations of the men who were fighting it. United Artists' production of *China Doll* told of a disillusioned AAF transport pilot who takes to the bottle to drown his twisted memories of the war; Columbia's *War Lover* swept aside all visions of wartime honor and gallantry in its study of an 8th Air Force bomber pilot who delights in the act of killing; and Paramount's *Catch 22*, the darkest and most cynical of all anti-war allegories, focused on the exploits of a World War II bomber group staffed by a crew of battle-crazed psychotics.

In addition to these more thought provoking studies of the war, the sixties and seventies marked the era of the big-budget combat epic: multi-million dollar, multi-national spectaculars that concentrated on entire battle scenarios instead of smaller specific combat actions. Among the largest of these was Twentieth Century-Fox's $25,000,000 production of *Tora! Tora! Tora!*, a blow-by-blow account of the December 7, 1941, raid on Pearl Harbor and the events which led up to it, and Universal's *Midway*, which detailed the most decisive and significant U.S. naval battle of World War II.

Hollywood also showed a continuing interest in dramatizing the story behind the bombing mission that ended the war and ushered in the atomic age. MGM's 1953 production of *Above and Beyond* described, in documentary fashion, the preparations for and execution of the first A-bomb attack on Hiroshima through the eyes of its commander Colonel Paul W. Tibbets. This was followed, twenty-seven years later, by Viacom's 1980 production of *Enola Gay*, a technically superior but dramatically inferior sequel to Tibbets' story.

The World War II combat films of the last thirty years have earned themselves an enduring nitch in the history of the American cinema and the culture of the American people. No war in the history of modern man has been given as much media attention as World War II. It was a conflict whose issues and dangers were clear-cut and well defined and, unlike Korea and Vietnam, there was never much doubt as to why we were fighting or whether victory was worth the price we had to pay for it. Despite the post World War II reconsiderations and the disillusionments of the Cold War, it was a period in our history that summoned up the best in us as a nation and as a people.

FLYING LEATHERNECKS

R.K.O.

— 1951 —

CAST

Dan: JOHN WAYNE; Griff: ROBERT RYAN; Cowboy: DON TAYLOR; Joan Kirby: JANIS CARTER; Clancy: JAY C. FLIPPEN; Dr. Curan: WILLIAM HARRIGAN; Colonel: JAMES BELL; General: BARRY KELLEY

CREDITS

Director: NICHOLAS RAY; Producer: EDMUND GRAINGER; Screenplay: JAMES EDWARD GRANT; Original Story: KENNETH GAMET; Cinematographer: WILLIAM E. SNYDER; Air Operations: PAUL MANTZ; Art Direction: ALBERT S. D'AGOSTINO, JAMES W. SULLIVAN; Set Decoration: DARRELL SILVERA, JOHN STURTEVANT; Film Editor: SHERMAN TODD; Musical Score: ROY WEBB; Sound Technician: FRANK MC WHORTER, CLEM PORTMAN

The declaration of war in Korea brought about a marked change in Hollywood's pictures about World War II. While filmmakers continued to explore various aspects of the conflict, their treatment of the theme was noticeably more jingoistic in tone and closely paralleled the gung-ho "flag-wavers" that were made from 1939 to 1945. Typical of the films produced during this period was RKO's Technicolor air epic *Flying Leathernecks,* released in 1951, and starring John "Duke" Wayne.

The story, by James Edward Grant (*Sands of Iwo Jima*) and Kenneth Gamet (*Flying Tigers*), recounts the exploits of a tough Marine air officer, Major Dan Kirby (John Wayne), who arrives in Hawaii to take command of one of the first F4F units to be sent to Guadalcanal. His appointment is at first met with resentment, since the men of the squadron expected their executive officer, Captain Carl Griffin (Robert Ryan), to be promoted to the job.

John Wayne addresses the men of his new squadron prior to shipping out for Guadalcanal.

During the difficult months that follow, Kirby whips the group into an effective combat unit, exacting a heavy toll from the enemy and in turn absorbing quite a few casualties himself. While Griffin openly rallies the men behind their new C.O., he privately resents Kirby's rigid discipline and what he feels is Kirby's indifference toward the well-being of his fliers. In time, the unit regroups and is given the newer, more deadly, F4U Corsair to take into combat. Winning approval for close air support of ground troops, Kirby boldly leads his squadron through the bloody campaigns on Leyte, Tarawa, Iwo Jima, and Okinawa. When his tour of duty comes to an end, Kirby decides the time is right to hand over command of the group to his deserving executive officer. It is then that Griffin finally realizes that his former C.O.'s stern methods and tough facade was designed with only one thought in mind – to save the lives of his men.

While *Flying Leathernecks* stays in the air and concentrates on the development of Marine air power in the Pacific, it remains an interesting film. The aerial sequences are impressively staged and skillfully integrated with a great deal of exciting combat footage shot during World War II. Unfortunately, a substantial part of the story is bogged down on the ground using the old *Dawn Patrol* theme about the subordinate who comes to hate his C.O., as a heartless butcher, until he himself is placed in that same unrewarding position; and it is here that the film's credibility comes to an abrupt halt.

Pre-production planning for the picture began in early 1950. In an effort to capitalize on John Wayne's successful performance in *Sands of Iwo Jima,* RKO boss Howard Hughes decided to cast him again as the unpopular Marine Corps officer who must send his men out to fight and die (Wayne reportedly netted a record $300,000 for his role in the film). Using their many close ties with military officials in Washington, Hughes and producer Edmund Grainger arranged to shoot the bulk of the film at the USMC's facility at Camp Pendleton, California, where the necessary troops and equipment would be available for all of the action sequences.

Wayne leads the first complement of F4F fighter planes to arrive on the battered island of Guadalcanal. In actuality these are F6F Hellcats roaring over RKO's airbase constructed on the north side of the Camp Pendleton facility. By 1950, few Wildcats had survived the scrapper's torch, forcing the producers of the film to use its bigger brother, the F6F, in its place.

John Wayne and Robert Ryan are given the official welcome to Guadalcanal by William Harrigan.

Actual filming got underway in late November 1950. Director Nicholas Ray and his production company set up operations on a seventy-five acre tract of land on the North side of the Pendleton facility, which had been transformed into a typical wartime Marine air base. This included camouflaging the base's existing blacktop runway with over ten tons of sand and crushed coral, planting hundreds of palm trees and other types of south sea fauna, and pitching a massive tent city with a myriad of sand bag bunkers.

Wayne prepares to climb into one of VMT-2's Hellcats for a close-up shot. Prior to its temporary role in the movies, the squadron had been using its aircraft for training replacement pilots for the fighting in Korea.

All of the planes and pilots used during the three months of filming were provided by Marine Training Squadron VMT-2 and Marine Fighter Squadron VMF-232, stationed at nearby El Toro Marine Corps Air Station in Santa Ana, California. This included a mixed complement of some forty-five fighter aircraft, composed primarily of F6F-5 Hellcats, to stand-in for the F4F's used in the early sequences of the film, and F4U-4 Corsairs, which were used throughout the remaining portions of the story. Noted stunt pilot Paul Mantz handled all the air-to-air photography from one of his twin-engined B-25 camera ships.

It was while working on the film that Mantz had one of his closer brushes with death. In an attempt to obtain a birds-eye view of an actual dive-bombing attack, director Ray requested Mantz to fly in low over an enemy stronghold, trailing a group of F4U's that supposedly had just bombed the target with napalm. The resulting explosions from the attack would be provided by ten cases of dynamite hidden inside the enemy structure.

Having had a number of "previous experiences" with nervous powder men, Mantz cautioned the director that timing was of the utmost importance in an operation of this sort, and not to set off the charge until he had passed over the target; a cameraman would film the explosion from the extreme tail end of the aircraft.

As agreed, Mantz made his run over the target at approximately 100 feet altitude and at about 200 knots indicated airspeed. Much as he had feared would happen occurred; the dynamite was prematurely detonated just as he passed over the enemy structure. The concussion of the

Wayne's squadron ultimately regroups and equips with the newer, more deadly, F4U Corsair. VMT-2 and VMF-232 provided all the F4U's used in the picture.

blast was so great, it threw the cameraman positioned in the tail into the waist compartment of the B-25. All of the windows in the aircraft were either blown-out or smashed, and the blast popped rivets all over the fuselage. Struggling to regain control of the ship, Mantz and co-pilot Cort Johnson pulled up and away from the explosion and headed for an emergency landing at nearby Orange County Airport. Although Mantz and his crew came through the incident unhurt, a quick check of the aircraft indicated it would need to be completely rebuilt before it could fly again.

By February of 1951, director Ray and his crew had completed all of their exteriors, and the group returned to the RKO-Pathe Studios in Culver City to complete the remaining sound stage sequences of the film. *Flying Leathernecks* premiered nine months later on October 3, 1951, at the Pantages Theater in Hollywood. Reviews of the film were generally mixed with most critics noting the flaws in Wayne's performance as compared to his award-winning characterization in *Sands of Iwo Jima.*

NEW YORK TIMES

"As long as it stays in the air, 'Flying Leathernecks', is an exciting thing to watch. Since this new war drama is a Howard Hughes presentation from R.K.O. and co-stars those battered stalwarts, John Wayne and Robert Ryan, any customer can rightly assure that he'll get his money's worth in the way of uniformed virility and battle casualties. Mr. Hughes, pictorially speaking, has taken no chances. He has photographed his man's-man package in brilliant Technicolor and turned over the directorial reins to Nicholas Ray, who has crammed a lot of sound and fury into his flying assaults. These sequences, in fact, are so fast, furious and picturesque and so adroitly spliced in with spectacular news reel footage that any combat hardened Marine pilot should justifiably tingle with pride . . ."

Howard Thompson
September 20, 1951

Wayne orders his men to remain in formation until they've sighted the target. At the time of filming "Flying Leathernecks," Wayne was under contract to RKO and reportedly received a record $300,000 for his role in the picture.

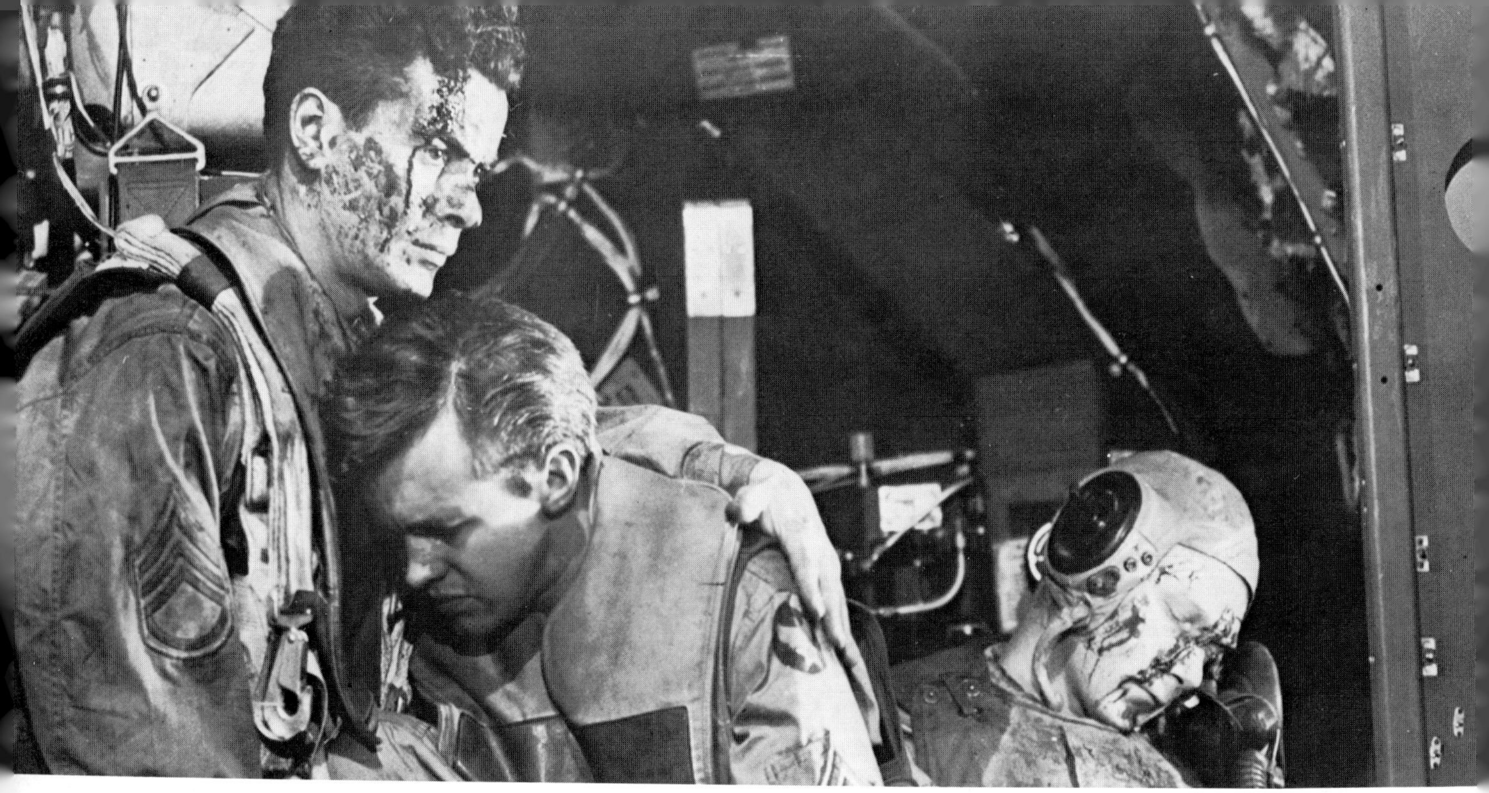

WILD BLUE YONDER

Republic

—1952 —

CAST

Captain Harold Calvert: WENDELL COREY; Lt. Helen Landers: VERA RALSTON; Major Tom West: FORREST TUCKER; Sergeant Hank Stack: PHIL HARRIS; Major Ida Winton: RUTH DONNELLY; Lt. Ted Cranshaw: WILLIAM CHING; Sergeant Shaker Shuker: HARRY CAREY, JR.; Connie Hudson: PENNY EDWARDS; Sergeant Pulaski: WALLY CASSELL; Sergeant Pop Davis: JAMES BROWN; Corporal Frenchy: RICHARD ERDMAN; Sergeant Tony: PHILLIP PINE; Peanuts: MARTIN KILBURN; Nelson: HAL BAYLOR; O'Hara: JOE BROWN, JR.

CREDITS

Director: ALLAN DWAN; Producer: HERBERT J. YATES; Screenplay: RICHARD TREGASKIS; Original Story: ANDREW GEER, CHARLES GRAYSON; Cinematographer: REGGIE LANNING; Art Direction: JAMES SULLIVAN; Set Decoration: JOHN MC CARTHY, CHARLES THOMPSON; Special Effects: HOWARD LYDECKER, THEODORE LYDECKER; Film Editor: RICHARD VAN ENGER; Musical Score: VICTOR YOUNG; Sound Technician: DICK TYLER, HOWARD WILSON; Costumes: ADELE PALMER

Within three months of the release of RKO's *Flying Leathernecks* came yet another World War II air epic entitled *Wild Blue Yonder*. Based on a story by Andrew Geer and Charles Grayson, the film traces the development and deployment of America's World War II super-weapon, the Boeing B-29.

The opening of the film has Captain Harold Calvert (Wendell Corey) and his crew of B-24 "hotshots" reporting for duty at the Smokey Hill Army Air Force Base in Kansas, where they will learn the ins and outs of the new B-29 Superfortress. Much to their dismay, they soon find out that the man who will be training them will be Major Tom

Wendell Corey takes the controls of a B-29 for the first time. Note that his "fifty mission cap" is erroneously of postwar vintage.

West (Forrest Tucker), an officer who bears the mark of cowardice for turning back on the mission to bomb the Ploesti oil refineries. During the months that follow, West goes about the business of training the fliers to operate the new bomber, despite their quiet contempt. Ultimately, the entire group is transferred overseas, where the importance of the B-29 is proven in combat. When the group is ordered to Tinian, to prepare for one of the largest bombing raids of the war, West decides it is time to prove his mettle in combat, and accompanies Calvert and his crew on the mission. Although they successfully bomb the target, Calvert's ship is hit by anti-aircraft fire, seriously wounding him and several others in the crew. Forced to take over command of the plane, West performs his duties with valor and brings the crippled bomber in for a crash landing. Tragically, he is killed attempting to rescue a trapped crewmate in the wreckage of the burning plane.

Despite an earnest attempt on the part of the producers of the film, *Wild Blue Yonder's* cliche-ridden screenplay rarely ever rises above the mediocre level in its story of the men who manned the B-29 Superfortresses. What little

The 22nd Bomb Group, headquartered at March Air Force Base in Riverside, California, provided all the B-29's used in "Wild Blue Yonder." The group had just returned from combat in Korea at the time of filming.

Forrest Tucker addresses the new B-29 crew members he is to train. The B-29 behind him belonged to the 22nd Bomb Group and required a quick coat of watercolor paint, to hide its Korean War markings, prior to going before the cameras.

impact the film does achieve is contained in some truly excellent aerial combat footage of B-29's in action in the Pacific. To this the studio added its own footage photographed at March Air Force Base near Riverside, California. Republic's production crew spent nearly three weeks at the base shooting scenes in and around a number of B-29's assigned to the 22nd Bomb Group's 2nd Bomb Squadron. This included a limited number of aerial scenes of the group's Superfortresses making bombing runs over Catalina Island, which later doubled for Tokyo in the final portion of the film.

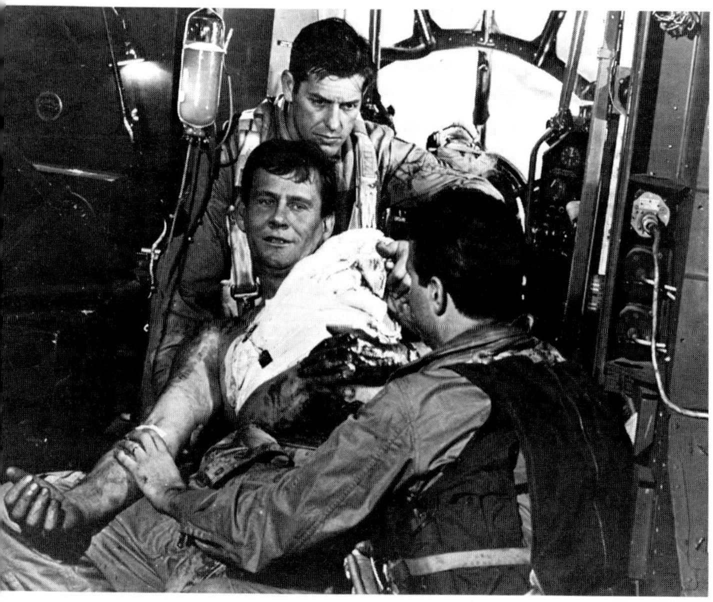

Wendell Corey is seriously injured during a bombing mission over Tokyo. The U.S. Air Force provided Republic with an actual B-29 for sound stage interiors such as these.

Wild Blue Yonder had its world premier at the Ritz Theater in Hollywood on January 24, 1952. Critical reviews of the film were, to say the least, disappointing.

NEW YORK TIMES

"Despite the ascendent title of the first film to open here this year, we regret to report that movies in 1952 aren't yet airborne. Republic's 'Wild Blue Yonder', which took the lead at Loew's State yesterday, goes the length of an oft-traveled runway without ever getting up off the ground. As a matter of fact, this soggy saga of bomber airmen in World War II plows monotonously through every cliche of aerial war films before it finally hits the mud and bogs down in the bathos of mawkish heroics and tears . . ."

Bosley Crowther
January 2, 1952

FLAT TOP

Monogram

— 1952 —

CAST

Dan Collier: STERLING HAYDEN; Joe Rodgers: RICHARD CARLSON; Red Kelley: BILL PHIPPS, Snakehips MacKay: JOHN BROMFIELD; Barney Smith: KEITH LARSEN; Longfellow: WILLIAM SCHALLERT; Commander: WALTER COY; Judge: TODD KARNS; Dorothy: PHYLLIS COATES; Willie: DAVE WILLOCK

CREDITS

Director: LESLEY SELANDER; Producer: WALTER MIRISCH; Original Screenplay: STEVEN FISHER; Cinematographer: HARRY NEUMANN; Art Direction: DAVID MILTON; Set Decoration: ILONA VAS; Special Effects: HARRY COSWICK; Film Editor: WILLIAM AUSTIN; Musical Score: MARLIN SKILES; Sound Technician: CHARLES COOPER

Hollywood continued pumping out a spate of Korean War engendered combat films well into the first half of the decade. Monogram Pictures jumped on the bandwagon in late 1952 with its own low-budget air epic about carrier warfare in the Pacific entitled *Flat Top,* starring Sterling Hayden and Richard Carlson.

The story, by Steven Fisher (*Destination Tokyo*), opens aboard the aircraft carrier *Princeton*, as she cruises off the coast of Korea, sometime in 1952. As Air Group Commander Dan Collier (Sterling Hayden) awaits the arrival of a new group of fliers aboard ship, his mind drifts back to a similar time and place in 1944 when he was stationed aboard this same ship awaiting another group of rookies. Standing on the bridge of the ship, he closely watches the green replacement pilots land one by one on the pitching deck of the carrier. When they report for duty, Collier gives them their first taste of discipline by grounding

The 2500 man crew of the USS Princeton (CVA-37) line-up on deck during change of command ceremonies in 1952. Monogram's crew spent nearly two weeks aboard the carrier, filming shots for use in "Flat Top."

Sterling Hayden leads his air group in an attack against Japanese targets in the Phillipines. Hayden had served with the U.S. Marines during World War II and was decorated for heroism in battle.

one of them, Lt. Barney Smith (Keith Larsen), for disregarding the orders of the Landing Signal Officer. At first the men resent their combat hardened C.O., and fail to understand his stern tactics. Even Collier's executive officer Joe Rodgers (Richard Carlson) attempts to intercede on their behalf, but to no avail. In time though, Rodgers and the young officer pilots gradually come to understand the whys and wherefores of their new skipper. The air group eventually distinguishes itself in combat throughout the Pacific theater, ending ultimately in the Invasion of the Phillippines, where even a reprieved Lt. Barney Smith is given another chance to prove himself, and emerges from the battle a hero.

While Monogram's *Flat Top* offers nothing new or stimulating in the way of its story (basically a lightweight version of *Dawn Patrol*), it does contain much interesting and here-to-fore unseen combat footage shot in the Pacific during World War II. Supplementing this, Monogram's film crew spent nearly two weeks aboard the USS *Princeton* (CVA-37) while it was enroute to Pearl Harbor, Hawaii, and its second tour of duty in Korea. Commander William Denton's Carrier Air Group 19 (CAG 19) provided the Hollywood cameramen with plenty of exciting shots of their F4U Corsairs during combat maneuvers at sea, all of which were later intercut with the stock combat footage

Carrier Air Group 19 (CAG 19) provided Monogram's camera crew with plenty of exciting shots during their stay aboard the "Princeton." At the time, the group was equipped with a mixed complement of F4U-4's and F4U-5's.

and sound stage sequences shot at the Monogram Studios in Hollywood.

Flat Top had its world premier November 11, 1952, aboard the USS *Princeton* while moored in San Diego Harbor. Among the many invited guests and dignitaries were all of the officers and men of CAG 19, which had just returned from its second tour of duty in Korea.

NEW YORK TIMES

". . . If this Monogram offering, featuring Sterling Hayden and Richard Carlson, becomes increasingly familiar with each reel, indeed it should. For Steve Fisher's scenario, full of hollow-sounding dialogue and cliches, focuses on a battered standby-the upper echelon end and its effect on a standard assortment of rookie pilots . . . . Dull though most of the film may be below decks, Monogram has had the gumption to splice in a generous compilation of official Navy photography. These awesome shots of our Pacific Fleet in action include some rousing battles by our dog fighters and the Japanese Zeros and a carefully technical coverage of the galvanized carriers in action . . ."

Bosley Crowther
December 6, 1952

"Flat Top" contained much interesting and here-to-fore unseen combat footage shot during the war. This particular scene was taken aboard the USS Enterprise in 1943.

ABOVE AND BEYOND

Metro-Goldwyn-Mayer

— 1953 —

CAST

Colonel Paul W. Tibbets: ROBERT TAYLOR; Lucey Tibbets: ELEANOR PARKER; Major Uanna: JAMES WHITMORE; Major General Vernon C. Brent: LARRY KEATING; Captain Parsons: LARRY GATES; Marge Bratton: MARILYN ERSKINE; Major Harry Bratton: STEPHEN DUNNE; General Samuel E. Roberts: ROBERT BURTON; Dr. Ramsey: HAYDEN RORKE; Dr. Van Dyke: LARRY DOBKIN; Dr. Fiske: JACK RAINE; Dutch Van Kirk: JONATHAN COTT; Thomas Ferebee: JEFF RICHARDS; Bob Lewis: DICK SIMMONS; Wyatt Duzenbury: JOHN MC KEE; Radio Operator: PATRICK CONWAY; Paul Tibbets, Jr.: CHRISTIE OLSON; Driver: WILLIAM LESTER; Mary Malone: BARBARA RUICK; General Curtis E. LeMay: JIM BACKUS

CREDITS

Directors: MELVIN FRANK, NORMAN PANAMA; Producers: MELVIN FRANK, NORMAN PANAMA; Screenplay: BEIRNE LAY, JR., MELVIN FRANK, NORMAN PANAMA; Original Story: BEIRNE LAY, JR..; Cinematographer: RAY JUNE; Air Operations: PAUL MANTZ; Art Direction: CEDRIC GIBBONS, MALCOLM BROWN; Set Decoration: EDWIN B. WILLIS, RALPH HURST; Special Effects: A. ARNOLD GILLESPIE, WARREN NEWCOMBE; Film Editor: COTTON WARBURTON; Musical Score: HUGO FRIEDHOFER; Sound Technician: DOUGLAS SHEARER; Wardrobe: HELEN ROSE

One of the more thoughtful and ambitious film projects of the early nineteen-fifties was MGM's production of *Above and Beyond*, released in January of 1953. Based on an original screenplay by Bierne Lay (*Twelve O'Clock High*), Melvin Frank and Norman Panama, the film sensitively depicts the story of USAAF Colonel Paul W. Tibbets, the pilot chosen to lead the first atomic bomb strike against Japan.

Tibbets' (Robert Taylor) story begins in the summer of 1944, when USAAF Commanding General "Hap" Arnold selects the twenty-nine year old pilot to organize

Robert Taylor is ordered home for a special assignment he knows little about.

the special combat group that will drop the bomb. The ultra-secret nature of the project calls for military personnel of the highest caliber. Of the more than 2000 applicants interviewed, over a third are rejected. Many of the men chosen for the mission are former members of Tibbets' 97th Bomb Group, having served with him in Europe and Africa; others are hand-picked for their outstanding military records and specialized skills. The crews are told only that they are to drop a new sort of weapon, nothing more. Tibbets alone knows the true purpose behind their mission.

In the interest of security, all of the unit's flight training operations are undertaken at remote Wendover Field in Utah. Members of the group, now formally known as the 509th Composite Group, are cautioned to limit their contact with the outside world, or even with other USAAF personnel on the base. While the rigid security regulations are highly successful (as events would later prove), they bring Tibbets into a great deal of conflict with not only his men but also his wife Lucey (Eleanor Parker), who mistakes his taciturn behavior for vanity. In June of 1945, after nine months of intensive training, the 509th is ordered overseas to North Air Field on Tinian to prepare for its intended mission. By the first week in August, all is in readiness; the main strike force consists of three B-29's: Colonel Tibbets' "Enola Gay" carrying the bomb, Captain George Marquart's "Necessary Evil" as observation aircraft, and Major Charles Sweeney's "The Great Artiste" carrying the scientific monitoring instruments. In the early morning hours of August 6, 1945, Tibbets lifts the "Enola Gay" off of North Air Field's floodlit runway and points her nose toward Japan. The other two aircraft follow suit. Five hours into the flight Tibbets receives word that weather over Hiroshima is clear at all altitudes. The report effectively seals the fate of that sprawling industrial complex. At 9:15 AM, bombardier Major Tom Ferebee (Jeff Richards)

Eleanor Parker has a brief reunion with her husband prior to his leaving for Wendover Field, Utah. Lamentably, too much of the film's plot revolved around the Tibbets' marital difficulties during the preparations for the mission.

Taylor is shown the bomb for the first time, as scientists Larry Dobkin, Larry Gates, and Hayden Rourke look on.

toggles the bomb on target. The explosion that follows instantly obliterates more than half the city. Shocked by the intensity of the blast, Tibbets and his crew watch in awe as the raging mushroom cloud rises 50,000 feet over

Taylor's Commanding Officer Larry Keating asks him if he is willing to live with the responsibility of dropping a bomb that may kill or injure over 100,000 people.

the target. News of the successful mission is flashed to Tinian and then to the President who announces it to the world. The dawn of the atomic age had arrived and with it the beginning of the end of the most devastating war in history.

Although somewhat dated when viewed today, MGM's *Above and Beyond* still ranks as one of Hollywood's finest aviation films. Its superb, almost documentary-like depiction of the A-bomb mission, with all of its technical and psychological explications, effectively dramatized one of history's most momentous events. The film's only flaw lies in its somewhat tedious preoccupation with Tibbets' marital problems during the preparations for the raid.

Oddly enough, it was at the U.S. Air Force's urging that this aspect of the story was given so much play in the picture. During the early fifties, General Curtis LeMay's Strategic Air Command (SAC) was experiencing a very high rate of divorce among its crewmembers. Duty in SAC was highly demanding and due to the nature of its mission, flight crews were away from their families for weeks at a time. It was not the type of life that lent itself to stable marriages.

When Metro approached the Air Force with its idea for

Taylor and his crew return from one of their numerous training missions over Utah. All of the Wendover and North Field sequences were shot at Davis-Monthan Air Force Base outside of Tucson, Arizona.

the film, the USAF suggested that it might help SAC's problem if the studio did a story that focused on the stress the A-bomb mission put on personal relationships and how one man handled the problem. When approached with this concept, Colonel Tibbets concurred with the idea and agreed to lend his full support to screenwriters Lay, Frank, and Panama in scripting the story. He later recalled the experience in his autobiography *The Tibbets Story:*

"Although sensitive at first when I found the movie makers taking certain liberties with the facts, I soon came to learn that this approach was routine. When history is transformed into entertainment its not unusual to jazz things up a bit to heighten suspense and excitement – but usually within the framework of probability . . . They [the screenwriters] explained to me that some of the incidents had to be rearranged to make the story flow better; and I agreed that the changes didn't detract from the basic honesty of the story . . . They also asked me to be technical advisor throughout the making of the picture, but I felt that would be about the worst thing I could do. The fact that I was still in the Air Force might influence my decisions. I also didn't believe I could take an objective view of the story that was primarily about my life . . . For the job I recommended [Lt. Colonel] Charley Begg, who had been commander of the ordnance squadron that assembled the bomb. He had been with us all the time and had a good opportunity to observe the stresses and strains at work on the flight crews and their families. He was an intelligent and perceptive officer who had occupied a front-row seat to the entire development."[1]

Davis-Monthan's 43rd Bomb Group provided most of the B-29's and KB-29's used in the air and ground scenes appearing in "Above and Beyond."

Taylor explains the nature of the weapon to his crew before the bomb run over Hiroshima.

The real Colonel Paul Tibbets gives his Hollywood counterpart, Robert Taylor, a few quick tips on flying the B-29 during a visit to the MGM Studios in 1952.

Joining Lt. Colonel Begg as technical advisor to the studio was Air Force Major Norman Ray, an accomplished B-29 pilot who had been an aircraft commander in the original 509th Composite Group. While Begg concentrated his efforts towards advising the filmmakers on details about the bomb, it was Ray's duty to oversee all of the flying aspects in the picture. Strangely enough this would be the second time he had participated in a film about the Hiroshima mission; having flown in a number of aerial sequences for MGM's original A-bomb effort *The Beginning or the End* in 1946.

Production got underway on February 5, 1952, at the Metro-Goldwyn-Mayer Studios in Culver City, California. It was here that all of the tense aerial close-up scenes were shot of Tibbets and his crew piloting the "Enola Gay" to Hiroshima. The sectionalized B-29 fuselage that had originally been used in *The Beginning or the End* was again taken out of storage and put back into action for these sequences.

In early March, Metro's cast and crew transferred filming operations to Davis-Monthan Air Force Base outside of Tucson, Arizona, to begin work on the exteriors for the picture. During their two-week stay, the base doubled not

The now familiar mushroom cloud rises 50,000 feet over Hiroshima. The blast obliterated more than half the city and killed or injured over 120,000 of its occupants.

only as the 509th's training facility at Wendover Field, Utah, but also as North Air Field on Tinian from whence the group staged its history making raid. Davis-Monthan's 43rd and 303rd Bomb Groups provided all of the B-29's used in these latter sequences. Paul Mantz handled the air-to-air filming operations from his specially modified B-25 camera ship "The Smasher."

Production of the film officially came to an end on March 26, 1952. *Above and Beyond* premiered nine months later on January 8, 1953, at the Egyptian Theater in Hollywood. Critical reviews of the film were excellent and the Academy of Motion Picture Arts and Sciences nominated the picture for two Oscars, including Best Original Motion Picture Story (Beirne Lay, Jr.) and Best Scoring of a Dramatic Picture (Hugo Friedhofer).

NEW YORK TIMES

"Having already dramatized the story of the development of the atomic bomb and its fateful delivery on Hiroshima in 'The Beginning or the End', Metro is now concentrating on a personal aspect of that history in 'Above and Beyond', a fervent romance that arrived at the Mayfair yesterday . . . So long as attention is directed to the strictly technical activities of preparing for and delivering the mysterious atomic bomb, this tediously long and earnest picture has substance and plausibility with the greatest emotional stimulation in the account of the Hiroshima trip . . ."

Bosley Crowther
January 31, 1953

BATTLE STATIONS

Columbia

— 1956 —

CAST

Father Joe McIntyre: JOHN LUND; Buck Fitzpatrick: WILLIAM BENDIX; Captain Tom Matthews: RICHARD BOONE; Chris Jordan: KEEFE BRASSELLE; Ensign Pete Kelly: WILLIAM LESLIE; "Squawk" Hewitt: JAMES LYDON; Marty Brennan: CLAUDE AKINS; Patrick Mosher: GEORGE O'HANLON; Tom Short: EDDIE FOY, III; William Halsey: JACK DIAMOND; Archie Golder: CHRIS RANDALL

CREDITS

Director: LEWIS SEILER; Producer: BRYAN FOY; Screenplay: CRANE WILBUR; Original Story: BEN FINNEY; Cinematography: BURNETT GUFFEY; Art Director: CARY O'DELL; Film Editor: JEROME THOMAS; Recording Supervisor: JOHN LIVADARY; Sound Technician: DONALD MC KAY; Musical Score: MISCHA BAKALEINIKOFF

In 1956 Columbia Studios released what was to become one of the last Hollywood film productions to deal with Naval carrier operations in the Pacific during World War II. Entitled *Battle Stations*, the picture is a semi-fictional account of the aircraft carrier USS *Franklin* (CV-13) during the battle for Okinawa in 1945.

The story of the carrier and its men is told through the eyes of her Chaplain, Lt. Commander Joseph McIntyre (John Lund), who arrives aboard ship in early February 1945. A few days later the *Franklin* leaves the United States bound for Vice Admiral Mark Mitscher's Task Force 58 (TF-58) in the Pacific. Captain Tom Matthews (Richard Boone) orders round-the-clock drills to keep the crews alert during the long cruise. Chief Bosun Mate Buck Fitzpatrick (William Bendix) drives his men to the point of exhaustion during this time, knowing that the exercises might save their lives in the thick of battle. On March 13th, they join the other ships of TF-58 in Ulithi Anchorage to prepare for the amphibious invasion of Okinawa. For the

Chief Bosun Mate William Bendix drills his men during the long cruise to the Pacific.

Franklin, it proves to be one of the deadliest campaigns of the war. During the battle, some 400 Japanese aircraft fling themselves at the fleet in a series of mass suicide attacks. Hit by two 500 pound armor piercing bombs, the *Franklin* is turned into a cauldron of flame, exploding bombs, and rockets. Despite orders to the contrary, Captain Matthews and his crew refuse to abandon their valiant ship. Father McIntyre and Chief Fitzpatrick are among the many brave men who pitch in to help the wounded and dying, organize fire-fighting parties, and help jettison live ammunition from below decks. When the veil of smoke and fire finally lifts, "the fighting lady" is still afloat. Listing badly and gutted by flame, the *Franklin* makes for port under her own power, a graphic tribute to the gallant officers and men who fought to save her.

Columbia's *Battle Stations* remains of interest when it concentrates on the USS *Franklin's* battle for survival during the invasion of Okinawa. The film's primary fault lies in a rather pedestrian storyline that uses every stock service character and cliche in the book. Fortunately, a number of the characters in the story, such as Richard Boone's Captain Matthews and John Lund's Chaplain Mc Intyre, were based on actual persons, Captain Leslie Gehres and Medal of Honor winner Lt. Commander Joseph O'Callahan, giving the film some added credibility.

Columbia's cast and crew spent nearly a week at sea aboard the USS Princeton shooting scenes for use in "Battle Stations." At the time of the filming (July 1955), the "Princeton" was one of the last U.S. Navy aircraft carriers still equipped with a handful of World War II vintage fighters and torpedo bombers.

Two 500 pound bombs turn the "Franklin" into a flaming inferno. A great deal of stock wartime footage, such as this, was used in the final cut of the picture.

Cameramen catch one of VS-23's Avengers as it prepares to land aboard the USS Princeton.

Fire-fighting crews attempt to extinguish some of the fires aboard ship. This particular scene was recreated aboard the "Princeton" using one of VC-3's F4U-5's.

In order to minimize the production costs inherent in a project of this sort, the entire film was shot aboard the World War II Essex class carrier USS *Princeton* (CVS-37), based at Naval Air Station North Island in San Diego, California. At the time (July 1955), the *Princeton* was one of the few U.S. Navy carriers still equipped with a handfull of WWII vintage aircraft. During the four weeks of filming aboard ship, Navy Composite Squadron VC-3 provided a mixed number of F4U-4 and -5 Corsairs, and Anti-Submarine Squadron VS-23, a complement of TBM-3S Avengers, for use in the picture. These scenes were later integrated with a great deal of stock wartime combat footage for the final effect.

Battle Stations had its world premier in February of 1956. Critical reviews of the film were generally poor due to the picture's weak storyline and slow directorial pacing.

LOS ANGELES TIMES

"Battle Stations" is filled with stock footage of war scenes and stock characters of all kinds. Unfortunately the former outshines the latter by a country mile . . . The time of the feature is World War II; the place, a carrier of the Essex class; the characters, stereotyped . . . Outside of the battle sequences, the main interest [in the film] lies in a very complete tour of a huge Navy aircraft carrier and the training scenes aboard ship . . ."

John Scott
February 17, 1956

CHINA DOLL

United Artists

— 1958 —

CAST

Cliff Brandon: VICTOR MATURE; Shu-Jen: LI LI HUA; Father Cairns: WARD BOND; Phil Gates: BOB MATHIAS; Dan O'Neill: STUART WHITMAN; Ernie Fleming: KENNETH PERRY; Ellington: DANNY CHANG, Steve Hill: JOHNNY DESMOND; Alice Nichols: ELAINE CURTIS; Mona Perkins: ANN MC CREA; Dave Reisner: STEVE MITCHELL; Carlo Menotti: TIGE ANDREWS

CREDITS

Director: FRANK BORZAGE; Producer: FRANK BORZAGE; Screenplay: KITTY BUHLER; Original Story: JAMES NABLO, THOMAS KELLY; Cinematographer: WILLIAM CLOTHIER; Art Direction: HOWARD RICHMOND; Special Effects: DAVID KOEHLER; Film Editor: JACK MURRAY; Musical Score: HENRY VARS; Sound Technician: PAUL HOLLY; Wardrobe: WESLEY JEFFRIES, ANGELA ALEXANDER

By the late 1950's, World War II was fast becoming, for most of mainstream America, but a fleeting memory. While Hollywood's moviemakers continued to explore various aspects of the war in their films, they began to look at the conflict in a different, more cynical, light. In United Artists' 1957 release, *China Doll*, director Frank Borzage *(Flight Command)* set aside the phony heroics to examine the darker side of the war and its impact on the individuals caught up in it.

The story, by Kitty Buhler, centers on a disillusioned Army Air Force Captain, Cliff Brandon (Victor Mature), who commands a small transport squadron flying supplies over the "Hump" (Himalayas) to China. A lone-wolf, Brandon has seen too many of the cruelties of war, and spends most of his non-flying hours drowning his bitterness in a local Kunming bar. During a particularly heavy drinking spree, he gives an old Chinese beggar some money and unknowingly buys his daughter, Shu-Jen (Li Li Hua). The next morning, when he realizes what he has done, he

Victor Mature and Bob Mathias prepare for another supply mission over the "Hump."

Johnny Desmond and Tige Andrews discuss an upcoming mission while working on one of the squadron's C–47 transports. This was one of two "Gooney Birds" acquired from Mercer Airlines for use in the film.

wants nothing to do with the young waif. In time though, he grows fond of Shu-Jen and ultimately makes her his wife. Tragically, a Japanese bombing raid ends both of their lives soon after the birth of their baby girl. Years after the war, this sole remaining symbol of their love is brought to the United States and adopted by the family of one of Brandon's flyers.

While *China Doll's* screenplay has some winning merits, it is obviously long on pathos and short on action. Aside from a few well-staged aerial sequences, most of the film's scenario takes place on the ground in the form of a long drawn out romance between Victor Mature and Li Li Hua.

Taking a mere five weeks to complete, Borzage and his crew shot most of the picture in and around the rural Saugus-Newhall area of Southern California. A pair of C–47 transports were temporarily leased from Mercer Airlines of Burbank for use in the air and ground sequences of the film. In addition to the "Gooney Birds," a small number of F4U Corsairs were obtained from a local surplus dealer to stand-in as the Japanese Zero's in the final battle sequences of the story.

Transport pilot Stuart Whitman and Red Cross Volunteers Ann McCrea and Elaine Curtis survey the bombing damage done to their Kunming airfield.

Released in September of 1958, *China Doll* received surprisingly good reviews from most of the critics, who welcomed Frank Borzage's return to motion pictures after a long absence.

NEW YORK TIMES

"China Doll," an Army Air Force tale of 1943, is a modest war picture of modest impact, directed and produced by, of all people, Frank Borzage . . . The scenario, written by Kitty Buhler, frankly substitutes ground sentiment for aerial bloodiness . . . as quietly piloted by a professional like Mr. Borzage (remember the first "Seventh Heaven") a familiar war drama has some winning aspects . . ."

Howard Thompson
December 4, 1958

A shocked Victor Mature finds that his wife Li Li Hua has been killed in the Japanese bombing raid.

THE WAR LOVER

Columbia

— 1962 —

CAST

Buzz Rickson: STEVE MC QUEEN; Ed Bolland: ROBERT WAGNER; Daphne: SHIRLEY ANNE FIELD; Lynch: GARY COCKRELL; Junior Sailen: MICHAEL CRAWFORD; Brindt: BILL EDWARDS; Lamb: CHUCK JULIAN; Handown: ROBERT EASTON; Prien: AL WAXMAN; Farr: TOM BUSBY; Bragliani: GEORGE SPERDAKOS; Haverstraw: BOB KANTER; Emmet: JERRY STOVIN; Vogt: EDWARD BISHOP; Murika: RICHARD LEECH; Randall: BERNARD BRADEN

CREDITS

Director: PHILLIP LEACOCK; Producer: ARTHUR HORNBLOW, JR.; Screenplay: HOWARD KOCH; Original Story: JOHN HERSEY; Cinematographer: BOB HUKE; Aerial Cinematographers: RON TAYLOR, SKEETS KELLY; Air Operations: JOHN CREWDSON, GREG BOARD, TIM CLUTTERBUCK, LARRY RONACORS, DON HACKETT; Art Direction: BILL ANDREWS; Special Effects: WALLY VEEVERS, TED SAMUELS; Film Editor: GORDON HALES; Musical Score: RICHARD ADDINSELL; Sound Technician: NORMAN BOLLAND, RED LAW; Wardrobe: ELSA FENNELL

Led in part by the success of Fox's epic production of *The Longest Day*, the sixties became one of the most prolific decades for World War II films since the end of that conflict in 1945. Combat spectaculars of all shapes and sizes, rolled off the Hollywood conveyor belts by the dozen. One of the best and most underrated of these was Columbia's 1962 release, *The War Lover*, starring Steve McQueen and Robert Wagner.

Adapted from the Pulitzer Prize winning novel by John Hersey, the film is a probing psychological study of a mal-

"The Body" heads for "Festung Europa" with another B-17 close behind. A total of four B-17's were acquired for use in the film.

adjusted bomber pilot who has difficulty reconciling life away from the air war over Germany.

The story begins in late 1943 at a typical 8th Air Force base in the midlands of England. Captain Buzz Rickson (Steve McQueen) methodically runs through the preflight checklist, as the crew of his B-17, "The Body," settle into position for take-off. A cold calculating type, Rickson exults in war and has seen his crew through twenty-three missions with nary a scratch. In contrast, Rickson's co-pilot, Lt. Ed Boland (Robert Wagner), abhors the war and sees his C.O. as a dehumanized personality who revels in the act of killing. It is on this, their twenty-fourth mission together, that Rickson's luck finally runs-out. As the bombers near the target of Leipzig, a swarm of German fighter planes intercept the formation. "The Body" lurches under repeated air attacks by the Luftwaffe fighters. With two engines shot out and several crewmen dead, Rickson reluctantly decides to turn back for the coast of England. Assured of his invinceability, he orders Boland and the rest of the crew to bail out over the Channel, while he fights to save the life of his bomber alone. His frenzied attempt ends in failure though, as the doomed flyer and his crippled aircraft crash in flames against the white cliffs of Dover.

Of the many films produced about the air war over Europe, *The War Lover* ranks as one of the finest and, in

Steve McQueen and Robert Wagner slog through the English mud on their way to a mission briefing.

Former RAF flying officer and motion picture stunt pilot John Crewdson (left) discusses an upcoming flight with his crewmates. Crewdson was responsible for much of the technical excellence seen throughout the film.

Robert Wagner looks on in shock as Steve McQueen prepares to buzz their airfield following a "leaflet raid."

its anti-war context, the most disturbing. Steve McQueen's depiction of the twisted 8th Air Force bomber pilot who cannot adjust to life on the ground is graphically absorbing and, so long as the film concentrates on this aspect of the story, it excells. Lamentably, too much of Howard Koch's screenplay is wasted on the "menage a trois" between McQueen, Wagner, and their English girlfriend, Shirley Anne Field, and it is here that the film grinds to a screeching halt.

Much of the credit for the technical and historical veracity that is seen throughout the film is directly attributable to former Royal Air Force flying officer and motion picture stunt pilot, John Crewdson, who coordinated all air operations for the production. Columbia (in the summer of 1961) assigned Crewdson and his Film Aviation Services, Ltd. organization the enviable task of locating, restoring, and ferrying to England, the three B-17G Flying Fortresses needed for the film. Accomplishing the feat in little more than four months, Crewdson and his crew of mechanics unearthed three of the veteran bombers in Tucson, Arizona, where they were overhauled and then flown on a 6000 mile ferry flight to Bovingdon Airfield, north of London.

British director Phillip Leacock discusses an upcoming scene with Steve McQueen.

In what later became the highlight of the film, Crewdson buzzes Bovingdon Airfield at near zero altitude.

There the aircraft were restored to their full wartime configurations, including the installation of power gun turrets, fixed and flexible .50 caliber machine guns, and application of appropriate 8th Air Force bomb group markings (specifically the 91st Bomb Group, to blend in with the stock footage that was later borrowed from *Memphis Belle* and *Twelve O'Clock High*).

Production of the film officially got under way at Bovingdon Airfield on October 10, 1961. A former 8th Air Force (92nd Bomb Group) training facility, Bovingdon had been shared jointly by personnel of the U.S. and Royal Air Forces since the late 1940's. With most of its World War II buildings largely intact, the base provided a perfect atmosphere for shooting most of the air and ground sequences needed for the film.

For nearly seven weeks, the skies above Southern England were filled once again with the distinctive drone of Flying Fortresses as Columbia's production crew, under the direction of Phillip Leacock, breathed life into Hersey's prize-winning novel.

Among the many outstanding sequences that were filmed at this time was the scene in which Rickson and his crew defiantly buzz their airfield following a "leaflet raid" over Germany. In recreating the scene, Crewdson was called upon to fly his B-17 at near zero altitude across Bovingdon Airfield. Opting to fly the dangerous sortie alone, he later recalled his impressions of the flight in Martin Caiden's book *Everything But the Flak*:

". . . it was perhaps the most exhiliarating flying I've ever done. For nearly five minutes I beat the hell out of everybody and everything on that air field. The director [Phillip Leacock] said he wanted close-ups of the staff in

Incensed at him for buzzing the airfield, McQueen's C.O. gives him a few words of "sage" advice as Robert Wagner looks on.

Columbia's "bomb group" taxies into position for take-off at Bovingdon Airfield, October 1961.

"The War Lover" included a limited amount of combat footage from "Memphis Belle" and "Twelve O'Clock High." Paul Mantz's classic belly landing scene was among those resurrected for the film.

A stunned Robert Wagner finds his bombardier friend has been killed in the crash of his B-17.

the control tower reacting to the sight of the B-17 roaring straight at them and then screaming by at a height below the tower – with the wing only inches away . . . I asked that old girl to give me all she had and she gave it to me in full . . . I pounded along inches away from the tower and nearly scraped the ball turret off on the runway. Pulling up was out of the question a few times, so I just flew between the hangars . . . I understood later that several people fainted . . ."[2]

In mid-December, director Leacock and his crew transferred filming operations to the Royal Air Force's Manston Airfield (on the east coast of England) from whence all of the overwater sequences were to be shot. Script requirements called for Crewdson and his pilots to fly numerous low-level missions over the English Channel with engines "shot out" and propellers feathered. Smoke pots installed in the wings were used to simulate engine fires while cannon and flak damage were effected by riveting jagged pieces of sheet metal to the bombers' fuselage.

It was while the company was based at Manston that the only fatality of the production occurred. During one of the low-level bomber sorties over the English Channel, British sky-diving champion, Mike Reilly, jumped to his death in a parachuting accident. The twenty-eight year old school teacher was doubling for Robert Wagner at the time he bailed-out of what was supposedly Buzz Rickson's combat-striken bomber. Although rescuers reached him less than ninety seconds after he impacted the water, it is believed he drowned when the blossoming canopy of his parachute dragged him under the chilled waters of the channel.

In early January, Leacock an his crew returned to the Shepperton Studios, in Surrey, to complete the remain-

A wounded Steve McQueen chooses to stay with his bomber as Robert Wagner prepares to bail-out.

ing sound stage sequences of the film. It was there that all of the "aerial" close-ups were shot of Steve McQueen and his crew flying through the flak-filled skies over Germany. The remains of a former Israeli Defense Force B–17G (a combat veteran of the IDF's No. 69 Squadron) had been located and shipped in from Tel Aviv specifically for these purposes.

Sadly, only one of the four Flying Fortresses that were acquired for the film would survive to return to the United States. Heavy customs duties and various mechanical problems prevented the others from returning and they were dismantled soon after the end of filming.

Production of the film officially came to a close on February 9, 1962. *The War Lover* had its world premier nine months later, in October of 1962, and was greeted with generally favorable response from film critics and movie audiences.

VARIETY

". . . Arthur Hornblow's production of John Hersey's 'The War Lover' is accomplished in all respects save one. Lamentably, that one flaw happens to be a major one: lack of proper clarification of or penetration into the character referred to by the title. This single conspicuous shortcoming strips the film of its potential "prestige picture" appeal for more discerning audiences, leaving it to be claimed by less choosy buffs of the war picture. Since its action scenes have been meticulously and expertly mounted, an air of authenticity pervades the film that, coupled with its earnest, skillful performances, gives the Columbia release some promise as a contender for the action market . . ."

October 24, 1962

Rickson's crew abandons their crippled B–17 in the final sequence of the film. British parachuting champion Mike Reilly was tragically killed during the re-enactment of this scene.

THE THOUSAND PLANE RAID

United Artists

— 1969 —

CAST

Colonel Greg Brandon: CHRISTOPHER GEORGE; Lt. Gabrielle Ames: LORAINE STEPHENS; General Cotten Palmer: J.D. CANNON; Wing Commander Trafton Howard: GARY MARSHALL; Group Commander Leslie Hardwicke: MICHAEL EVANS; Lt. Archer: BEN MURPHY; Major Varga: JAMES GAMMON; Sergeant Kruger: GAVIN MAC LEOD

CREDITS

Director: BORIS SAGAL; Producer: LEWIS J. RACHMIL; Screenplay: DONALD SANFORD; Original Story: ROBERT VINCENT WRIGHT; Cinematographer: WILLIAM SPENCER; Air Operations: FRANK PINE, JIM APPLEBY, FRANK TALLMAN, DON LYKINS, SKIP MARSH, J.E. BOYLES, JAMES STUMPF, ROBERT GRIDER; Art Direction: HAROLD MICHELSON; Set Decoration: BILL CALVERT; Special Effects: JUSTUS GIBBS, HENRY MILLAR, JR.; Film Editor: HENRY BATISTA, JODIE COPELAN; Musical Score: JAMES HASKELL; Sound Technician: ROBERT MARTIN

Hollywood's war films continued to flourish well into the latter half of the 1960's. Unfortunately, in many cases, quantity, not quality, had become the keyword. United Artists' 1969 release, *The Thousand Plane Raid*, starring Christopher George and Loraine Stephens, was typical of the many low-budget combat films produced during this period.

Loosely based on Ralph Barker's book *The Thousand Plane Raid*, the screenplay, by Donald Sanford, centers on the brash, bull-headed leader of the 103rd Bomb Group, Colonel Greg Brandon (Christopher George), who has devised a plan to wipe out one of Germany's principal airplane works in a brazen 1000 plane daylight bombing raid. Despite many repeated attempts at convincing "the brass" of his ideas, Brandon's superiors feel the plan would be suicidal. Only his girlfriend and his chief confidant, Lieutenant Gabrielle Ames (Loraine Stephens), feel his farsighted concepts have merit. It is to Brandon's complete surprise then that his plan is finally approved. Despite some initial misgivings, Brandon leads the wing in the largest bombing mission of the war. While there are numerous casualties, the target is clobbered, and for Bran–

Christopher George briefs his men prior to the first thousand plane raid over Germany.

don and his comrades, the war shortened by several months.

It would seem that *The Thousand Plane Raid's* only redeeming asset lies in the fact that it is the only Hollywood production depicting the activities of an 8th Air Force bomb group to be filmed entirely in color. Past that, the picture has little to offer the aficianado. The obvious low-budget production values (i.e., poorly tinted and grainy out-takes from *Twelve O'Clock High* and *Memphis Belle*) and cliche-ridden storyline (that borders at times on the ludicrous), combine to destroy what little credibility the film projects.

Although not readily apparent from the finished product, a good deal of time and effort did go into producing the authentic flying sequences for the film. All of the exterior scenes were filmed on location in the northern California town of Santa Maria (chosen for its English-like appearance) during the winter of 1968. The local airfield there had been completely camouflaged to look like a typical wartime 8th Air Force base, including period maintenance shops, operations center and World War II style control tower. Completing the illusion were three privately owned B-17 Flying Fortresses that had been

Stunt pilots Jim Appleby and Skip Marsh fly Frank Tallman's B-17G "Balls of Fire" during air-to-air filming off the coast of Northern California.

Don Lykins and Bob Grider land the Air Museum's B-17G "Bucking Bronco" following a filming session over Santa Maria's airport.

WAC Lieutenant Loraine Stephens and fellow members of the 103rd B.G. await the return of their bomb group from Germany.

flown in for the production. These included a B-17G from Ed Maloney's Air Museum in Ontario, California, another "G" model from stunt pilot Frank Tallman's collection in Santa Ana, California, and lastly, a rare B-17F from Aircraft Specialties Inc., an aerial tanker firm, in Phoenix, Arizona.

Director Boris Sagal and his crew spent nearly two weeks at the airfield shooting all of the air and ground scenes needed for the film. This included a good deal of air-to-air formation footage of the B-17's shot off the coast of California from Frank Tallman's B-25 camera ship. The balance of the six-week shooting schedule was completed at the Samuel Goldwyn Studios in Hollywood and the American Film Institute's Greystone Mansion in Beverly Hills, which had been temporarily converted into 8th Air Force headquarters for the film.

The Thousand Plane Raid had its world premier in Portland, Oregon on June 18, 1969. Critical reviews of the film were, in general, disappointing.

VARIETY

"The Thousand Plane Raid" dealing with the first of the massive air strikes over principal German targets in 1943, appears to have had potential for an exciting film, but turns into little more than a stereotyped adventure yarn . . . for those acquainted with this era of history, the B-17's will provide some rememberance, but little more . . ."

July 17, 1969

CATCH 22

Paramount

— 1970 —

CAST

Captain Yossarian: ALAN ARKIN; Hungry Joe: SETH ALLEN; Captain Orr: ROBERT BALABAN; Colonel Cathcart: MARTIN BALSAM; Major Danby: RICHARD BENJAMIN; Dreedle's WAC: SUSANNE BENTON; Captain Mc Watt: PETER BONERZ; Sergeant Towser: NORMAN FELL; Captain Nately: ARTHUR GARFUNKEL; Dr. Daneeka: JACK GILFORD; Aardvark: CHUCK GRODIN; Lt. Colonel Korn: BUCK HENRY; Major Major: BOB NEWHART; Colonel Moodus: AUSTIN PENDLETON; Chaplain Tappman: ANTHONY PERKINS; Nurse Duckett: PAULA PRENTISS; Lt. Dobbs: MARTIN SHEEN; Milo Minderbinder: JON VOIGHT; General Dreedle: ORSON WELLES; Nately's Whore: GINA ROVERE; Luciana: OLIMPIA CARLISI

CREDITS

Director: MIKE NICHOLS; Producers: MARTIN RANSOHOFF, JOHN CALLEY; Screenplay: BUCK HENRY; Original Story: JOSEPH HELLER; Cinematographer: DAVID WATKIN; Aerial Cinematographers: JOHNNY JORDEN, NELSON TYLER, HAROLD WELLMAN; Air Operations: FRANK TALLMAN, JAMES APPLEBY, FRANK PINE; Art Direction: HAROLD MICHELSON; Set Decoration: RAY MOYER; Special Effects: LEE VASQUE, ALBERT WHITLOCK; Film Editor: SAM O'STEEN; Musical Score: JOHN HAMMELL; Sound Technician: LARRY JOST; Wardrobe: LAMBERT MARKS

The year 1970 saw the premier of one of the blackest, and perhaps bleakest, cinematic satires about the air war ever to reach the silver screen. Adapted from the best-selling novel by Joseph Heller, Paramount's *Catch 22* is a decidedly anti-military look at the exploits of a none too-typical World War II bomb squadron by the unit's battle-crazed bombardier.

The story, as written by Buck Henry and directed by

The 256th Bomb Squadron moves into position for take-off. A total of eighteen B-25's were used in the film.

Mike Nichols, begins in 1944, on the tiny Mediterranean island of Pianosa. It is here, on this shriveled piece of real estate, that the 256th Bomb Squadron is based and from which the somewhat "flak-happy" Captain John Yossarian (Alan Arkin) is plotting his escape. Far from your average hero, Yossarian has flown more than fifty combat missions over Italy, and has decided he doesn't like the war anymore, on the grounds that it might kill him. In fact, Yossarian is convinced that everyone wants him dead, including the group's C.O., Colonel Cathcart (Martin Balsam), who is continually raising the number of bombing missions required before an airman can rotate home. Out of desperation, Yossarian asks flight surgeon "Doc" Daneka (Jack Gilford) to certify him insane so he can stop flying. This prompts the doctor to recite the Army Air Force's little known "Catch 22" regulation which states: "In order to be grounded, you've got to be crazy. And you must be crazy to keep flying. But if you ask to be grounded, that must mean that you're not crazy anymore, and you've got to keep flying." It is just this sort of circular logic that finally pushes Yossarian off the deep end. In one final act of triumphant madness, he climbs into his one-man rubber life raft and paddles off to Sweden, happy to be rid of the war, Pianosa, and the Army Air Force for good.

Alan Arkin ponders his fate prior to taking off on another bombing mission. His co-pilot is actor-singer-songwriter Art Garfunkel.

Despite two years of effort, a budget of $17 million dollars, and the combined talents of its large and multifaceted production crew, *Catch 22* became one of the major artistic and financial failures of the 1970 film season. While Nichols' cinematic translation attempted to remain faithful to Heller's work, it sadly lacked much of the humor, wit, and pathos contained in the original novel, and became little more than a convuluted, and at times grotesque, series of black-out sketches. Once in the air though, the picture does come alive with some of the finest aerial footage of the B-25 Mitchell bomber ever captured on film.

Preliminary work on the picture began in early 1968 under the guidance of producer John Calley and director

One of the most exciting and certainly most dangerous scenes in "Catch 22" involved this mass take-off of all eighteen B-25's over the Gulf of California.

Mike Nichols. Initially it had been planned to photograph the entire picture on location in Tunisia, Sicily, and Sardinia (the original setting for the book), utilizing an entire bomb group of B-25's. After scouting these locales however, the filmmakers found the areas so drastically changed from what they had been in 1944, that they were of very little use to the production. After numerous months of searching, an alternate site was eventually located twenty miles north of the remote fishing village of Guaymas, Mexico. It was there, along the Golfo de California, that Nichols and his production crew built (at a cost of $1,000,000) the island airbase of Pianosa, complete with barracks, ready rooms, control tower, revetments, and a 6000 foot operational runway.

The complex task of assembling Nichols' air group of B-25 bombers and the crews to fly and maintain them was turned over to famed stunt pilot Frank Tallman of Tallmantz Aviation in Santa Ana, California. A former Navy flight instructor, Tallman had joined forces with Paul Mantz in 1961 to supply planes and pilots to all the major motion picture studios. In little time, the two flying impresarios had quickly captured most of the business the film capitol had to offer. *Catch 22* would prove to be one of the most difficult assignments of Tallman's long and varied career.

In all, a total of eighteen B-25's were eventually acquired for use in the film. A mixed bag of wartime "J" and postwar "N" models, they came from as far as New York, Wyoming, Illinois, Texas, and Arizona. Tallmantz's Santa Ana headquarters soon looked like a World War II air depot, as mechanics converted the vintage bombers back to their full wartime configurations, complete with upper gun turrets, bombsights, nose, waist and tail armaments, and operational bomb bays. Along with the aircraft came over $50,000 worth of spare parts (everything from R-2600 engines to spare tires) to support the upcoming film operations.

Frank Tallman (center) poses for an official portrait with some of the pilots and mechanics that made it all possible.

"Catch 22" contained some of the most impressive B-25 formation footage ever captured on film. Each of the airplanes was carefully restored to its full wartime configuration, including the installation of upper gun turrets and nose, waist and tail armaments.

The selection and training of the flight crews that would man the bombers became the responsibility of Tallmantz's Director of Operations, Frank Pine, and General Manager and Chief Pilot, Jim Appleby. A group of thirty-six pilots were initially chosen for the job: eighteen aircraft commanders and eighteen co-pilots.[3] All of the fliers had had prior military experience, many with combat records. "Quite a few of the guys had flown B-25's either during World War II, after the war or in Korea and were seasoned military types," recalls Appleby. "We knew it was going to be a military type operation with a lot of tight, possibly dangerous, formation flying, so we wanted people who knew all the signals, that we could rely on in a pinch, and who we didn't have to train from the ground up."[4]

Despite whatever prior flying experience they had, Appleby ran each of the men through a week-long B-25 refresher course that included formation take-offs, formation practice flights, in-flight filming techniques, and a military style ground school. By the time production began, each of the pilots had received their B-25 type ratings and were ready for whatever lay ahead.

By early January 1969, Paramount's construction crews had completed work on the Pianosa set and Nichols' "troops" began arriving from California. As the various B-25's flew in from Santa Ana, studio artists set about applying the final touches of "make-up" needed for their upcoming roles in the film. This included a bogus set of 12th Air Force markings (Heller's novel was based in part on his exploits with the 12th Air Force's 340th Bomb Group) and the now familiar World War II nose art adornments, which ranged from the gaudy "Free, Fast and Ready" to the patriotic "Berlin Express".

Filming began in earnest on January 11, 1969. Among the first scenes to be shot in Mexico was the impressive early morning montage that opens the film. In what was perhaps the most dangerous aerial stunt ever attempted for a motion picture, Tallman's fliers executed a mass side-by-side take-off of all eighteen B-25's from the narrow Pianosa airstrip. Jim Appleby led the flight that day and describes what it was like:

"I can't remember exactly whose idea this scene was, but I remember telling him, in no uncertain terms, that no military commander, in his right mind, is going to make a mass launch of eighteen airplanes, fully loaded with fuel and bombs, like you saw in the movie." Despite his objections, the scene was ordered shot by studio officials. Appleby continues: "I told the guys in the briefing that day that no matter what happened, they had to keep going – or get out of the way quick – or they'd have eighteen B-25's flying right up their ass! On that particular morning I was positioned about half way down the formation with Frank Pine behind me, with cameras rolling. On cue [a red flag in the tower], we all went to METO power [maximum continuous take-off power – thirty inches of manifold] and started rolling down the runway at two second intervals. It took every bit of strength of both pilots to keep the airplane under control and get it in the air, but we all managed to get through it and live to tell about it. They [the movie people] told us later that the prop wash was so strong behind us that it blew a military weapons carrier with a 800 millimeter lens mounted on it end over end, destroying both the vehicle and the camera."[4]

Nearly four months of filming and 1500 hours of flying time followed without any serious incidents. Ironically, all but a small portion of the stunning B-25 footage that Tallman's fliers worked so hard to get, would ever find its way into the completed film.

By mid-April, all of the location filming in Mexico had been completed and the cast and crew began preparations for the return trip to Los Angeles. Another twelve weeks of studio work lay ahead in Rome, for the elaborate Fellini-like bordello scenes, and in Hollywood, for the aerial process shots, before the film would be completed. Production finally came to an end on August 15, 1969.

Catch 22 had its Los Angeles premier on June 26, 1970, at the National Theater in Hollywood. With few exceptions, critical and audience response to the film was poor, making Nichols' anti-war allegory one of the biggest box-office disappointments of the year.

Cameramen catch stunt pilot Frank Pine at the controls of B-25N "Laden Maiden" during a filming session over the Gulf of California. Nearly four months of filming and 1500 hours of flying time was accumulated by Tallman's fliers during their stay in Mexico.

LIFE

"... Mike Nichols' movie version of (Heller's) novel is, in tone, as hot and heavy as the original was cool and light. Charitably, one might say that he was seeking the visual equivalent of the book's verbal style. But he failed abysmally and in the process he and writer Buck Henry have mislad every bit of humor that made the novel emotionally bearable and esthetically memorable, replacing it with desperately earnest proof they hate war. Part of their failure was probably inevitable. So much of the book's effectiveness stemmed from the rich matrix of relationships between its characters, the endless range of their responses to the situations they shared. Even so, these movie people seem to be only the ghosts of their former selves, more evidence of Nichols' desire for the conspicuous consumption of acting talent than a gift for skillfully employing it in large numbers."

Richard Shickel
July 3, 1970

Much of the credit for the film's excellent aerial scenes must go to veteran stunt pilots Frank Pine (far left) and Jim Appleby (far right), seen here preparing for another "mission" over Guaymas.

TORA! TORA! TORA!

Twentieth Century-Fox

— 1970 —

CAST

Admiral Kimmel: MARTIN BALSAM; Admiral Yamamoto: SOH YAMAMURA; Henry Stimson: JOSEPH COTTON; General Short: JASON ROBARDS; Commander Genda: TATSUYA MIHASHI; Lt. Colonel Bratton: E.G. MARSHALL; Lt. Commander Fuchida: TAKAHIRO TAMURA; Admiral Halsey: JAMES WHITMORE; Admiral Nagumo: EIJIRO TONO; Lt. Commander Kramer: WESLEY ADDY; Ambassador Nomura: SHOGO SHIMADA; Lt. Commander Thomas: FRANK ALETTER; Prince Konoye: KOREYA SENDA; Frank Knox: LEON AMES; Admiral Yoshida: JUNYA USAMI; Captain John Earle: RICHARD ANDERSON; Foreign Minister Matsuoka: KAZUO KITAMURA; General George C. Marshall: KEITH ANDES; Admiral Stark: EDWARD ANDREWS; Lt. Kaminsky: NEVILLE BRAND; Mrs. Kramer: LEORA DANA; General Tojo: ASAO UCHIDA; Cordell Hull: GEORGE MACREADY; Major Truman Landon: NORMAN ALDEN; Captain Theodore Wilkinson: WALTER BROOKE; Lt. George Welch: RICK COOPER; Doris Miller: ELVEN HAVARD; Miss Ray Cave: JUNE DAYTON; Cornelia: JEFF DONNELL; Colonel Edward F. French: RICHARD ERDMAN; Lt. Commander William Outerbridge: JERRY FOGEL; Kameto Kuroshima: SHUNICHI NAKAMURA; Lt. Kenneth Taylor: CARL REINDEL; Rear Admiral Bellinger: EDMON RYAN; Saburo Kurusu: HISAO TOAKE

CREDITS

Directors: RICHARD FLEISCHER, TOSHIO MASUDA, KINJI FUKASAKU; Second Unit Director: RAY KELLOGG; Producer: ELMO WILLIAMS; Associate Producers: OTTO LANG, MASAYUKI TAKAGI, KEINOSUKE KUBO; Screenplay: LARRY FORRESTER, HIDEO OGUNI, RYUZO KIKUSHIMA; Cinematographers: CHARLES WHEELER, SINAKU HIMEDA, MASAMICHI SATOH, OSAMI FURAYA; Aerial Cinematographers: DAVID BUTLER, MICHAEL BUTLER; Air Operations: LT. COLONEL ART WILDERN, CAPTAIN GEORGE WATKINS, JACK CANARY, DAVID JONES; Art Direction: JACK SMITH, YOSHIRO MURAKI, RICHARD DAY, TAIZOH KAWASHIMA; Set Decoration: WALTER SCOTT, NORMAN ROCKETT; Special Effects: L.B. ABBOTT, A.D. FLOWERS, ART CRUICKSHANK; Film Editors: JAMES NEWCOM, PEMBROKE HERRING, INOUE CHIKAYA; Musical Score: JERRY GOLDSMITH; Sound Technicians: JAMES CORCORAN, MURRAY SPIVACK, DOUG WILLIAMS, TED SODERBERG, HERMAN LEWIS, SHIN WATARAI; Wardrobe: COURTNEY HASLAM, ED HYNIGEAR; Makeup: DAN STRIEPEKI, LAYNE BRITTON

Japanese sailors snap to attention during change of command ceremonies aboard the carrier "Akagi."

In an attempt to emulate the phenomenal box-office success of its 1962 blockbuster, *The Longest Day*, Twentieth Century-Fox Studios decided to bring to the screen, for the first time, the full story of the surprise Japanese air attack on Pearl Harbor on December 7, 1941. The result was a 1970 release entitled *Tora! Tora! Tora!*, which re-enacts, in great detail, the raid and the events which led up to the "date that will live in infany" for all Americans.

Based on a screenplay by Larry Forrester, Hideo Oguni, and Ryuzo Kikushima, the story opens in September of 1939, as Admiral Isoruku Yamamoto (Soh Yamamura) takes command of the Japanese Imperial Fleet. It is Yamamoto who first conceives of the raid on Pearl Harbor, realizing that he must eliminate the U.S. Pacific Fleet, if Japan is going to realize its goal of Asian conquest. Months of strategic planning and preparation are devoted to what will become the most audacious attack in military history. By late 1941, the United States and Japan are veering inexorably toward war. Although U.S. Army intelligence officers have succeeded in cracking the Japanese diplomatic code and know they will ultimately strike somewhere in the Pacific, few, if any, feel the attack will take place at Pearl Harbor.

At a little past dawn, on Sunday, December 7th, two waves of 353 bombers, torpedo planes, and fighters roar off the pitching decks of Vice Admiral Chuchi Nagumo's (Eijiro Tono) carrier task force (positioned 230 miles north of Oahu) and head south toward the unsuspecting U.S. Naval facility. At 0755 hours, the first bombs fall on the air bases at Hickam, Wheeler, and Ford Island. Within minutes, half of the island's defensive air power has been wiped out. Simultaneously, "Battleship Row," the heart of the American naval fleet, receives a series of devastating blows from attacking Japanese torpedo bombers. By battle's end, some two hours later, the once powerful Pacific fleet lay a smoldering wreck. A total of eighteen ships have been severely damaged or sunk, 188 aircraft destroyed and most appalling of all, 3581 servicemen have been killed or wounded. In one fell swoop, control of the Pacific has shifted to the hands of the Japanese, and the United States unwillingly catapulted into the Second World War.

Taking three years to plan and eight months to film – at a cost of over $25,000,000 – Fox's *Tora! Tora! Tora!*

Takahiro Tamura greets some of the pilots of his Pearl Harbor attack force as they arrive aboard the "Akagi."

The Pearl Harbor attack force is given the signal to take-off, December 7, 1941. These scenes were filmed aboard a full scale mock-up of the "Akagi" built along the perimeters of Ashiya Air Force Base on the island of Kyushu.

remains one of the finest and most technically accurate dramatizations of the Pearl Harbor tragedy ever to reach the screen. Utilizing the same cross-cutting techniques as *The Longest Day*, the film uniquely tells the story of the attack from the point of view of both nations, without presenting any value judgments of its own. While the screenplay drags periodically in leading up to the attack, the battle itself and the special effects that produced it are nothing less than spectacular.

Takahiro Tamura gets his first glimpse of the sleeping Pearl Harbor Naval Base.

Pre-production planning for the film began in 1966 under the guidance of veteran producer Elmo Williams (*The Longest Day, The Blue Max*). Using source material from two contemporary works on the subject, Dr. Gordon Prange's *Tora! Tora! Tora!*, and Ladislas Farago's *The Broken Seal*, Williams elected to emphasize the Japanese point of view, specifically "the airmen's point of view," in his cinematic retelling of the Pearl Harbor attack. Consequently, it was decided to film two separate versions of the story, one in Japan and one in the United States, under directors Richard Fleischer, Toshio Masuda, and Kinji Fukasaku, and integrate them into one motion picture for the final effect.

Department of Defense approval was secured to film most of the American sequences at the original military installations that had been involved in the December 7th attack. These included Oahu's Ford Island Naval Base, Wheeler Air Force Base, the Schofield Barracks, Fort Shafter Army Base, and most importantly the original anchorages along Pearl Harbor's "Battleship Row." The Japanese sequences would primarily be filmed at the JASDF's Ashiya Air Force Base on the island of Kyushu, in Tokyo, for exteriors of the Imperial Palace and the United States Embassy, and along Kyushu's Kagoshima

A flight of Zero fighters move in for their attack on the U.S. Pacific Fleet. These World War II destroyer escorts were among the half-dozen U.S. Navy vessels leased for use in the film.

Bay, the original site of pilot rehearsals for the mission.

The scarcity of ships and aircraft from the Pearl Harbor era forced Williams to use several different expediencies in recreating the naval and air forces that were involved in the battle. Fox's miniature department constructed as many as nineteen Japanese warships and ten American warships (as well as the Pearl Harbor docks and surrounding land areas) for use in the picture. Averaging forty feet in length, the ships were built on a scale of either one-half inch to a foot or three-quarter inch to a foot, depending upon whether they were to be blown-up on screen (the larger the scale the more realistic the explosion). For key scenes involving the actors, the studio constructed three full-scale replicas (two in Japan, one in Hawaii) of the Japanese battleship *Nagota*, aircraft carrier *Akagi* and American battleship *Arizona*, which would also double for the USS *West Virginia, Oklahoma,* and *Nevada* at various stages of the filming.

In addition to these screen combatants, the Navy Department loaned Fox six actual warships for the duration of their filming schedule. These included the USS *Philip* (DD498), *Sproston* (DD577), *Brister* (DE329), *Newell* (DE322), *Sheldrake* (AM62), and the "Fighting Lady" of World War II, the USS *Yorktown* (CV10), which would double for the carrier *Akagi* in the early morning take-off sequences scheduled to be filmed off the coast of California.

Some thirty World War II AT-6 and BT-13 training aircraft were modified to represent the 353 Japanese aircraft of Vice Admiral Nagumo's carrier strike force. Refitted with larger engines, three-bladed propellers and numerous other modifications, the group consisted of twelve Mitsubishi A6M2 "Zeroes" (AT-6's), nine Aichi Type 99

Bomb explosions aboard the USS West Virginia hurl a group of sailors overboard.

A flight of incoming Japanese Zero's surprise an Army gun emplacement on Opana Point.

Explosions envelope a pair of P-40's on the Wheeler Field flight line.

Few of the Army's P-40's are left intact following the air raid on Wheeler.

"Vals" (BT-13's), and nine Nakajima Type 97 "Kates" (an AT-6/BT-13 combination). In Japan, another twenty-one AT-6's, declared surplus by the JASDF and turned over to the studio, were similarly modified for use in the carrier sequences filmed at Ashiya AFB.

To represent the American air forces that were stationed at Pearl Harbor, the studio leased or purchased another forty-three aircraft of various types, including two P-40 pursuits, one B-25 medium bomber, one SBD dive bomber, one flyable and five non-flyable PBY patrol planes, five B-17 heavy bombers, and twenty-seven expendable fiberglass P-40 replicas for use in the air attack scenes filmed at Wheeler Air Force Base. Add a lone PT-17 trainer, and Williams had at his command one of the largest assemblages of World War II ships and aircraft ever gathered for use in a single motion picture.

Production officially got under way on December 4, 1968, aboard the USS *Yorktown*. It was on this historic ship that some of the most impressive scenes in the film were made; those of the pre-dawn carrier take-offs of Lt. Commander Mitsuo Fuchida's air group from the carrier *Akagi*. Capturing the excitement of the moment perfectly, Navy Captain George Watkins (chief pilot and technical advisor for the *Yorktown* operation) led the thirty-plane contingent of Fox's newly-formed air group, as it roared off the wooden decks of the *Yorktown* and into the early morning skies above the Pacific Ocean. Accomplished without a hitch, the beautifully-staged sequence was later integrated with the static carrier footage shot on the *Akagi* set in Japan to complete the effect.

From a production standpoint, the restaging of the actual air attacks on Pearl Harbor and its surrounding airfields proved by far to be the most complex and difficult operation in the entire filming schedule. Taking over three

Japanese Zero's destroy an Army P-40 as it attempts to take-off during the raid.

months to complete, at a cost of $8,000,000, the scenes were photographed at the original locales of Ford Island (which also doubles for Hickam Field in the film), Wheeler Field, and in and around the docks of Pearl Harbor's naval facility.

USAF Lt. Colonel Art Wildern (Retired), chief of air operations for the Pearl Harbor sequences, personally led all of the low-level air attacks during this period. A former World War II fighter pilot, Wildern had flown 106 combat missions with the Ninth Air Force's 362nd Fighter Group in England and France. With nearly 2000 hours of flying time in AT-6's alone (as a pilot and instructor), he was emminently qualified to lead the studio's IJN air group. "When they [representatives from the U.S. Navy and Fox Studios] first interviewed me for the job I think they were taken back a bit when I told them I also had a good deal of experience in blowing up ships – if that's what they needed," recalls Wildern. In August 1944, Wildern's unit received its first Distinguished Unit Citation (DUC) for a fighter-bomber mission against Brest Harbor, in which they sank an enemy cruiser and submarine, beached another cruiser, and set afire a dozen other naval and merchant ships caught in the harbor.

After receiving his assignment from producer Elmo Williams, Wildern was given reasonably free rein over all flying aspects of the Pearl Harbor filming. Of the over 400 applicants who applied for the piloting jobs, only forty-seven were eventually chosen.[7] Ranging in age from their late twenties to their mid-fifties, all were either retired or off-duty service pilots from the Navy, Air Force, Marine Corps, or Air Guard. "I had the final say on every pilot chosen for the film," remembers Wildern. "I knew we would be spending a lot of time in tight formations or

Little of the Army's air fleet is left intact following the surprise air raid.

George Macready delivers a tongue-lashing to Japanese ambassadors Shogo Shinada and Hisao Toake for delivering their ultimatum after Pearl Harbor had already been bombed.

Fox camera crews watch as the "Tora! Tora! Tora!" air group sweeps in for its attack on Pearl Harbor.

Studio firemen hose down a group of P-40's following the "attack" on Wheeler Field.

'down on the deck,' so we screened them closely for how much military flying experience they had, their AT-6 and SNJ flight time, and total amount of 'tail dragger' experience. After we had picked all the pilots, I got the studio to go along with a twenty-six hour transition training program to get the 'rust' off of everybody. I really do think it paid off in the end. There was a great espirit de corps among the fellas and I think it showed in our work on the screen."[8]

Temporarily headquartered at NAS Barbers Point, on the southern tip of Oahu, Wildern and his fliers logged more than 4000 flying hours during their "bombing" and "strafing" missions over Pearl Harbor. "We flew most of the missions the same way we had in World War II – 'flat-ass' on the deck," recalls Wildern. "Daily briefings were held at 4:30 in the morning, where we'd go over that day's shooting schedule and what the movie people expected of us. During the filming, I had one of my people in a FAC (forward air controller) position on the ground, coordinating our 'air strikes' with the director and special effects people who were setting off the explosions we had to fly through. [About one-and-a-quarter tons of explosives and 120,000 gallons of gasoline and diesel oil were employed in the battle scenes shot at Pearl Harbor.] Once we got into the actual air attacks, it might as well have been for real, because that's just the way we flew it."[9] And indeed it showed. Over thirty-five hours of combat footage was shot during the filming in Hawaii. Although only a fraction of it appears in the final cut of the film, the scenes remain classics of their kind.

By May of 1969, all of the location filming had been completed and Williams' crew returned to California for an additional six weeks of backlot and miniature photography at the Fox studios in Los Angeles and Malibu. Production of the film officially came to a close on June 10, 1969. Given the complexity of the post-production editing processes needed to put the film together, over a year passed before the picture was ready for release to the public.

Tora! Tora! Tora! had its world premiere at the Criterion Theater in New York City on September 23, 1970. Despite all the effort and capital that went into making the film, critical reviews (in the United States) were mixed and

Second unit production manager, Jack Stubbs (front row-center), poses with some of the "Tora! Tora! Tora!" flight crews at Wheeler AFB, Hawaii.

The USS Arizona comes under attack in one of the many excellent miniature scenes filmed at Fox's Malibu ranch. A total of twenty-nine miniature warships were constructed for use in the film.

One of the "Tora" Zero's lands at NAS Barbers Point following a day-long filming session over Pearl Harbor. A total of twelve of these replica fighters were used in the sequences filmed in Hawaii.

box-office results disappointing. One can only assume that since the film had been made within the shadows of a real war in Vietnam, a war that had grown progressively unpopular with many Americans, that this had a negative effect on the reception of the film. Regardless, *Tora! Tora! Tora!* won the Academy Award for Best Special Visual Effects of 1970 (A.D. Flowers, L.B. Abbott) and was nominated for five additional awards: Best Cinematography (Charles Wheeler, Osami Furuyu, Sinaku Himeda, Masamichi Satoh); Art Direction (Jack Smith, Yoshiro Muraki, Richard Day, Taizoh Kawashima); Set Decoration (Walter Scott, Norman Rockett, Call Biddiscombe); Sound (Murray Spivak, Herman Lewis); and Film Editing (James Newcom, Pembroke Herring, Inoue Chikaya).

LOS ANGELES TIMES

"To put its first strength first, 20th Century-Fox's 'Tora! Tora! Tora!' contains some of the most spectacular war action sequences I've ever seen. Pearl Harbor on the Sunday morning of December 7, 1941, cannot have looked or sounded or felt greatly different from this . . . to put its second strength second, 'Tora! Tora! Tora!' really consists of two pictures, one American-made, one Japanese-made, which have been intercut for maximum suspense and for maximum separation of the two national streams . . . Elmo Williams produced this enormously elaborate and difficult work, at a reported cost of $25 million, and Richard Fleischer was the overall director . . . 'Tora' advances no argument, it will not comfort militarists at the expense of the pacifist, or vice-versa . . . it makes war spectacular, as war undeniably can be, but it can hardly be said to glorify war . . ."

Charles Champlin
September 23, 1970

Director of "Tora" air operations, Lt. Colonel Art Wildern (left), discusses an upcoming scene with producer Elmo Williams (center), and director Richard Fleisher (right).

MIDWAY

Universal

— 1976 —

CAST

Captain Matt Garth: CHARLTON HESTON; Admiral Chester W. Nimitz: HENRY FONDA; Captain Vinton Maddox: JAMES COBURN; Rear Admiral Raymond A. Spruance: GLENN FORD; Commander Joseph Rochefort: HAL HOLBROOK; Admiral Isoroku Yamamoto: TOSHIRO MIFUNE; Admiral William F. Halsey: ROBERT MITCHUM; Commander Carl Jessop: CLIFF ROBERTSON; Lt. Commander Ernest L. Blake: ROBERT WAGNER; Rear Admiral Frank J. "Jack" Fletcher: ROBERT WEBBER; Admiral Harry Pearson: ED NELSON; Vice Admiral Chuichi Nagumo: JAMES SHIGETA; Haruko Sakura: CHRISTINA KOKUBO; Commander Max Leslie: MONTE MARKHAM; Captain Miles Browning: BIFF MC GUIRE; Ensign George Gay: KEVIN DOBSON; Lt. Commander C. Wade McClusky: CHRISTOPHER GEORGE; Lt. Commander John Waldron: GLENN CORBETT; Captain Elliott Buckmaster: GREGORY WALCOTT; Ensign Tom Garth: EDWARD ALBERT

CREDITS

Producer: WALTER MIRISCH; Director: JACK SMIGHT; Original Screenplay: DONALD S. SANFORD; Cinematographer: HARRY STRADLING, JR.; Air Operations: FRANK PINE; Art Direction: WALTER TYLER; Set Decoration: JOHN DWYER; Special Effects: JACK MC MASTER; Film Editors: ROBERT SWINK, FRANK J. URIOSTE; Musical Score: JOHN WILLIAMS; Sound Technicians: ROBERT MARTIN, LEONARD PETERSON

By the early seventies, America's growing disillusionment with the Vietnam conflict had resulted in a dearth of Hollywood war films on the silver screen. In fact, it was not until 1976, six years after the release of Fox's *Tora! Tora! Tora!,* that American moviegoers saw the rebirth of the war epic in the form of Universal's multimillion dollar production of *Midway*. Based on the book of the same name, by Donald S. Sanford, the film is an at-

Henry Fonda discusses battle strategy with some of his junior officers, Robert Wagner, Charlton Heston, and James Coburn.

times perceptive cinematic study of the Battle of Midway, considered by historians to be the most decisive and significant naval battle of World War II.

The story begins in May of 1942, as Imperial Japanese Headquarters issues the following orders to Admiral Isoruku Yamamoto (Toshiro Mifune): "Commander in Chief Combined Fleet will, in cooperation with the Army, invade and occupy strategic points in the Western Aleutions and Midway Island." It was perhaps the boldest undertaking in the history of Japanese naval warfare, the purpose of which was to push Japan's defense perimeters further from its shores and to lure what remained of the U.S. Pacific Fleet into a final, all-out, battle. Yamamoto's strike force consisted of over 150 ships, including eleven battleships, sixty destroyers, twenty-three cruisers, and four aircraft carriers. The U.S. Pacific Fleet, under the command of Admiral Chester Nimitz (Henry Fonda), consisted of less than sixty ships, the aircraft carriers *Yorktown, Enterprise* and *Hornet* and a combined complement of 230 carrier airplanes.

The "Blue Ghost" of World War II, the USS Lexington (CVT-16), during one of her regular training cruises in the Gulf of Mexico Some fifty members of Universal's production company spent a week aboard ship filming scenes for use in "Midway."

James Shigeta discusses battle plans with members of his staff, Pat Morita, Lloyd Kino, and Robert Ito.

Though woefully outnumbered, the U.S. Navy had succeeded in breaking the Japanese radio code and knew the Imperial Fleet was converging on Midway Island. In the early morning hours of June 4, 1942, aircraft from the three U.S. carriers launched their attacks against Yamamoto's unsuspecting invasion force. In little more than five minutes, the Japanese had lost three of its carriers, the *Soryu, Kaga,* and *Akagi,* and all air groups aboard those ships. Hours later, in a vicious exchange of carrier air strikes, the *Yorktown* was so severely damaged she had to be abandoned and the

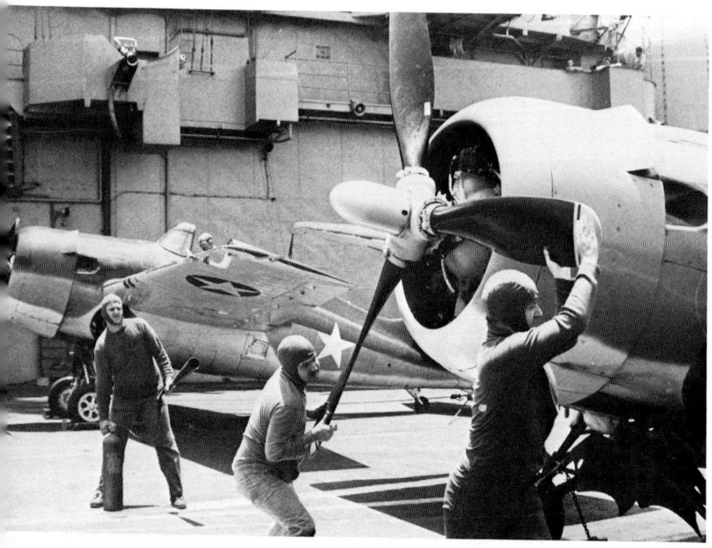

Navy crewmen prepare a pair of F4F Wildcats for battle aboard the USS Yorktown. This scene was actually filmed aboard the "Lexington" using ship's personnel as extras.

last of the Japanese carriers, the *Hiryu,* disabled and sunk. By battle's end, the Americans had lost only one aircraft carrier and one destroyer; the Japanese all four of its aircraft carriers, many of its experienced pilots, a heavy cruiser, and sustained major damage to six other warships. For Japan, her long sweeping offensive in the Pacific had come to an abrupt end; the tide of battle had finally shifted in America's favor.

While Universal's production of *Midway* is an interesting and generally accurate account of the Battle of Midway, it loses much of its credibility to the confusing and highly improbable histrionics that are played out between actual events. The introduction of such fictional characters as Captain Matt Garth (Charlton Heston) and his son Ensign Tom Garth (Edward Albert), for dramatic effect, do little to aid the film and serve only to confuse an already complicated screenplay.

In deference to producer Walter Mirisch and his film crew, it must be acknowledged that the problems encountered in transferring a story of this magnitude and complexity to the screen were immense. Given the relative scarcity of period warships and aircraft to re-enact the battle sequences, Mirisch had no choice but to use several different production expediencies to make his film. Primarily, this consisted of using a great deal of stock Navy combat footage from World War II and combining it with out-takes from several different motion pictures and documentaries including: *Tora! Tora! Tora!, Thirty Seconds Over Tokyo, Dive Bomber, Flying Leathernecks, Admiral Yama-*

Kevin Dobson prepares to launch his torpedo attack against the carrier Kaga. His TBD Devastator is actually a modified SNJ-5.

moto, The Fighting Lady, and John Ford's wartime documentary *The Battle of Midway.* To this, Mirisch added his own studio dramatizations filmed on Universal's backlot, at various locations in California, and most importantly those photographed aboard the last active World War II aircraft carrier in U.S. Naval service, the USS *Lexington* (CVT-16), off the coast of Florida.

Chief pilot and aerial coordinator for the production, Frank Pine, of Tallmantz Aviation, was given the task of rounding up the few World War II aircraft that were actually used in these sequences. Pine's "air group" ultimately consisted of one PBY-5A, posing as twelve different Catalinas in the film; two privately owned FM-2 Wildcats, to stand-in for the seventy-nine F4F-3's of VF-3 (*Yorktown*), VF-6 (*Enterprise*) and VF-8 (*Hornet*); and a small number of Japanese "Zeroes", "Vals", and "Kates" resurrected from Fox's production of *Tora! Tora! Tora!*. In addition to these flyable aircraft, the studio also acquired the use of a number of non-flyable museum pieces for use in the sound stage process shots. These aircraft included an SBD-5 Dauntless, another FM-2 Wildcat and an SNJ-5 training plane modified to look like a Douglas TBD Devastator.

Formal production of the film was begun on May 15, 1975, under the direction of Jack Smight. The first week of filming was spent aboard the USS *Lexington*, (during one of her regular training cruises in the Gulf of Mexico) shooting interior and exterior "atmosphere" shots in various parts of the ship. During this time, some 500 members

Vintage aircraft collectors Rudy Frasca (above) and Junior Burchinal (below) provided the two flyable FM-2's used in the film.

Charlton Heston instructs his pilots to launch their attack on the Japanese carrier "Hiryu." Heston's SBD is actually sitting on terra firma inside Universal's Sound Stage 22.

Some of Universal's acting troupe gather on deck upon completion of filming aboard the "Lexington." Glenn Ford and Charlton Heston were both World War II veterans, having served in the U.S. Coast Guard and U.S. Army Air Force respectively.

of the *Lexington's* 1500 man crew volunteered to serve as extras in various scenes with the studio's actors.

Despite the fact that the two FM-2's brought aboard ship were airworthy, Navy regulations prohibited them from being flown off the carrier. Therefore they were used strictly as props for the actors to climb in or out of or in various background scenes filmed above or below decks. It was only after the *Lexington* had docked at NAS Pensacola, and the Wildcats off-loaded, that the planes were flown in a short air-to-air filming session prior to the production company's return to Los Angeles.

The balance of the nine-week shooting schedule was spent filming scenes at various locations in California, including the U.S. Army's facility at Fort MacArthur, the Long Beach Naval Base on Terminal Island, the Pt. Mugu Naval Base, Huntington Library's Japanese Gardens in Pasadena, and on Universal Studio's Sound Stage 22. It was there that all of the intricate in-flight process scenes were filmed, along with numerous shipboard sequences staged on sets made up of actual parts of World War II aircraft carriers (i.e., the USS *Hancock*) that had been earmarked for scrap by the U.S. Navy.

Production of the film officially ended on July 20, 1975. *Midway* had its world premier in Los Angeles, Cali-

The USS Yorktown comes under attack during the Battle of Midway. This particular scene first appeared in John Ford's wartime documentary "The Battle of Midway," and was later resurrected for use in Universal's film.

fornia, nearly one year later, on June 18, 1976, during America's Bicentennial Celebration. While critical response to the film was mixed, popular audience response to the picture was overwhelming, making *Midway* the sixth largest grossing film of the year.

LOS ANGELES TIMES

". . . the principal strength of 'Midway' as written by Donald S. Sanford and directed by Jack Smight is that it keeps the lines of battle both straight and suspenseful in the viewer's mind. The camera looks in constantly on battle maps and strategy talks on both the U.S. and Japanese sides, and the screen is full of captions telling us what ships and aircraft are which and whose . . . it is the action, the exploding planes, the floating holocausts, the black plumes arcing into the sea, the cannons roaring, which carry the picture for those who care . . ."

Charles Chaplin
June 18, 1976

Retired Navy officer George Gay (right), who participated in the Battle of Midway, acted as one of the film's technical advisors. Here he assists director Jack Smight (left) in recreating his wartime rescue.

HANOVER STREET

Columbia

— 1979 —

CAST

Lt. David Halloran: HARRISON FORD; Margaret Sellinger: LESLEY-ANNE DOWN; Paul Sellinger: CHRISTOPHER PLUMMER; Major Trumbo: ALEC MC COWEN; Lt. Jerry Cimino: RICHARD MASUR; Lt. Martin Hyer: MICHAEL SACKS; Harry Pike: MAX WALL; Lt. Wells: KEITH BUCKLEY; Phyllis: SHERRIE HEWSON; Colonel Bart: SHANE RIMMER; Sarah Sellinger: PATSY KENSIT

CREDITS

Director: PETER HYAMS; Producer: PAUL LAZARUS; Screenplay: PETER HYAMS; Cinematographer: DAVID WATKINS; Air Operations: JOHN HAWKE; Art Direction: MALCOLM MIDDLETON, ROBERT CARTWRIGHT; Production Designer: PHILLIP HARRISON; Special Effects: MARTIN GUTTERIDGE; Film Editor: JAMES MITCHELL; Musical Score: JOHN BARRY; Sound Technician: ROBIN GREGORY; Wardrobe: JOAN BRIDGES

The box-office appeal of Universal's production of *Midway* prompted yet another rash of films about World War II during the late 1970's. Among the worst of these combat epics was Columbia's 1979 release *Hanover Street*, a film which reduced the air war to little more than an endless series of bombing, briefing, and bedroom scenes.

The story, by writer-director Peter Hyams (*Capricorn One*), has 8th Air Force bomber pilot, Lt. David Halloran (Harrison Ford) meeting pretty Red Cross volunteer Margaret Sellinger (Lesley-Anne Down), during a German air raid over London's Hanover Street district. In little time, the two strangers become lovers, at which point, Halloran learns, to his dismay, that Margaret is married to famed British intelligence officer Paul Sellinger (Christopher Plummer). Despite this ominous note, the star-crossed lovers continue to meet secretly, between regular bombing jaunts over "Festung Europa." In a queer twist of fate, Halloran and Paul Sellinger are thrown together on a dangerous intelligence mission into occupied France. Barely escaping

Harrison Ford and his bomber crew pose before their "8th Air Force" B-25J "Gorgeous George-Ann." This particular aircraft had previously appeared in "Catch 22" as "Laden Maiden."

with their lives, the pair return to England, where the battle-scarred Halloran does the only honorable thing he can do by convincing Margaret to forget him and return to her loyal husband and family.

Hanover Street's sudsy storyline pretty much speaks for itself. Aside from some brief, but truly excellent, flying sequences involving Halloran's B-25 squadron (a little dramatic license here since the 8th Air Force had no B-25 combat units during World War II), the film offers little in the way of wartime reality.

Taking over four months to complete, the film was shot entirely on location in England during the spring and summer of 1978. All of the interior scenes, including those shot on the elaborate Hanover Street set, were filmed at the EMI-Elstree Studios outside of London. The remaining air and ground scenes were staged at the former Royal Air Force facilities at Bovingdon and Little Rissington, north of London, where director Hyams and his film crew had gathered five privately owned B-25's for use in the 8th Air Force sequences of the story.

Hanover Street had its world premier at Mann's Chinese Theater in Hollywood, California, on May 18, 1979. Critical reviews of the film were decidedly mixed.

NEW YORK TIMES

"Every now and then a film comes along of such painstaking, overripe foolishness that it breaks through the garbage barrier to become one of those rare movies you rush to see for laughs. What Peter Hyams has achieved with 'Hanover Street', his new film about a wartime romance set in London of 1943, is a movie that is almost as funny as Woody Allen's 'Whats Up, Tiger Lily?' . . . [it] looks as if Mr. Hyams had studied every popular romantic drama, from 'A Farewell to Arms' to 'Love Affair' and 'Love Story,' and then, when he left the screening room, had been hit on the head with a brick. When he woke up he remembered bits and pieces of things he'd seen but his judgment had fled . . ."

Vincent Canby
May 18, 1979

A pair of B-25's encounter enemy flak in one of the few battle sequences appearing in "Hanover Street."

ENOLA GAY

Viacom

— 1980 —

CAST

Lt. Colonel Paul Tibbets: PATRICK DUFFY; Captain Bob Lewis: GREGORY HARRISON; Major Tom Ferebee: GARY FRANK; Lt. Jacob Beser: BILLY CRYSTAL; Major Bud Uanna: STEPHEN MACHT; Lucy Tibbets: KIM DARBY; Captain Deak Parsons: ROBERT PINE; Captain Ted Van Kirk: STEPHEN BURLEIGH; T/Sergeant George Caron: GLEN MORRISSEY; M/Sergeant Wyatt Duzenbury: FRED NELSON; S/Sergeant Joe Stiborek: DAVID COLOSINO; Sergeant Robert Shumard: MATHEW HAGGERTY; Dr. Robert Oppenheimer: ROBERT WALDEN; President Truman: ED NELSON

CREDITS

Director: DAVID LOWELL RICH; Producer: FRANKLIN LEVY, STANLEY KALLIS; Screenplay: JAMES POE, MILLARD KAUFMAN; Original Story: GREGORY THOMAS, MAX GORDON WITTS; Cinematographer: ROBERT MORRISON; Air Operations: CLAY LACY, CARTER MC GREGOR, WILLIAM BECKER, RANDY SOHN, ART STAGG, RALPH JOHNSON; Art Direction: JACK DE SHIELDS; Set Decoration: TOM PEDIGO; Special Effects: GUNTER JENNINGS; Film Editor: BYRON CHUDNOW; Sound Technician: COYE VANOVER; Wardrobe: MICHAEL HOFFMAN

The fall of 1980 saw the release of yet another film treatment of the atomic bomb story. Covering much the same ground as its MGM predecessors, *The Beginning or the End* and *Above and Beyond,* Viacom's production of *Enola Gay* describes, through the eyes of its participants, the preparations for and execution of the first A-bomb attack against Japan.

Based on the best-selling book by Gregory Thomas and Max Gordon Witts, the film recounts the story of Lt. Colonel Paul Tibbets (Patrick Duffy) and the ten-man crew of the B-29 "Enola Gay" (named after Tibbets' mother) as they

Duffy and his crew pose for the cameramen prior to taking off on the Hiroshima mission, August 6, 1945.

Patrick Duffy watches as the first of the 509th Bomb Group crews arrive at Wendover Field, Utah.

prepare for the bombing raid that changed the course of history. Nearly nine months of intensive ultrasecret flight training precedes the crew's arrival on the island airbase of Tinian that hot summer in 1945. It is not until the men have settled in, that Tibbets gives them the full details of their upcoming mission and the destructive power of the weapon they will carry. In the early morning hours of August 6, 1945, Tibbets lifts the "Enola Gay" and her lethal cargo, off of Tinian's floodlit runway and points her nose toward the heart of Japan. Little more than six hours later, at approximately 9:15 AM, bombardier Major Tom Ferebee (Gary Frank), releases the bomb over their objective, the port city of Hiroshima. The blast that follows destroys over fifty percent of the city, kills or injures over 120,000 of its occupants, and ultimately brings about the long awaited end to World War II.

Aside from some minor historical concessions, Viacom's production of *Enola Gay* is technically quite good. Adhering closely to the facts presented in the Thomas-Witts book of the same name, the film follows the crew of the "Enola Gay" from the time of their flight training at remote Wendover Army Air Force Base in Utah, to the

The Confederate Air Force's B-29 "FiFi" arrives in Tucson, Arizona, to begin work on the filming of "Enola Gay."

Film crews capture the action during the first day of shooting at Davis-Monthan Air Force Base, outside of Tucson, Arizona.

moment they dropped the bomb and became world renowned figures. Unfortunately, the film's scenarists, James Poe and Millard Kaufman, chose to make the same mistake as their predecessors had in *Above and Beyond*, by placing too much of the screenplay's emphasis on Lt. Colonel Tibbets' marital woes, instead of the mission itself. This fact, combined with the shallow acting performances by many of the film's principal performers, ultimately weakened the overall impact of an otherwise excellent motion picture.

Pre-production planning for *Enola Gay* began in 1977. Nearly three years and $4.5 million dollars would be needed to transform the film into a finished motion picture. One of the greatest problems facing producers Franklin Levy and Stanley Kallis during this time was the acquisition of three B-29's to re-enact the original Hiroshima mission. A country-wide search by the filmmakers revealed that, of the 4000 Superfortresses built, only a handful still remained intact, and all were preserved in museums. Luckily, two of these aircraft, "FiFi," from the Confederate Air Force Museum in Harlingen, Texas, and "Fertile Myrtle," from the American Air Museum in Oakland, California, were maintained in flyable condition and could be made available for use in the film. A third, non-flyable example, "Sentimental Journey," was located at

The island of Tinian is a beehive of activity as maintenance crews prepare the "Enola Gay" and her sister ships for the Hiroshima mission.

the Pima County Air Museum in Tucson, Arizona, and was made available for use in fleshing-out various background scenes.

Arrangements were made with the Department of Defense to use Davis-Monthan Air Force Base in Tucson, Arizona, as the primary site for filming most of air and ground sequences needed for the picture. Established in 1927, this sprawling 11,000 acre airbase, with its multitude of World War II buildings, ultimately proved invaluable in providing the proper atmosphere for the many varied locales depicted throughout the film. These included, among others, the 509th Composite Group's training facilities at Wendover Army Air Force Base in Utah, the atom bomb test site at Alamogordo, New Mexico, and even the Army Air Force's lush island airbase on Tinian, from which the original mission was staged.

In early May 1980, director David Lowell Rich and his film company arrived in Tucson to begin work on the exteriors. Studio technicians soon had turned the airfield's clock back some thirty-five years with the over thirty tons of World War II equipment (everything from inkwells to radio receivers) that had been convoyed in from Hollywood. Most important among the "props" of course were the three B-29 Superfortresses that lined Davis-Monthan's ramp. Each had emerged from the base's paint shop bearing

Stephen Macht (right) goes over some last minute script changes with director David Lowell Rich (left).

A far cry from the open cockpit camera ships used by Paul Mantz, this Learjet Model 23 was used for filming all of the impressive air-to-air sequences featured in "Enola Gay."

the special unit markings of the 509th Composite Group – circa 1945. For their temporary roles as film stars, "FiFi" had become Lt. Colonel Paul Tibbets' "Enola Gay," "Fertile Myrtle" had become Major Charles Sweeney's "The Great Artiste," and "Sentimental Journey" had become Captain George Marquardt's "Necessary Evil," the latter two having been special observation aircraft on the mission. Joining them for the filming were a number of other museum pieces, including a pair of vintage C-47 transports and a rare Lockheed P-38 fighter plane.

Brigadier General Paul Tibbets (center) poses with his Hollywood counterpart, Patrick Duffy, during filming at Davis-Monthan Air Force Base.

For nearly three weeks the base once again resounded to the throaty roar of B-29's, as the Superforts did their bit for the filmmakers. Assisting Rich (himself a former B-29 navigator) with the many technical and historical aspects of the story was retired Brigadier General Paul W. Tibbets, Jr. Now an executive with an Ohio-based Lear Jet firm, Tibbets had at one time become the object of scorn in the 1950's and 60's for the role he played in the A-bomb mission. Expressing his views to one reporter during the filming, he said:

"I just wanted to finally set the record straight. I'm here to provide guidance and be of any help in making this film into an authentic and true representation of what happened with the mission and in the training of the 509th Group. I'm not a technical advisor nor do I have any official position with the movie – I haven't the time, I have a business to run. But I did want to come down and talk to these young actors and give them a sense of what the world was like then and what the war was like."[10]

By the third week in May, filming at Davis-Monthan had been completed, and the production company began packing for the return trip to California. Accompanying them would be the two flyable B-29's and their respective flight and maintenance crews. Once there, another three weeks of shooting lay ahead, including four days of indoor process filming at Burbank Airport, a day and night shooting session at Point Mugu Naval Air Station, and some additional air-to-air photography over the Mojave Desert Bombing Range.

Smoke engulfs the port city of Hiroshima following the dropping of the bomb.

Production of the film officially ended on May 22, 1980. *Enola Gay* had its world premier six months later, on November 23, 1980. Critical reviews of the film were mixed with most critics noting the screenplay's lack of depth and superficial treatment of the individuals involved on the mission.

LOS ANGELES TIMES

"Although 'Enola Gay' is the story of the B-29 bomber that dropped the A-bomb on Hiroshima and ushered in the nuclear age, the film [of the same name] is rather pedestrian . . . the script by the late James Poe and Millard Kaufman from the factual book by Gordon Thomas and Max Gordon Witts, follows Tibbets, a brilliant career Army pilot, from the time he is assigned to the Manhattan Project, to assembling and training his elite squadron, through the actual mission itself from the Island of Tinian . . . [unfortunately] it never really probes very deeply into the men or the mission . . . the performance of Patrick Duffy as Tibbets never really involves you in his inner turmoil. Kim Darby is agreeable as his wife but the sequence seems mere padding . . . [as] do others . . ."

Cecil Smith
November 21, 1980

Notes

CHAPTER ONE

1. Mike Steen, *Hollywood Speaks* (New York: Putnam Books, 1974), p. 288.
2. *New York Sun,* January 14, 1941.
3. Letter from Colonel Winton Miller to author, August 16, 1978.
4. David Chierichette, *Hollywood Director* (New York: Curtiss Books, 1973), pp. 154–160.
5. Elmer Dyer, "Shooting Technicolor in the Air," *American Cinematographer,* February 1942, pp. 60-61.

CHAPTER TWO

1. Triffy interview. Lawrence Suid, *Guts and Glory* (Reading, Massachusetts: Addison-Wesley, 1978), p. 44.
2. Letter from Lt. Colonel Edward Hillery to author, September 29, 1978.
3. Ibid.
4. Interview with Henry Hathaway, May 16, 1978.
5. Letter from Robert Middleton to author, May 29, 1979.
6. Letter from Robert Middleton to author, June 17, 1979.
7. Interview with Winston Green, July 9, 1978.
8. Mike Steen, *Hollywood Speaks* (New York: Putnam Books, 1974), p. 296.
9. Interview with Major James Davis, June 12, 1980.
10. Interview with Captain James Brown, May 15, 1979.
11. Letter from Brigadier General Robert Lee Scott to author, November 18, 1978.

CHAPTER THREE

1. William Wyler, "No Magic Wand," *The Screen Writer,* February, 1947, pp. 102–116.
2. Letter from Colonel John deRussy to author, October 30, 1978.
3. Interview with Bob King, August 27, 1978.
4. Ibid.

CHAPTER FOUR

1. Paul Tibbets, *The Tibbets Story* (New York: Stein and Day, 1978), pp. 262–267.
2. Crewdson interview, Martin Caiden, *Everything but the Flak* (New York: Duell, Sloan and Pearce, 1964), pp. 201–202.
3. James Appleby, Wayne Berg, I.N. Burchinal, Wayne Burtt, John Bagley, Ray Burkhead, Odel Burton, Frank Blaha, Jack Biven, Willis Fritts, Richard Fischer, Dick Gillespie, Hal Gray, Barney Green, Dan Hill, Les Hall, Don Hackett, Marvin Jackson, Danny Johnson, Jenner Knight, Steward Kunkee, Skip Marsh, Mike McDonald, Thomas Mooney, Edward Mitrani, Don Ornbaum, Frank Pine, Wendell Reid, Terry Rossi, Charles Rector, Jim Speers, Len Stonich, Frank Tallman, Rick Wilson, Forrest Watson, David Viviano, David Voltz.
4. Interview with Major James Appleby, September 5, 1983.
5. Ibid.
6. Interview with Lt. Colonel Art Wildern, July 6, 1983.
7. *Zero/Kate/Val:* James Ashford, Coy Austin, Joseph Beno, Burton Berglund, Leroy Bruflat, Robert Bumgarner, Louis Cislo, Dennis Clark, Ralph Clark, Greg Corliss, Kenneth Costa, Arthur Daegling, John Darby, Guy Davis, William Doak, Warren Dukes, George Duncan, Clinton Effinger, Frank Eger, Henry English, Padraic Evans, Fred Farrell, Frank Hall, William Klopp, Peter Krueger, Ira Lewey, Dean Laird, James Loughmiller, David MacArthur, Robert Maguire, Robert Maycock, John McDaniel, Kenneth Milam, Lewis Mitchell, E.R. Modzelewski, John O'Neil, William Ritzmann, Alfred Seol, Guy Strong, Joseph Tully, Jerry Thompson, Carl Ward, Art Wildern, Eugene Williams, James Williamson; *P-40:* Henry Davis, William Lacy, Lucien Parish; *B-17:* Allen Mosley, Dave Haines, Don Clark, George Burnette, Bill Benedict, Jim Stumpf, Sam Steele, Bill Groomer, Gary Pylant, Don Fletcher; *PT-17:* Janet Hitt, Chuck Young; *PBY:* Bill Buxton, Lloyd Goodyear.
8. Interview with Lt. Colonel Art Wildern, July 6, 1983.
9. Ibid.
10. *The Desert Airman,* April 25, 1980.

Selected Bibliography

Alexander, Charles. *Nationalism in American Thought, 1930-1945.* Chicago: Rand McNally and Company, 1969.

Amberg, George, ed. *New York Times Film Reviews.* New York: Quadrangle Books Inc., 1972.

Baxter, John. *Hollywood in the Thirties.* San Diego: A.S. Barnes, 1968.

Bowen, Ezra, ed. *This Fabulous Century: 1940-1950.* New York: Time-Life Books, 1969.

Brosnan, John. *Movie Magic.* New York: St. Martin's Press, 1974.

Caiden, Martin. *Everything but the Flak.* New York: Duell, Sloan and Pearce, 1964.

Chierichetti, David. *Hollywood Director.* New York: Curtiss Books, 1973.

Culhane, John. *Special Effects in the Movies.* New York: Ballantine Books, 1981.

Dickens, Homer. *The Films of James Cagney.* New York: Citadel Press, 1972.

Dimmitt, Richard. *Title Guide to the Talkies.* Metuchen, New Jersey: Scarecrow Press, 1965.

Dwiggins, Don. *Hollywood Pilot: The Biography of Paul Mantz.* New York: Doubleday, 1967.

Dyer, Elmer. "Shooting Technicolor in the Air." *American Cinematographer,* February, 1942.

Essoe, Gabe. *The Films of Clark Gable.* New York: Citadel Press, 1970.

Farber, Manny. "Movies in Wartime." *New Republic,* January 3, 1944.

Farmer, James. "The Making of Twelve O'Clock High." *Journal of the American Aviation Historical Society,* Winter, 1974.

Gow, Gordon. *Hollywood in the Fifties.* London: Tantivy Press, 1971.

Griffith, Robert and Mayer, Arthur. *The Movies.* New York: Simon and Schuster, 1970.

Grossman, Edward. "Bloody Popcorn." *Harper's.* December, 1970.

Guy, Rory. "Hollywood Goes to War." *Cinema,* March, 1966.

Halliwell, Leslie. *Filmgoers Companion, 5th ed.* New York: Avon Books, 1975.

Higham, Charles. *The Art of the American Film.* New York: Anchor Books, 1974.

Higham, Charles and Wallis, Hal. *Star Maker: The Autobiography of Hal Wallis.* New York: MacMillan Publishing, 1980.

Hughes, Robert, ed. *Film: Book 2-Films of Peace and War.* New York: Grove Press, 1962.

Jablonski, Edward. *Flying Fortress.* New York: Doubleday, 1965.

____________. *Tragic Victories.* New York: Doubleday, 1971.

Jacobs, Lewis, ed. *The Documentary Tradition.* New York: Hopkinson and Blake, 1971.

____________. "World War II and the American Film." *Cinema Journal,* Winter, 1967/68.

Jeavons, Clyde. *A Pictorial History of War Films.* New York: Citadel Press, 1974.

Jones, Dorothy. "Hollywood Goes to War." *Nation,* January 27, 1945.

____________. "Is Hollywood Growing Up?" *Nation,* February 3, 1945.

____________. "War Films Made in Hollywood, 1942-1944." *Hollywood Quarterly,* October, 1945.

Jones, Ken and McClure, Arthur. *Hollywood at War.* New York: A.S. Barnes, 1973.

Kagan, Norman. *The War Film.* New York: Pyramid Books, 1974.

Lingeman, Richard. *Don't You Know There's A War On?* New York: G.P. Putnam's Sons, 1970.

Look Magazine, The Editors of. *Movielot to the Beachhead.* New York: Doubleday, Doran, 1945.

Manvell, Roger. *Films and the Second World War.* New York: A.S. Barnes, 1974.

McCullough, David, ed. *The American Heritage Pictorial History of World War II.* New York: American Heritage Publishing Co., 1966.

Morella, Joe. *The Films of World War II.* New York: Citadel Press, 1973.

Nugent, Frank. "Hollywood Waves the Flag." *Nation,* April 8, 1939.

Price, James. "Smoke Tinted Spectacles: War Films." *London Magazine,* February, 1966.

Rotha, Paul. *Documentary Film. Rev. ed.* London: Faber and Faber, 1952.

Rubin, Steven. *Combat Films: 1945 - 1970.* North Carolina: McFarland and Company, 1981.

Shale, Richard. *Academy Awards.* New York: Unger Publishing, 1978.

Shindler, Colin. *Hollywood Goes to War.* London: Rutledge and Kegan Paul Ltd., 1979.

Skogsberg, Bertil, *Wings on the Screen.* San Diego: A.S. Barnes, 1981.

Steen, Mike. *Hollywood Speaks.* New York: G.P. Putnam's Sons, 1974.

Suid, Lawrence. *Guts and Glory.* Reading, Massachusetts: Addison-Wesley, 1978.

Thomas, Tony, Behlmer, Rudy and McCarthy, Clifford. *The Films of Errol Flynn.* New York: Citadel Press, 1969.

Thomas, Tony. *Films of the Forties.* New York: Citadel Press, 1977.

Tibbets, Paul. *The Tibbets Story.* New York: Stein and Day, 1978.

Warner, Jack. *My First Hundred Years in Hollywood.* New York: Doubleday, 1964.

Wyler, William. "No Magic Wand." *The Screen Writer,* February, 1947.

Index of Film Titles